She Walked for *All* of Us

She Walked for *All* of Us

One Woman's 1971 Protest Against
An Illegal War

Louise Bruyn

Foreword by Bernard Lown, MD

Afterword by Olivia Ames Hoblitzelle

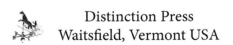

Distinction Press
Waitsfield, Vermont USA

Distinction Press
354 Hastings Road
Waitsfield, Vermont 05673-7117
United States of America

802.496.3271
www.distinctionpress.com
kitty@distinctionpress.com

© 2013 Louise Bruyn

Foreword © 2013 Bernard Lown, MD

Afterword © 2013 Olivia Ames Hoblitzelle

Cover and author photos © 1971 Kathryn Abbe

Interior photographs @ the various news organizations
and photographers as mentioned

Designed and typeset by Kitty Werner, RSBPress

Published 2013

PERMISSIONS: Page 28: "Atlas," by Rod McKuen, from *Love's Been Good To Me* © 1969 by Rod
McKuen & Pocket Books. "With Love, © 1969 by Rod McKuen & Stanyan Books, "A Book
of Days & A Month of Sundays," © 1981 by Rod McKuen & Harper & Row. All copyrights
renewed. Used by permission.
Page 32: Ginsberg, Allen. "Song." Selected Poems: 1947–1995. New York, NY: Harper Collins,
1996. Permission given.
Page 137: "Air Support," by Maida Follini, permission given by author.
Page 192: *This is the American Earth,* © 1960, Nancy Newhall, ©2013, the Estate of Beaumont
and Nancy Newhall. Permission to reproduce courtesy of Scheinbaum and Russek Ltd., Santa
Fe, New Mexico
Page 236: "Pieta for Today," by Virginia Bates, used by permission of Abecedarian Books, Inc.

ISBN 978-1-937667-12-2

Library of Congress Control Number 2013937152

The day before Louise Bruyn left to walk from Boston to Washington, D.C. as a witness against the Vietnam War, a *Boston Globe* interviewer asked her,

"Who are you doing this for?"

Moved deeply by the question to the edge of tears, she replied,

"I'm doing it for us—I'm doing it for all of us."

Louise had responded to an inner call. Inspired and courageous, her response reflected the feelings of countless others—nationwide—who had become numb to the horrors of the war, apathetic in the face of inability to affect a change. Her walk was an act of hope. She walked alone, but as the title reflects, her action was on behalf of all of us. She didn't want people to follow her; she only wanted others to find their own ways to act for peace.

Published over 40 years later, Louise's chronicle of her journey carries the same timeless message: one person can ignite the hearts of many and help to change the course of events. As with her walk, may her book inspire others to continue their work for a more peaceful and sustainable world.

— O.A.H.

To the Vietnamese people,
who suffered so during the French and
American Wars

And especially to Mme. Ngo Ba Thanh,
whom I will never forget

Contents

Foreword

When Louise Bruyn asked me to write a foreword, I welcomed her esteem but wished she had selected someone else. I suspected the book would be a bore. How could a long forgotten tale of a solitary walk from Boston to Washington by an ordinary middle-aged suburbanite be of interest? I shared Louise's outrage of the unrelenting high tech maiming and killing of Vietnamese. I could not conceive, though, how recalling a monotonous lonely trudge in mid winter could be a compelling or an even interesting story. What could a reader learn that is relevant to the roiling issues of our times?

I agreed to accept the assignment, but intended to short shrift it. Skim a few pages and then craft some praiseworthy banalities. Something unexpected followed. It rapidly became evident that Louise was no ordinary "Quaker peace activist." The more I read the unpretentious story, the greater my curiosity as to what motivated her trying venture. When Louise began the walk she had no preconceived agenda, there was no strategic plan how best to reach people, nor did she foster the illusion that this act would hasten an end to the Vietnam carnage. As she intones, "The walk is like a prayer." What was she praying for? Certainly not for self-redemption. There comes a time when confronted with outrage, we must act to remain human. Not just any deed, but focused action floating the injustice to the level of public visibility. How she achieved this became a page-turner for me.

The transformation of Louise and the fulfillment of her prayer is what drives the book. At the outset she had a choice of carrying posters proclaiming her mission. It would have helped emotionally and physically to be surrounded by family, friends and supporters. She refused both. Louise believed that being accompanied and hoisting placards might discourage engagement with strangers. She craved forging conversations, not preaching to the choir. Her aim was to help breach the universe of silence about Vietnam.

Louise learned that walking alone in this grueling track could be transformative. The visible self-sacrifice and loneliness of it evoked empathy, steered curiosity, raised questions and led to conversation. Others, seeing her self-inflicted pain, asked, "why are you doing it?" The curiosity of strangers led to discussion, which began to instill doubt and questioning about our actions in Vietnam. By walking alone, she was no longer alone.

Albert Schweitzer wrote, "I decided that I would make my life my argument." Louise made this pilgrimage her argument. When people learn that there is no disjuncture between word and deed they are more likely, not only to listen, but also to hear. To gain and project such moral clarity was ultimately her mission. As Louise writes, "I was speaking from the deepest part of me to the deepest part of everyone on the way."

What did Louise's walk achieve? The war in Vietnam continued. Atrocities multiplied. American military might proved wanting against an aroused populace. We brutalized Vietnam with ever-mounting mindless ferocity. Ultimately we were ignominiously defeated and kicked out. Worse still, the so-called "lesson of Vietnam" of avoiding such foreign military misadventures was soon forgotten. Since then we have had the catastrophe of Iraq and the quagmire of Afghanistan. Yet our government is readying Americans for the worst of possible misadventures, an assault against Iran.

Since Vietnam our military expenditures doubled, currently exceeding the combined spending of all our putative enemies worldwide. We are now waging a hundred years war against Islamic jihadists. In former times the civilized response would have been a calibrated police action against terrorists. Democratic institutions are fragile against the demands of unending war. Increasingly the USA is being transformed into a militarized national security state. Did Louise then walk in vain?

This would be a wrong conclusion. Let me explain. Over 30 years ago, during the height of the cold war, we organized an international medical movement demanding the abolition of nuclear weapons. We were persuaded that these were instruments of genocide. Our research convinced us that nuclear war would constitute the final epidemic for humankind. We deemed that silence was a betrayal of the fundamental commitment of doctors to preserve the life and health of their patients.

The International Physicians for the Prevention of Nuclear War (IP-PNW) was unique in that the leadership included Soviet doctors. At the time the staccato drumbeat of propaganda from Washington was that Russians were our mortal enemies threatening our very survival. Collaborating with them, as we did, bordered on treason. We faced a frightened and fear-anesthetized public. The chance of IPPNW prospering seemed nil.

Like Louise we were compelled to act. Like her we believed that there was no greater force in modern society than an educated public, aroused and angered to effect change. Like her we were driven by a moral imperative.

IPPNW reached millions with a simple message, "Americans and Russians either live together or die together." The involvement of multitudes in the antinuclear movement compelled governments to begin serious negotiations. Within a mere four years of its founding we received the ultimate accolade, a Nobel Peace Prize.

Reading *She Walked for All of Us* made me reflect that without the "Louises" of the world who engaged in the anti-Vietnam struggle, we would not have succeeded two decades later in helping put an end to the nuclear arms race.

Howard Zinn, the great American historian, captured the essence.

And if we do act, in however small a way, we don't have to wait for some grand utopian future. The future is an infinite succession of presents, and to live now as we think human beings should live, in defiance of all that is bad around us, is itself a marvelous victory.

Bernard Lown, MD
Co-Founder of IPPNW
Co-recipient Nobel Peace Prize (1985)
Author, *Prescription for Survival:A Doctor's Journey to End Nuclear Madness*,
2008, Berrett-Koehler Pub.

* Howard Zinn last paragraph of *No One is Neutral on a Moving Train*. Beacon Press. Boston. 1994.

Acknowledgments

When I returned from the walk, I had to record what I had experienced. During the summer of 1971, from my notes in red ink and my tiny red notebook, I transferred everything into a typewriter. Had I really been on this walk? Did I really have all those experiences? I needed to remember. I needed to confirm it to myself. I did not intend to write a book.

A few times in the 70s and 80s, however, I submitted it to a publisher. It was rejected and I had other things to do: a job, involvement in anti-nuclear work, in environmental work, more important in my opinion. Retired in 1999, I began to think again about the manuscript. Two summers ago, using microfilm at the Newton Free Library, I selected quotes from *The New York Times* for each day of walking. I wanted young people to know what was going on in the country during the year 1971. On the walk, I hadn't read any of the quotes. They are there for the reader. But still I hadn't moved ahead on the publishing search.

In the Spring of 2012, however, I decided that if it were ever going to be published it had to be now. I was 82. I also felt it was an obligation. With the world having so many problems, the story might convince others of the importance of becoming active, even in a small way. By then, I knew myself well. I had to reach out for help. I couldn't do it alone. I needed someone by my side to keep me focused and on task. An impossible-to-fill need. Who could do that?! I made a very conscious declaration to myself to reach out for help…but I didn't ask anybody.

Only a few weeks later a young friend, **Katherine Gekas**, told me she had decided that instead of volunteering at a local institution, she wanted to volunteer for me, to just help me do whatever I needed, an hour and a half, once a week. I accepted her generous offer, and the first day, not thinking of my declaration and not knowing how to best use her help, we just cleaned out a file drawer. Before she left, though, I thought to ask if she would like to help me with the book. She had the skills I needed. Task-oriented, organized, good with computers, highly intelligent and had a thoughtful, gentle spirit. She said, "Yes." Honestly, I could not have finished this book without Katherine at my elbow almost weekly from last Spring to this. Somehow, my silent declaration must have reached her. I am forever indebted to her.

Readers will recognize **Olivia Hoblitzelle**, in many places in the story. Though we didn't see each other for many years in between, we connected easily whenever it happened. She meanwhile had published her beautiful book, *A Thousand Joys, A Thousand Sorrows*, a record of her life with Hob, her husband, in his waning years of Alzheimer's disease. She extended such love and encouragement to me to tell my story, always available during this last year to the computer to read the manuscript and to give welcome, good advice. And she let us include her amazing story of the work she and others did to light fires across the country.

As a published author of children's books, **Sarah Lamstein** had been in touch soon after my walk to see if she could make the story appropriate for children. The endeavor brought us close and we kept in touch over the years. I believe she kept her book in reserve until I had published mine. Sarah, I hope, will finally publish that book. During this last year she contributed enormously to the manuscript by reading and commenting.

The above three women were "the wind beneath my wings."
This book wouldn't have taken off if it hadn't been for them.

My dear friend, **Martha Penzer**, poet and librarian and Quaker, was such a special help in the early years. She encouraged me in the 1980s to publish this story and always had faith in me. Her mother Stella had even helped my family during the walk with household needs. Martha spent long hours during the early 2000s putting all the news clips and photos into notebooks in acrylic sleeves, helping me to be more organized.

I thank **Louise Lown** for an invitation to tea last Spring. She had reason to ask me more about the walk. It afforded a lovely opportunity to get to know her better and her husband, Bernard Lown. Louise read the manuscript, made comments, and it led to a warm connection between our two families, for which I am most grateful.

Paul Shannon was the go-to person for the data I needed. A dear friend, my "partner in crime," one with whom I could share memories of Vietnam, having gone there with others to demonstrate against the war in January 1975. I thank him for his continued openness to helping me with details of events I had forgotten or didn't know at all.

My loving thanks to my computer-whiz nephew, **Lloyd Muenzer**, who, on a visit to Newton from California, strung together all the daily entries into one computer entity, so that I was able to go into the whole story without having to reclick for each day.

I thank dear long-time friend **Valerie Kreutzer** for her encouragement, and shared joy when things were going right for either of us. She is an elegant writer. I wish I could have written this with her gift. She published her book, *Maria,* about her experience raising her Columbian daughter. She read my manuscript more than once, I'm sure, and offered sound advice.

Thank you to **Claire Gorfinkel** with Intentional Productions for her reading of part of the manuscript while in the Sierras and commenting on her return. Many thanks to **Marcia Yudkin**, owner of Creative Ways Publishing, who read the manuscript. Unasked, she edited it in many places, which helped me learn certain writing pitfalls. And she praised the book. **Kitty Werner**, owner of Distinction Press, respecting Marcia's words and work, picked it up for publishing, sight unseen! Kitty has continued to work with me to design and get right the text and photos, all while staying human in email interchanges that at times were either wonderfully warm or zany. Kitty was always willing to listen and yet to hold to her point of view when she felt it important. I thank her for a great publishing experience.

A special thank you to **Kathryn Abbe**, the photographer who took the front and back photos in 1971. She accompanied Alice Lake who wrote the *Good Housekeeping Magazine* article. These were not used, so she gave me the slides, 42 years ago.

I appreciate the generosity of many of those companies and individuals holding the copyrights to the poems in this book, who gave me permission to include them with little or no fee. They are listed on the copyright page.

I thank my husband, **Severyn**, for his constant support in this endeavor. For years he urged me to publish this story. From the first mention of the idea of the walk to the final look and content of this book he has been with me, giving his helpful input when asked. He has been my 61-year-Love.

And to our daughters, **Rebecca** and **Susan**, I thank them for their help in trying to find a title and locating pictures to include. They even asked their friends to help. I am very grateful for the fine women they have become, regardless of the walk or the book. They had a bit of cynicism that I would ever get this finished, but now that it is a reality, they are excited with me. I am likewise grateful for the fine man our son **George** is. He did miss all the excitement of the walk itself, so knowing the details when he gets a copy of this will be a surprise to him.

I hope I have not forgotten to thank anyone who has been helpful on this book. If so, I am deeply sorry. I apologize to all the people I had met and who had walked with me whose names I had to take out of this narrative. There were just too many for the readers to navigate. I hope there are not too many as it is; I resisted removing many of them.

I welcome readers to share this journey with me.

The Beginning

"Vietnam Village wipeout proof of how deeply the nation is sunk in anesthesia." It was February 6, 1971.

The opinion piece in the op-ed section of the *Boston Globe* caught my eye. I was sitting in the kitchen having my morning cup of coffee, reading the newspaper as I did every day. We were in about the 6th year of the Vietnam War. The article spoke of a project of our government to relocate hundreds of thousands of Vietnamese from the five northernmost provinces of South Vietnam to southern provinces. It spoke of the previous U.S. attacks on individual villages, the forced relocations, the bombing, the torture of those who refused to leave their homes, the destruction of their homes, the killing. And now, the "social engineers" had come up with their "final solution." They would do to whole provinces what they used to do to one village at a time. The writer said that even though this project had been reported in the *New York Times*, the press and television had failed to comment on it. And the writer concluded that the nation was "sunk in anesthesia."

I was aware that the U.S. had just invaded Laos and there was a news blackout. The previous year, we had invaded Cambodia and it was all over the news. The reaction was loud and clear. Protest demonstrations happened across the country. At Kent State University in Ohio four students were killed and nine wounded by National Guard riflemen, and

1

a week later at Jackson State University in Mississippi, two were killed and many more wounded. Now, less than a year later, silence.

I walked into the living room with my coffee and paper and sat on the sofa. The room was full of sunshine.

I went on with other reading, but an unsettled feeling was going on just below the surface. I had been taking a theater history course and so was reading *The Act and the Image*, by Raymond Ben Avram. I had read his section about *dramatic action*, which was italicized. I looked up Webster's definition of "action": "the act or process of producing an effect or performing a function; the doing of something. The effecting of an alteration by means of force; a thing done…"

And I looked at the news article again. And then I could see. I, too, was anesthetized. I was not responding.

My husband, Sev, walked into the room. I handed him the editorial. We talked about the war and I went back to reading Ben Avram, but I was unable to focus on the text. We spoke more about the war and the absurdity of the inaction in the face of the war's expansion. And I said something like, "Someone ought to walk to Washington to tell the government to stop this war!" I don't remember if those were the exact words. Perhaps the words were, "I feel like walking to Washington to tell them to stop!" I spoke with intensity, but I knew it was a ridiculous idea. I threw it out to Sev as an expression of my frustration, my anger. After a quiet pause, he said, "You know, that's the kind of thing that would help people to feel what is happening. That's the kind of thing it might take."

I tried to return to my reading, but my brain would not let the idea go. The italicized words *dramatic action* kept jumping off the page at me. I put the book down and hurried into the dining room where we kept the maps, pulled out one that showed the Eastern Seaboard, Maine to Florida—and there was the section Boston to Washington, D.C. It was 450 miles! I walked back into the living room, felt the sunshine, the warm golds, yellows, browns of the room. But something unrelated to that comfort was churning inside me.

All day I moved between the reality of my tasks, overseeing a children's dance in a theater production, housecleaning, preparing dinner—and that preposterous idea. It would take me twenty-three days, I thought. I could do 20 miles a day. Twenty-three days. Winter vacation was coming up. I had planned to paint my kitchen, but that certainly could be laid aside.

While fixing dinner that night, I said to my fifteen-year-old daughter, Susan, "Guess what, I'm thinking of walking to Washington, D.C."

Sue had mayonnaise poised on a knife. She stopped her motion, then said, "Sure, Mom, when are you leaving?"

I told her I was serious, but only at the stage of thinking about it. I was sharing only the bud of an idea. It was too personal yet, too insane, too ridiculous to trust to anyone outside the family.

Susan and Becky, 16, had both participated with us in peace demonstrations, vigils, leafleting, and working for peace candidates since we had moved from Jacksonville, Illinois to Newton, Massachusetts in 1966. (Our older son George had by this time moved out of the house. He was living in Illinois.) While in Illinois we had joined the Society of Friends (Quakers), and now, living in Newton, we had joined Friends Meeting at Cambridge. The children knew the depth of our caring and understood.

However, that night I had to call some very close friends, Betty and Chuck Woodbury, who were also members of the Friends Meeting at Cambridge. Chuck had been Presiding Clerk. I trusted both for their judgment on such an undertaking as this would be. Besides having a deep faith in the Quaker testimonies, they were hikers; they knew the practical aspect of walking. Unfortunately they had company that night (Jim and Jerilyn Prior, who were also hikers) so they didn't have time for me to run over, but because of the nature of the call, the sound of my voice, Betty asked if something were troubling me, if it were a crisis. I explained that it could certainly wait until morning, but that it concerned an idea I had...walking to Washington, D.C. We agreed to drive to Meeting together the following morning.

The next morning, the Woodburys and Priors came to pick us up. We slipped right into gear. The Priors were completely enthusiastic. Jerilyn, who was a physician, commented, "It's so great to put your body where your mind is." She mentioned, too, the meaning that a walk had for people. A quest. A search. A combination of real and symbolic.

Betty and Chuck were a little more reserved. They put the question to me, "But isn't there something *else* you could do, that would be just as strong? Isn't there another form of protest that would be better, more meaningful?"

I said I had thought about that. I tried. But I could think of nothing as strong. When I said I could do it in 23 days, 20 miles a day, Jim countered with advice. I should consider 10 miles a day.

"Ten miles a day? That would take 45 days!" My insides knotted up.

During Friends Meeting for Worship I can only remember feeling tight inside. I tried to hold the idea up to the Light, but I wasn't getting any help. I just knew that soon I would have to make a decision. Does one do something like this, or doesn't one? I knew something was working inside me that wouldn't let go, that soon it would have to resolve itself, because I couldn't go on living in this state of suspension.

One of the suggestions from the Woodburys and the Priors was to discuss this idea with several other people who had had experience in non-violent action. When I got home from Meeting, the only ones I could reach immediately by phone were Marjorie and Bob Swann of the Committee for Non-Violent Action in Voluntown, Connecticut. We explored by phone many of the possibilities, but decided that it would be good to talk face-to-face. I told Marj I could arrive in Voluntown about 1:00 p.m. on Monday to talk with them.

Sunday night we had company for dinner—three of our closest friends from Illinois– Pat Simon, Valerie Kreutzer, and Lois Foersterling. It was a birthday celebration for Valerie. I really didn't have dinner prepared ahead of time nicely like I had intended. I explained my preoccupation. And we all thought about this undertaking. Valerie and Pat and Lois could understand my feelings, but it seemed so preposterous, so mad. They were not enthusiastic, only thoughtful.

Lois came out with the strongest opinion: "Louise, no! I don't think you should do it. There are other ways a person can work for peace. A person's relationships with other people are very important. You are affecting your dance students. In your everyday life you are affecting the people with whom you come into contact. No, I don't want to hear another word about it!"

I knew we affected people in our everyday life. I taught modern dance to children and adults at the All Newton Music School and elsewhere around the Boston area. I performed in several small modern dance companies. Surely this did not speak to others of stopping this war.

I argued with her. I said that in order for the insanity of this Vietnam conflict to stop, people had to go *beyond* their ordinary lives to exert the power to stop it. It was not enough to "do one's thing" from day to day. A maximum effort had to be exerted by the people of this country to stop the forward momentum of this "machine of destruction." I could only compare our situation with that of Germany. How ready we were to blame the Germans for allowing the gassing and cremation of 6 million Jews in the 1930s and '40s. We had the term: "good Germans." They were the ones who didn't agree with the policies of the Nazi government but didn't raise a finger to stop the slaughter. Their excuse was so much stronger than ours. They were faced with a fascist government, a very dangerous structure against which to take action. Many said they "didn't know."

Our government was a democracy. It was supposed to be responsive to the will of the majority, and certainly supposed to be moral in its decisions. How could we justify our inaction in the face of the unspeakable destruction of a people and a country halfway around the world on the grounds that we were "saving them from Communism." No, if people felt our course in Vietnam, Cambodia, and Laos to be unjust, if they felt it to be immoral, then they had a duty to speak out against that course in the strongest way they could. It was a solemn responsibility, not just on the grounds that the government should be responsive to the will and moral convictions of the people, but that human life was precious, that each person is sacred, each life important.

Fine words. Where was my action?

———

Monday morning I left for Voluntown. The countryside was covered with snow, the highway slushy with rain.

Marj and Bob and I talked for several hours. I had not realized that a group had walked from Boston to D.C. four years earlier. Bob had the itinerary. It went through all the major cities, down through Providence, across to New Haven, down to New York City, etc. They had walked to call for a ban on nuclear testing. But they were a group. If one got sick, they could drop out and catch up later. It wouldn't stop the walk. Bob's spirit was so great. He said in his quiet, practical way, "It isn't a question of whether you can do it or not. It's just *how* do you want to do it. Do you want other people to go with you? Do you want to carry leaflets? Will you wear or carry a sign? Do you need a station wagon to go along with you carrying supplies like sleeping bags? When would you think of starting?"

Such good questions. I had so much formulating to do. But first, of course, I still had to make the decision of whether to do it or not.

Bob gave me so much confidence. Marj and I spent a few hours going over her old files of people who might be able to help along the way, and some maps of the areas I might be going through. I took all the information I could with me about the walk they had done before, and the lists of helpful people. It was getting dark. I had to leave. I told them both that I would give myself a deadline for deciding. I would make up my mind by Wednesday, yea or nay. I would call them.

The children were not home yet when I got home. They were having one of their last rehearsals for "Oklahoma!," the musical being put on by their high school. Becky was doing the choreography for it with a friend and Susan was one of the dancers. They were so happy, involved, and excited about the production.

Tuesday morning I had one last adult dance class to teach at the All Newton Music School before the end of term. Before the class, I asked to talk for a bit with the head of the school, Anne Gombosi. I confided my possible action to her, knowing it would impact the school's schedule. Her response was very thoughtful and gracious.

"I know you have to do it, Louise. I understand."

At the end of that morning's class I mentioned that something might come up that would keep me from teaching at the beginning of the second semester. I didn't know yet whether it would be so, I said, but I would know by the next day. They would find out through the music school.

Tuesday afternoon we got a call from someone at the Legal In-Service Program. Someone needed housing for that night. Could we help?

That evening, a returned African-American soldier named Doug (no last name offered) came over to the house. He had thought about going AWOL because he didn't want to get sent back to Vietnam, but then had decided to try to get out of the army legally. After dinner, we sat in the living room talking about the war. Doug had witnessed some of the atrocities committed by U.S. troops. While in Vietnam, he himself had worn a "necklace" of eighteen Viet Cong ears, he said. He called them a "set." He saw heads impaled on stakes. He told us he heard a commander tell a soldier who had killed a Vietnamese not to return without the person's ears. The soldier didn't have a regular knife, so he used a little plastic knife with the serrated edge to do the job.

When I mentioned the possibility that I would walk to Washington, Doug expressed his sense that there would be power in it.

As we continued sharing in the living room, Sev commented that he thought the walk idea was a good one, but he really didn't want me to leave so soon. It was still winter. Later in the spring it would be safer, not so much risk in the weather. But the urgency inside me said if I did it at all I had to do it as soon as possible. How could I justify "waiting for nice weather"? I wanted to leave on Sunday. Yet, I hadn't even decided whether I would do it.

Doug had more to say about the weather. He told us how he had hitched rides across the country with a friend in January, how cold it had been, how his friend's toes did get frost-bite and how the friend finally took the bus because they were so bad. I knew blizzards might come, but I also knew that we were one-third through February. Maybe the really bad weather had spent itself. For some reason, even though the thought of zero-degree weather and storms frightened me, it didn't seem relevant. It was something I would face one day at a time...if I were to go.

I had never had trouble sleeping. However, since the first glimmerings of this idea, I could hardly sleep. I would wake up in the middle of the night. I would awake early in the morning. Questions within me would rise up.

"Where will you stay at night?" I would ask myself.

"Well, I'll stay in hotels or inns along the way."

"What if there are no hotels or inns?"

"I'll seek out a church. Find a minister and ask to be put up."

"What if there are no churches at the end of each day's walk?"

"Well, I'll just go up to any house and ask them to put me up." That solved that issue.

Another question: "Friends have said it would be dangerous. Awful things might happen to a woman walking alone. How can you be safe?"

"I'm not afraid to walk in my own neighborhood. I'll just make everywhere my neighborhood." That took care of that.

Finally Wednesday came. I had said I would make a decision on Wednesday. But I hadn't said what time Wednesday.

I went to the house of a friend, Nancy Strong, with whom I had shared my intense feelings about the need for the walk. Her friend, Don Patterson, joined our conversation. I came for a final consultation on the action. I had begun to see how it might take shape and Nancy helped me clarify some thoughts. I would go alone, hoping that by doing so I would be urging others to take the strongest actions which they felt they could take wherever they were. The walk would not try to accumulate more people and therefore divert people from other activities. I would only carry on my back what I needed. No car would go with me, and I would carry no leaflets or signs. I had finally thought through what there was about signs that I didn't like. For me, for this action, a sign would separate me from the person with whom I was in contact. It would be dehumanizing. I would be a little less than a whole person. Leaflets would put something between the other person and me. While they had dropped their eyes to read, I would have lost a precious moment. Yet, I felt I needed something. I decided a black armband would be the visible symbol of my inward state of grief over the horrors of the war. Still, in talking about it with Nancy and Don, there was something unanswered about the whole project.

Then Don said, "In a way, the walk is like a prayer."

When I heard him say that, something hit me so deeply. The tears streamed down my face, and I said yes, yes, that was it. From that point on, I felt I had made the decision. Yes, I was going. Yes, I might fail, be stopped by the weather, be a fool in the eyes of many, but none of that mattered. I was speaking from the deepest part of me to the deepest part of everyone along the way, and that was all that mattered. I would proceed as the way opened, trusting that I would be shown the way.

————

When I had returned home on Wednesday, Becky walked into the living room, hesitantly, delicately.

"Well," she said, "have you decided?"

Looking at her, I nodded "yes."

"Are you going to do it?"

I nodded "yes" again.

She came over to me and put her arms around me. "I thought so," she said. "I told some of my friends about it and they think it's wonderful."

Wednesday night I attended the first of the three performances of "Oklahoma!" at the high school. Now that I knew what I was about to do, everything took on different overtones. The joy, lightheartedness, simplicity of the story was on such a different level than my inner state. Yet, there was so much vibrancy in the performance that it carried me right along. I was especially moved watching Becky and Susan dance together on stage for the first time. Never had I seen lovelier movement by high school students in an amateur performance. Not just our girls, but *all* the dancers really moved. They *danced*. They were full of joy. In a sense I looked at that play as a fulfillment. I knew the girls would be fine if I left them. I watched these two sisters moving in such harmony after years of my saying things like, "Stop hitting your sister, share that with her, stop calling each other names, you mustn't be jealous," etc., "advices" given equally to both, without much effect. And now this. My heart expanded until it was about to pop.

————

With the decision made to go, I now had to solve the problems of the trip itself. When would I leave? What would I do when I got there?

Sev and I had a long talk about the timing and the form of the walk. He was a Professor of Sociology at Boston College and had his teaching duties. He finally agreed to my sense that I had to do it now or never. If I were to wait, the urgency would leave me. So together we figured that maybe I could start on February 17th, the following Wednesday. But he stated, more than once during the next week, that if I found that I couldn't continue, for whatever reason, I should not hesitate to give it up and come home. I should not feel that I had failed.

We tried to imagine what form the walk would take. What would I do when I got to Washington? I said I wanted to take my concern to my congressmen. I would try to see them when I got there.

"What about the President?" he asked.

"Yes, the President." I would try to see him, too. Was I hearing myself right?

Sev kept saying, "This can't just be a walk against something; it has to be *for* something." For years he, especially, had been an advocate of World Law, of a strengthened United Nations, and we both had been members of the United World Federalists (now called World Federalists, U.S.A.). Often, we talked about the need for greater cooperation between nations. The United States had been trying for too long to police the world by itself and this could only get it into deeper and deeper trouble.

After retreating down to his study, Sev came upstairs, paper in hand. He had put together "Five Theses," five imperatives for our foreign policy in relation to Vietnam and to the world. We talked of the way Martin Luther had nailed his ninety-five theses to the door of a church in Germany when he was protesting church domination in the 16th century. Working over the wording together and later asking for the advice of friends, we finally assembled the following:

FIVE THESES ON UNITED STATES FOREIGN POLICY

In 1517, Martin Luther made public his protest against church domination by nailing ninety-five Theses to the door of the All Saints Church in Wittenberg, Germany.

In this year of 1971, I make this protest against state domination by nailing five theses to the door of the United States Congress. I carry this message written by my family and friends who support my mission.

Louise Bruyn

We love our nation for its ideals but we condemn its war policies. We oppose the fact that we must support the war through our taxes or be forced to go to prison.

We demand that the foreign policy of the United States be directed toward creating the foundations of world peace and law. The following five Theses convey our beliefs about the imperatives of U.S. Foreign policy today.

1. The American troops and air forces must be withdrawn immediately and totally from Southeast Asia.
2. An international commission composed of major capitalist and communist nations should be established to aid Vietnamese people to develop their nation and protect the lives of all people in Southeast Asia.
3. A Study Commission must be created immediately within the United Nations to review its Charter, looking toward the establishment of enforceable international law and a democratically constituted world government.
4. International agencies must be created with the authority to allocate economic aid for national liberation and development, and to prohibit separate aid from stronger nations seeking control over weaker nations.
5. An international agency must be established to control the use of nuclear weapons and ultimately banish their national production for destructive purposes.

This was the document that I would carry with me during the walk, collecting signatures as I went.

Thursday night Sev and I went to the regular Meeting for Business of the Friends Meeting at Cambridge, when members take care of ongoing business of the Meeting. When most of the business was finished, I stood up with trepidation. With butterflies in my stomach, my heart pounding, and the firmest voice I could muster, I announced to the forty or so gathered how distressed I was by the war, and how I felt that I must take action in protest to our expansion of the war. "I am planning to walk to Washington, D.C. and am leaving on February 17." I asked their support in spirit and their help in finding housing with anyone they thought might put me up along the way. The support in spirit I felt immediately. (Jessie Jones who sat next to me in that meeting became essential in planning and carrying out the logistics that worked so beautifully for me. She said later that she "caught the Fire." More about her later.)

When the Meeting was over, people came up to us and handed us many, many names as possibilities. Many who were there wrote to friends within that next week to see if they would be willing to put me up.

Someone suggested that a Meeting for Worship be held the day I left, that it be in the Meeting House, and others agreed. Though I expressed my deep gratitude, I mentioned how important I felt it to be that the walk should begin from our front door. Somehow, for the walk to be the clearest expression of my protest, it had to leave from our house in Newton, Massachusetts. So they changed the suggestion to having a Meeting for Worship in our living room just before I left, Wednesday morning, February 17th, 9:00 a.m. I would leave at 10:00. I could not believe the support that was coming through.

———

Sunday night Sev and I went to a fund-raising party at a Newton resident's house. It was held for the "Spring Offensive," a planned campaign to bring people to Washington to protest the war. All the "peace people" of Newton and the surrounding area had been invited to hear the plans of the spring program. Noam Chomsky spoke on the bombing of Laos (which, I discovered, had been going on for six years!), Sidney Peck on the plans of the People's Coalition for Peace and Justice, and Jay Craven on the People's Peace Treaty. Donald Sutherland, the actor, read from *Johnny Got His Gun*, by Dalton Trumbo. The house was packed with many old friends and many people I had never met before.

Sev and I asked permission to announce what my plans were. Having been given the okay, I made my announcement. Sev added that we would welcome getting names of people along the way who might put me up. He also asked for anyone interested to sign up to help with publicity and housing. By now we were equipped with 3 × 5 cards for addresses. A number of people gave us their names. This was the beginning of any sense of organization or "committee."

At home, Sev and I talked about publicity. One of the channels of outreach open to me was the news media. It was important that we utilize every means we possibly could. Sev dropped his own work (though not his teaching) during the time I was to be gone in order to work on publicity for this action. He would try in every way he could to maximize the coverage.

He wrote the following letter to the three major newspapers in the Boston area, the *Record-American*, the *Herald Traveler*, and the *Boston Globe*.

14 February 1971

To Whom It May Concern:

My wife, Louise, has decided to walk from Newton, Massachusetts to Washington, D.C. as a protest against the spiraling effects of the war in Vietnam and against the war itself. She is a housewife, a dance instructor at the All Newton Music School, a mother of teenage children, a person whose home means a great deal to her. I believe her protest is noteworthy because she is willing to give up the comforts of her home, her family, her artistic involvements, in order to make an action statement against the war; furthermore, her protest is one which should be communicated to those who have felt it impossible to be articulate about the developing holocaust in Southeast Asia.

Her reasons are simple. They augur a change in the temper of protest. The war has developed into a system of such devastating proportions that there is no longer time to debate its morality. The time has come for a fundamental kind of action which will bring it to a halt. It is the kind of action in which ordinary people who lead ordinary lives—housewives, businessmen, teachers, mailmen, bus drivers—can stop their routines and say that the war has become a seven year massacre. It can no longer be tolerated by any measure of humanity. Debate has ended. This must be the year of citizen action.

If nonviolent means of protest are not exercised quietly and firmly across the nation to end the war—by halting work, by ceasing to perform housely duties, in order to engage full time in protest—then surely action as violent as that which the administration is perpetrating on the people of Vietnam, will take place. Ordinary, conscientious people must begin to take the leadership to bring this war to a forceful halt.

Soldiers have been in our home telling us about the many My Lais not open to public view. They have told us about the established practice of cutting ears and heads off Vietnamese by our own soldiers. The war is brutalizing American youth. Six million people have been forcibly relocated and close to a million people have been killed—according to our own Defense Department statistics. The massive air attacks on Laos, Cambodia, and Vietnam, the vast destruction of foliage and natural life with its horrendous effects on the people and the genetic consequences to their children are morally indefensible.

If China were moving troops into Canada in support of the Quebec Liberation Front, we would take extreme measures to protect this hemisphere from foreign invasion and ideology. Can China be expected to remain silent much longer? The American war in Southeast Asia must come to an end before extreme measures—a Chinese nuclear bomb with delivery power—enters into the framework of war or into negotiations.

The German people did not do anything collectively and openly to resist their war and the atrocities perpetrated against the Jewish people. This inaction was condemned by the Nuremberg trials. In the United States, many people have debated and talked against the war but little direct action to stop the war has occurred except for the bombings of a radical few. These bombings have been called outrageous by the public when they are directed against buildings and the offenders are hunted down and sentenced. What a twist of morality!

The amount of bombings over Vietnam released by American airborne to kill, burn, and ravage the land of a foreign people averages 2-1/2 Hiroshima bombs per month! The fact that the public should condemn rock throwing in store windows and at the same time support the administrative policy which brings massive human destruction is almost beyond belief! People then wonder why, after the futile attempts to change such morally outrageous war policies, youth turn to a rock or a bomb, or finally, violence against themselves with drugs. Where has the leadership of this nation gone?

My wife expects to leave next Wednesday, February 17th. We will miss her—but she goes with our full support and all our love. She will have the support of her friends in the area. She hopes that her walk will signal others to act nonviolently on a scale that will bring this monstrous policy of killing people in Southeast Asia to an end.

Severyn T. Bruyn

The response from the newspapers was almost instantaneous. They began phoning to find out more. They sent reporters out to cover the story.

Together Sev and Jim called all the radio stations in the Boston area. I spent most of Tuesday talking on the phone, telling the story over and over, making tapes that would be broadcast later. Sev and Jim contacted the television stations.

When Jim had finished making all of these contacts Tuesday, he said, "Louise, why don't you call the President and tell him you are coming."

I looked at him and my jaw dropped!

He said, "Really, I mean it. Why don't you call him?"

My first reaction of disbelief at the idea turned to "Why not?" In every way possible I must try to reach this man.

After pacing the floor awhile, and rubbing my sweaty palms, I picked up the phone and dialed O.

"Operator, I'd like to place a person-to-person call to the President of the United States."

"Would that be at the White House?"

"Yes, I guess so." My heart had turned to jelly. I knew I wouldn't be allowed to talk to him at this time. But somehow I had to let the White House know I was coming.

The operator got a response at the White House. To them she said, "I have a party who would like to speak to President Richard Nixon."

"Who is calling, please?"

"Who is calling?" the operator said to me.

"Louise Bruyn," I said as I cringed inside.

"Louise Bruyn," she said.

The White House voice said, "Well, the President is not available to the telephone. Please tell your party that she will have to write a letter or send a telegram."

Not content with her requirement, I asked, "Is there someone else I could talk to there?"

"I can give you an aide," she said, and I was handed over to a friendly, understanding voice.

I said, "I would like an appointment to speak with the President."

"And when would you like to see him?" the voice asked.

"Well, I live in Newton, Massachusetts. I am leaving tomorrow and should be there around April 2. I am walking."

Without missing a beat he said, "And what would you like to talk to him about?"

At this point I told him I would like to speak to him personally about my deep distress about the war and my reasons for walking. He listened politely, then said, "I'll see what I can do. And what did you say your name was?"

I repeated my name. He thanked me. We hung up.

And that was that. I had made my first contact with the White House. At least from that time on, *someone* knew I was coming!

The previous Sunday morning, in our silent meeting for worship in Newton at a friend's house, we had sat in a small circle. It is the custom among Friends for anyone who feels moved to speak, to share inner thoughts, prayers, and insights to do so. Out of the silence Becky spoke. It was the first time I had ever heard her speak in Meeting. She quietly read this poem by Rod McKuen:

Atlas

Do not be afraid
to fall asleep with gypsies
    or run with leopards.

As travelers or highwaymen
we should employ
whatever kind of wheels it takes
to make our lives
    go smoothly down the road.

And if you love somebody
    tell them.
Love is a better roadmap
for trucking down the years
than Rand McNally ever made.*

*see credits page

Later that Sunday, Eloise Houghton of the Committee of Responsibility, also a Friend, came over to the house. The Committee consisted of a group of doctors and others who brought war-damaged children from Vietnam to this country for reconstructive surgery. Eloise let me take along some 8 × 10 pictures of napalm-burned children. Yes, that was one of the things I needed—pictorial proof of the human devastation. We sat around the kitchen table, with Susan also present. Eloise let me choose among many. The sight of those poor disfigured children with their melted flesh, mouths permanently agape, distorted features, made me crumple inside. I looked anew at my daughter Susan, how whole she was, how beautiful. And how I ached for the mothers of those once-perfect children; how I ached for the plight of those children themselves.

Susan looked at those pictures, too. And then she went into the other room and wrote a letter to the editors of *Life* magazine. That letter follows:

14 February, 1971
Life
Rockefeller Center
New York, New York

Dear Sirs:
I write this letter to inform you that my mother, protesting the war in Indo-China, is walking to Washington, D.C. from Newton, Massachusetts. The distance is 450 miles and she is going alone. I have often asked myself how I deserved a mother like this. She is a beautiful woman, strong in her beliefs, and full of love and understanding. Yet, this war, she cannot understand.

Thousands of people have died without knowing why and yet we continue to further the massacres and self destruction to "save" the South Vietnamese. All we have been able to accomplish is to destroy a good portion of that same population which we are trying to "save." To decrease casualties, you pull out or never enter the war instead of finding new borders to invade. Thousands of beautiful Vietnamese children have suffered so incredibly because their skin has melted into grotesque distortions from American napalm. They could have lived normal lives.

We have protested, leafleted, signed petitions, and gathered in rallies. We cry for recognition—not for us—but for our country's mistakes. We are thrown in jails for getting exasperated enough to throw rocks, yet at the same time a soldier in Vietnam is being awarded a medal for killing innocent women and children. What has our country come to? Are we looking for a nuclear war with China? We must stop now in order to save the lives of husbands and sons who would have died in vain.

For these reasons my mother walks. What does she think it will accomplish? Perhaps nothing. But she wants people to realize that the war will not stop by itself.

My mother will leave February 17 th from Newton and hopes to arrive in Washington, D.C. on April 2. She needs support. My love and prayers walk with her. I ask for your support to help her through this difficult journey.

Thank you.

Susan Bruyn

Earlier on the Wednesday I had made the decision to walk, I had called Jim and Jerilyn to tell them I was going to do it. They were elated. Jim offered his services immediately to help plot the course and help contact the news media. When I arrived at the Woodbury's, Jim laid out a map that was specifically Boston to Washington—a National Geographic creation. He took a yo-yo out of his pocket and laid the string in a straight line between Boston and Washington, lifting it up slightly at New York City and Baltimore so I wouldn't try to walk across a piece of the Atlantic Ocean or the Chesapeake Bay. Referring to the string, he found the roads closest to that line and marked destinations at approximately ten-mile intervals. The destinations were then listed consecutively on paper. We now had an itinerary. My arrival time, counting 45 days to cover 450 miles, which included two rest days, would be April 2. I would be arriving in Spring.

ITINERARY OF TRIP TO WASHINGTON
(subject to local change, but essentially accurate)

The following towns are the points of destination to be reached on each date noted below (Unless otherwise indicated, numbers indicate route to the *next* stop.)

February 17—Wed—South Natick, Mass.:

18	Thu	Holliston Rt 16
19	Fri	Mendon Rt 16
20	Sat	E. Douglas Rt 16
21	Sun	Webster Rts 197, 169, 171 (Ct.)
22	Mon	W. Woodstock, Ct Rts. 171, 198 (Ct.) US 44
23	Tue	Warrenville US 44 (alt.)
24	Wed	Storrs Ct. 275, 32 US 6, US 6 (alt.)
25	Thu	Columbia US 6 (alt.)
26	Fri	Marlborough US 66 (alt.)
27	Sat	Cobalt US 66 (alt.) Ct. 17
28	Sun	Durham Ct. 17
March 1	Mon	Northford Ct. 17
2	Tue	New Haven
3	Wed	(Rest Day)
4	Thu	Milford US 1
5	Fri	Fairfield US 1
6	Sat	Westport US 1
7	Sun	Darien US 1
8	Mon	Port Chester, N.Y.
9	Tue	New Rochelle US 1
10	Wed	via Pelham Rd., Shore Rd. and Westchester Ave. to Harlem River, N.Y.C.
11	Thu	via 5th Ave., (Central Park), E.14th St., Lafayette St. Broad St. to Staten Is. Ferry to Saint George
12	Fri	via St. Pauls Ave., Amboy Rd. to lower S.I., possibly Huguenot
13	Sat	via Pleasant Plain Ave., 440 toll bridge, 35 to 127A to 514 to Nixon, N.J
14	Sun	via 514, 27 to Franklin Park below New Brunswick
15	Mon	Princeton in on 27, out on 206
16	Tue	(Rest Day)
17	Wed	Trenton (in on 206, joins alt. 1.)
18	Thu	Penndel, Pennsylvania alt.1, 1
19	Fri	Pennypack Pk, Pa. US 1
20	Sat	Philadelphia

21	Sun	Swarthmore Pa. 320, US 13
22	Mon	Claymont, Del US 13s
23	Tue	Wilmington US 40
24	Wed	Cocks Bridge US 40
25	Thu	Elkton, Md. US 40
26	Fri	Havre de Grace US 40
27	Sat	Belcamp US 40, Silver Spring Rd., 1
28	Sun	Overlea US 1
29	Mon	Baltimore
30	Tue	Waterloo US 1
31	Wed	Laurel US 1
April 1	Thu	College Park US 1
2	Fri	Congress—Office Buildings

It came to me that one of the ways we could extend the action was to write a letter to all of our friends, our "Christmas card list," and tell them what we were doing. (Though written in the first person, in a very real sense it was "we." The entire family was involved.) The letter follows:

Newton Centre, Mass.

14 February 1971

Dear Friends and Relatives –
I feel I must write each of you to tell you my plans.

This Wednesday, February 17, I am leaving our house in Newton, Massachusetts and walking to Washington, D.C. It should take about 45 days to get there. I may arrive around April 2nd, providing I make it.

I am moved to do this because I can no longer sit in the comfort of our beautiful home, knowing the death and destruction we are causing in another land. I cannot separate myself from this though heaven knows I am well insulated. But I know it is my money supporting the war machine, my senators and representatives in Congress approving war measures. People feel so trapped. I felt that I must break my own routine in order to make my protest heard. For me, this is what my action means. I am speaking as strongly as I know how. It is my deep hope that others will be moved to take some action which for *them* is right—as strongly as they know how—to end the war.

None of you needs to have the horrors of the war described. I know of no one who feels the war should continue. Many of you are already engaged in a total commitment to work toward peace. I am trying to reach those who have become anesthetized and feel there is nothing one person can do. I am asking them to look for alternatives, to actively say "*no*" to the death machine which is war, in *their own way*.

In hope, Louise

These documents, the five Theses, the poem "Atlas" read by Becky at our Friends Meeting, Susan's letter to *Life Magazine*, my letter to our Christmas card list, and the itinerary, became the "press packet." It's what would go to all media who inquired about my action and to organizers and hosts whom I would meet on the way.

——•——

Wednesday, right after making the decision at Nancy Strong's house, I began to think about the realities of the trip. What would I wear? What would I carry? How? On the advice of Betty Woodbury and Nancy I went to a mountain climbing supply store that afternoon to get suggestions about the best equipment. I looked at boots and jackets and ponchos and mittens and socks and hats and backpacks. I was told that the best way to plan for a trip that involves all kinds of weather is to dress in thin layers. They showed me their windbreaker—zipper front, attached hood, patch pockets and cuffs with nylon closings and a matching "down sweater" to wear under it. However, the jacket was pale green. It seemed to make the most sense to wear bright orange. If I were going to be walking on a highway, I didn't want to be hit by mistake. I would far rather be a *visible* target. And besides, the jacket and sweater were very expensive. The boots, too, were pricey, though when I told the store-owner what I needed this gear for, he offered to give me a 15% discount. (He, too, was against the war. This was the first evidence of outside support for my action.) However, in my judgment, I needed to look further.

The next day I went to two stores in Cambridge. In one store, I liked a pair of boots, but they were slightly small. The manager called their downtown store and they had the size I wanted. It was a good omen.

Friday I went downtown and bought the boots.

Finally I returned to the first store. I bought the bright orange poncho, three pairs of heavy wool socks, a blue wool cap called a balaclava, which could be pulled down over my face for warmth, and a plastic water bottle. I still couldn't decide about the jacket and "down sweater." It seemed so much to spend. And it wasn't orange.

At home I waltzed around in my new boots with 2" thick soles. I went upstairs to talk to Sev about the jacket and down sweater that were so expensive but had all those wonderful pockets and the hood and the nylon closings.

"Well, you should get them if you need them," he said.

"I don't know. It's just so much to spend...," I worried. "Wait a minute...."

For some reason I went down to the jacket-and-coat-packed closet in the front hall and began to carefully look through everything that was there. There, hanging way over to the right, was a windbreaker, exactly like the one in the store, zipper front, attached hood, patch pockets, and cuffs with nylon closings. And it was orange. I couldn't believe what I saw! How did this jacket get into our closet? I asked the girls. No one knew whose it was. It had apparently been left there early in the fall. I couldn't fathom the amazing coincidence!

And then in our upstairs closet I found my old orange mohair sweater, which I had bought years ago at the Boston Good-Will store for 69 cents. It was perfect, thick and fluffy, lightweight, easily rolled into a small space.

Susan's friend, Bob Beaser, had a lightweight aluminum frame back-pack—color, bright orange—which he offered to lend me for the trip. I was almost all together.

In all of this planning the awful assumption I was making was that I *could* keep walking for 450 miles. Here I had bought a pair of brand new boots! Boots need to be broken in. What if I got blisters? The foot has to toughen up to new boots.

On Sunday, taking the Woodburys' wise counsel, I tested the boots by walking in them for about half a mile around the neighborhood. I got a blister! The boots were too small! And Monday was a holiday!

Luckily a discount store was open on Monday so I bought a pair of sneakers, a size larger than usual to make room for the heavy wool socks that would keep my feet from freezing.

Tuesday I exchanged the boots for a larger size and bought the last item, thermal underwear. My gear was now ready.

———•———

Wednesday was almost upon us. I was leaving the next day. I began to think about the cars that might be around the house the next morning, with our friends from Friends Meeting and the TV trucks. It seemed a good idea to tell the police what was about to happen. I called Officer Charles Feeley, a Newton police officer with whom we had become friendly, to tell him about the traffic tie-up there might be the next morning. When I called him, he already knew about it. I was amazed. He said, "Would you like a few of the men to keep the traffic clear for your walk as you go through Newton?"

"That would be wonderful," I said.

"Since you're one of our people," he said, "we could help you and those walking with you across the intersections at Beacon and Centre Streets, Four Corners, and Washington Street. Then when you cross over to the Wellesley line, our men will radio to the Wellesley police and they can take care of you from there."

"Thank you," I said, my heart full.

Then he said, "Would you like a letter of introduction to any police department along the way? A letter telling who you are?"

I couldn't believe the support! "Yes," I said, "that would be beautiful!"

He said he would bring it the next morning.

"Proceed as way opens"
—An old Quaker saying

Week One

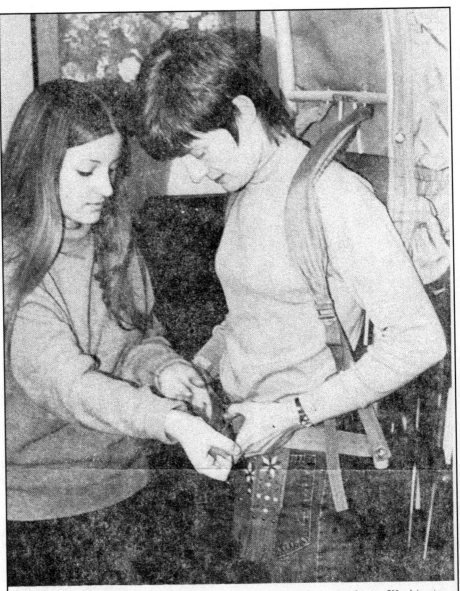

ОME HELP — Daughter Susan helps rs. Louise Bruyn with knapsack in preparation for march to Washington today. (Herb Capwell photo)

Boston Globe, February 17, 1971

Secretary of Defense Melvin R. Laird advised President Nixon and members of the Cabinet today to expect 'some tough days ahead' in the allied effort to cut the Ho Chi Minh Trail supply line in southern Laos....Missile sites in North Vietnam attacked for the 3rd day in a row.

—*New York Times, Wednesday, February 17, 1971*

Day

Newton to South Natick, Massachusetts

1

Wed, Feb 17

I was awake before six. The morning had finally come. I had slept pretty well with the help of an antihistamine pill, which Jerilyn had given me. Jim fixed a breakfast of scrambled eggs and toast. I tried to eat, but my stomach was in a knot. Somehow the food didn't want to go down. After breakfast I tried on my thermal underwear for the first time. It had been washed and dried in the dryer. Instead of shrinking, as I thought it would, the bottoms remained too long-waisted and the shirt hung too low, so about 8:00 a.m. I was at the sewing machine, adjusting the length. How typical, I thought: at the last minute doing something at the sewing machine.

I had packed my backpack the night before and just needed to tuck in the last few items that morning. It contained one change of clothes which amounted to one blue turtleneck T-shirt and underwear. I would be wearing my blue jeans. I had packed two pairs of wool socks and wore the third pair. I included a nightgown, toiletries, Band-Aids and moleskin for any blisters, scissors to cut the moleskin, the orange poncho and my water bottle. The Priors and Woodburys had given me some trail mix. Also, I had packed the pictures of napalm-burned children, the documents our family had put together with several copies of the Five Theses petition, and the map of the route to D.C. And I had packed my boots. I wasn't too worried about whether I would forget something. I knew I would not be too far from home the first night. Ten miles. That was only a fifteen-minute drive. But for me it would be an all day walk.

There was a knock at the door before 9:00 a.m. It was Officer Charles Feeley. He handed me the letter from the police department, signed by Chief Quinn. It read:

City of Newton Police Department

Office of the Chief of Police

TO WHOM IT MAY CONCERN:

This is to introduce MRS. LOUISE BRUYN of 48 Glenwood Avenue, Newton Centre, Massachusetts, who is of fine moral character—citizen, wife and mother, of our community.

Any consideration or assistance shown to MRS. BRUYN will be appreciated.

Very truly yours,

(Signed)

William F. Quinn
Chief of Police

I thanked him from the bottom of my heart. That treasured letter went into my pack.

When the Friends had planned a Meeting for Worship at our house, I had wondered to myself whether I could sit still for that hour before leaving. Yet, as the Friends began arriving at the house, I found that I was really looking forward to it. We sat in a circle in our living room with about 30 people from Meeting. When we all settled down into silence, I experienced such a sense of serenity. Instead of feeling nervous, I felt held by the Meeting. I felt a deep peace within me, a beautiful sense of an expanded spirit. I felt lifted up into a new awareness of what it meant to be human. It was like seeing the edge of an opening. I was not taking my humanness, or anyone else's, for granted—in that room or anywhere else in the world. I felt the unity of the whole spirit of humankind in a way in which I had never before been aware.

Out of the silence, in the tradition of Friends, Molly Gregory spoke. In her droll way, she said she was thinking about flies in a flytrap, how, in order to get out, the fly must find the small hole and walk out through the narrow way. "We are all in a flytrap and one of us has found a way out."

The silence continued until Elmer Brown offered a message based on the beautiful statement by George Fox, the founder of the Society of Friends, or Quakers, "…let us walk cheerfully over the world answering that of God in every one."

Other words I heard and remembered coming into that silence came from Barbara Cummings: "You have love enough."

After about forty-five minutes came the handshake that closes every Meeting.

The time had come. I must really leave. The media had pulled up outside and had waited there while we were Meeting, given Sev's insistence that they not press in. But now they were inside. I withdrew to the second floor to put on my "longies" under my jeans, to put on my jacket, pack, and blue hat. Susan had made my black armband during meeting, which she felt she couldn't sit through. She now helped me put it around my left arm. I was ready. Coming down the stairs with the TV cameras rolling and reporters asking questions, with everyone waiting in the first floor hall for me to appear, it was like being a bride. Someone even mentioned that it was like a wedding.

Finally I was out the door, accompanied by the many Friends, and friends who had joined in the Meeting for Worship. I had actually made it down the three steps to the walkway without slipping and breaking my ankle, a nagging fear I had had since I first announced my plans!

The weather couldn't have been more beautiful for February— sunny—a clear blue sky. There were mounds of snow-ice along the edges of the sidewalks and roads, but the walkways themselves were clear, except for some melting because of the sun's warmth.

The photographers from the newspapers took a few pictures in front of the house. Then as we were walking down Parker Street toward Beacon Street, one of them shouted at me, "Mrs. Bruyn, the sun's not in your face. Would you mind walking in the other direction?" Obligingly, I crossed the street and walked in the other direction for a few yards. It wasn't good enough. He wanted me to do it again. And again. I had had no experience with the way media people liked to set up their shots, even when action is underway. I was to learn a lot about them as I went along.

There were perhaps twenty to twenty-five people with us as far as Newton Centre. Then most of them turned back. Twelve to fifteen stayed with me as we proceeded west on Beacon Street. I dropped back in line after a few more blocks to walk with my friend, Pat Simon, and another newsman shouted at me, "Stay at the head of the line! Stay at the head of the line!"

I looked at him, shocked, and shot back, "Whose walk is this?" and kept walking with Pat.

We took our first rest break at Chestnut Street under the pines. The ground was damp, but it felt good to sit down. Suddenly, four members of the Legal In-Service Project drove up, Doug among them. They stayed just long enough to wish me well and went on.

Sandy Latner, a long time activist on issues of peace and justice, was one of those who was walking with me. He had been at the party the previous Sunday night when I had made the announcement of my intended walk. He had stung me with his comment, "Louise, why don't you immolate yourself as well." He was referring to the protest actions of Norman Morrison, a Quaker, who had burned himself to death in front of the Pentagon in 1965 and to several Buddhist monks in Vietnam as well, by pouring gasoline on themselves and lighting a match.

I had thought deeply about his comment. So now, with him walking beside me, I told him that I wanted him to know I did not feel I was being a martyr. I felt that this was a creative act, a positive response in the face of a need to act. Walking, after all, was a healthy thing. I was not destroying myself. I would not push myself further than I could go. I would be reaching out to others around me, trying to persuade them to take stronger actions than they had in the past. He seemed to be relieved; at least my explanation seemed rational. He was such a dedicated person himself, working just about full time for peace and civil rights, that he would not take anything false from anyone else. But I felt his support. He was, after all, walking with me.

At the intersection of Route 16 and Route 9 almost everyone left. There was just Pat and Wendy (her 16-year-old daughter), Louise Landy, Gail Woodbury (Chuck and Betty's daughter), and my Susan. Our press friends were still following us but soon stopped trying. They seemed bewildered at the logistics of keeping up with our progress while not walking themselves.

We stopped in Mister Donut for a coffee break and had our first

encounter with a young man at the counter who had been in the
Marines. He said our forces belonged in Vietnam to protect the South
Vietnamese from being overrun by the Communists. But though he
was saying these things, there was something in his manner that I felt
belied his words, that he felt deep down that we didn't belong there,
that it wasn't right for us to have helped keep the South from holding
elections in which Ho Chi Minh would have won. He was soft-spoken,
courteous, "patriotic," but when faced with the moral question of so
many lives, both theirs and ours, and for what, he was quiet. He didn't
know either. How does an ex-Marine protest?

We continued our walk. Passing a church in Wellesley we noticed a
sign on the outdoor announcement board: "Hope is the art of persever-
ance." Ah, yes, just what I needed.

I was beginning to feel the muscular strain of the continual pace. The
muscle that felt it the most was the one in front connecting my thigh
with my hip bone, the one that had to keep lifting the leg up, step after
step. I carried the pack some of the time, but my friends and daughter
carried it for me most of the time, so my initiation into the rigors of
managing it myself was gentle.

We arrived at our destination in South Natick. Rebecca met us there
with our VW bus and drove me to my first haven for the night. We
had arrived earlier than the Hams had expected, but they were most
cordial and welcoming. The evening was in a sense unique—being the
first in what was to become forty-five such evenings. I felt strange, out
of place, vulnerable. I took off my sneakers and padded around in my
heavy wool socks. I put the pack in the bedroom they had cleared for
me. It was while going through the pack that I found some of the nourishment packed for me by my friends. Food for the soul. Written on one
envelope:

Onward…!
    Our orange hope
        Our super lady-bug…
            Travel well, feel full of love—we love you.

And tucked inside the envelope, a poem:

> The weight of the world
> > is love.
> Under the burden
> > of solitude,
> under the burden
> of dissatisfaction
> the weight
> the weight we carry
> > is love.
>
> Who can deny?
> In dreams
> it touches
> the body,
> in thought
> constructs
> a miracle
> in imagination
> anguishes
> till born
> in human ——

"Song" by Allen Ginsberg

for your way... Carry on! Jerilyn

The Hams' children were so beautiful—preschool through upper grades—five of them. The house was charming, colonial, cozy, warm, clean. I couldn't help but think that what these children had was every child's right. All children should be raised as I sensed these were, fed with love and kindness and plenty of food, their thoughts and feelings listened to.

Sev arrived for a short stay with information about where I was to sleep the next night. When I left our house I knew where I would be the first and second nights, but there was still no third night's housing.

At six o'clock we watched the news. Now *there* was a strange feeling! We caught two of the three TV channels that had covered my walk. Each one handled it in a sensitive manner. Even though I looked strange to myself and sounded like someone else, I felt the message was getting across. The message was that the war had reached inhuman proportions, and that we had to begin acting human again. We had to be willing to change our pattern of living, to break out of the mold, to change our direction before any change would happen in our country.

Later that evening I made the promised call to Joe Clementi of WHDH for an interview, the first of the many interviews that would take place during the walk. I have no memory of what was said.

Bedtime soon arrived. I showered and bedded down for the night. I felt strangely alone, yet very held by those around me. I felt small but stronger than I had ever felt before. It didn't take long before I fell sound asleep.

First Lieutenant William L Calley, Jr. has been "charged with the premeditated murder of at least 102 unarmed men, women, and children in the tiny South Vietnamese hamlet three years ago..." [His] chief counsel...said today that the lieutenant did not feel he was killing 'humans' when he ordered and participated in the execution of two groups of Vietnamese civilians at Mylai. "...he believed he was following orders to destroy all living things in the village."

—New York Times, Thursday, February 18, 1971

Day

South Natick to Holliston, Massachusetts 2

Thurs, Feb 18

There was a light snow covering the ground when I got up. I wondered— how much snow would I have to walk through? It would be a good day for my boots. It was strange to again be putting on the thermal underwear, the blue turtleneck T shirt, the blue jeans, the clean pair of heavy wool socks. I had no choices to make in clothing. I brushed my teeth and took my Vitamin C. Rudman Ham cooked a breakfast of hotcakes, bacon, and syrup. But around the fringes of the pleasure was anxiety, both a sense of adventure and a fear of the unknown. The Hams then had to leave before I did.

Getting a plastic bag for each sneaker so I could store them in my pack, I saw a quote taped to their cupboard.

> *To thine own self be true,*
> *Baby, do thy thing.*

I read it as a confirmation of my action.

At 9:05 I put on the pack, walked out the door and began putting one foot before the other, leaving footprints in the light snow—the heavy tread of mountain boots.

Within a few short blocks I arrived at the South Natick Pharmacy on Route 16. There were the two newsmen—the reporter and the photographer from the *Herald Traveler*. They wanted a picture. I explained

34

that I had to put another Band-Aid on my foot because of a blister and would be taking off my boot in the pharmacy. "Ah," they said, "that will be our picture!"

My daughter Susan and Gail Woodbury arrived about 9:30 as planned. With about four men at the counter, a woman shopping in an aisle, and the three of us who had just entered, the pharmacist said, "We haven't had anything this exciting happen in ten years!"

One of the older men, perhaps about 60, said, "If you get into Holliston after 5:00 p.m. you could rest at the VFW where I work."

"Thank you," I said. "I would love to do that, but I will probably arrive there about 3:00."

I was applying more moleskin to my heel when the woman came up to me and handed me a package of moleskin, which she had just bought. "My contribution," she said, smiling.

The photographer took several pictures of my foot. "Hold it up this way, turn it out just a little, now smile." (click) "Let's get one more." (click)

Sue and Gail and I began walking on Highway 16 about 9:30. The newsmen followed in their car for two blocks. Next thing I knew the photographer was handing me a cup of coffee asking if I would sip it while he took a shot. I didn't want the coffee, but obliged while they took the picture that would make it seem as if he had caught me a couple of hours later. And now my blister was acting up. I needed more moleskin but couldn't find my scissors. I must have left them in the pharmacy. I waited while the photographer drove all of two blocks back to get them. He arrived some minutes later, not with *my* scissors, but with some new ones, which he said he talked the pharmacist into giving me as the pharmacist's "contribution."

With all the patching up of my feet, I still couldn't wear those boots more than a few more blocks. I had to put the sneakers back on. My heels were too sensitive and I didn't want to chance breaking the blisters.

Gail carried the pack much of that day. She had such a good long stride. She'd start at our pace and soon be far out in front, realize it, turn around and wait, getting in a few digs about what good shape *she* was in!

Ever since Susan was old enough to walk, she walked behind me whenever we went anywhere. If I slowed my pace she would slow hers. I could wait for her to catch up, we'd start together again, and she would slow down again. If I kept up my pace she would keep the same ten paces or so behind me. This time, when she told me she wanted to walk with me, she said, "Mom, you will never have to turn around and say 'Come on, Sue.'" And it was so. In all the days she walked with me, she either kept up with me or stayed ahead of me. She made it a point to never fall behind. And she didn't seem to mind slogging through the puddles from sun-melted snow with her too-long and dragging jeans. She had rain boots on.

At the intersection of Rts.16 and 27 a car filled with teenagers stopped. They wanted to know if I were "that lady walking to Washington." They wanted to know why I was doing it. I told them my feelings about the war, about how it had become so inhuman, and urged them to learn more about what was happening in Indo-China. They drove on, wishing me luck.

We all looked for the address of a place we were to have lunch, and finally stopped in the police station in Sherborn to make a phone call ahead. We found out we still had 45 minutes or more walking to do. Though I hadn't told the policeman who we were, he knew. We had a conversation, but not about the war… Somehow, I couldn't mention it. I kicked myself later for missing the opportunity. He was a returned Marine who really liked police work in a small community.

Finally, finally! we reached Betsy Johnson's house, the lunch stop for the day. It was about 1:15. Sue was so tired she actually fell asleep in the chair. We decided to call Gail's mother from there to pick up both girls and I would walk on to Holliston myself.

I wanted to communicate to Betsy how I felt about the war. Introducing the subject into a conversation was very difficult for me. I felt the most comfortable handing her a flyer I had with me from "Another Mother for Peace."

After Betty Woodbury picked up both girls, I left, striding on this time completely alone.

Two teenage girls ran out of their house as I passed. They asked if I were "that woman." Did I need a rest stop? A glass of water? Then, "But I don't understand. Why are you doing this?" I gave a similar answer as I had to the last group of teenagers and walked on.

It was then that I thought through the "whys" more carefully. I was walking first of all because it demanded a commitment from me. It involved physical and emotional energy focused for a period of 45 days on the war; during that time I would be growing. I would learn more facts, do more thinking, face the challenge of speaking to every kind of person. Secondly, I was affecting the people around me. By talking with them personally and through the news media, there was the possibility of influencing them to take stronger actions themselves against the war. And third, it was a visible protest to Washington. The government could *see* it, infinitesimal as it was. They knew *someone* was protesting.

I finally came into the town of Holliston. Meeting me were Norma Rae Wachs, my host for the evening, and her friend and her daughter. I walked about one block with them and we were at Norma Rae's house.

She had several friends in for tea and we chatted in an informal way. One of the friends handed me something she had written about the Blacks, in support of the Black Panthers against the "Super-rich." It was so full of hate. It was my first contact on this trip with the depth of hate that can exist in people. Though she didn't express it in the conversation with me, her writing fairly shouted with it. Though I understood, to the degree I could at the time, the depth of rage felt by African-Americans who had suffered such injustice over not just years, but centuries, the fanning of those flames by a white woman felt facile to me. The writing pointed to the "Super-rich" as the culprits of oppression rather than looking at our own role in continuing the racism, or the institutions perpetuating oppression. But...I didn't say anything. I just recoiled inside.

Finally I went upstairs about 5:00 for a hot shower and washed my hair. It felt so good. I put on some fresh Band-Aids and moleskin. Dinner was elegant—broiled chicken, rice, peas, wine, salad—a gourmet meal. Norma Rae's husband woke up for dinner; he worked nights. Sev came again for a few minutes. The big unknown remained: where would I stay the next night? We left the solution for the next morning.

Secretary of Defense Laird is concerned that… "the military at times has been overzealous in spying of anti-war and civil rights leaders…

United States command reported today that 51 Americans were killed in combat last week in Indochina, double of previous week's toll of 24. Wounded were 217, previous week 367. Since Jan. 1, '61 — 44,459 killed, 294,946 wounded. South Vietnamese battle deaths — 120,011. Reported enemy toll — 701,058.

—New York Times, Friday, February 19, 1971

Day

3

Holliston to Mendon, Massachusetts

Fri, Feb 19

After breakfast we called a number of places trying to find where I would stay in Mendon. Church numbers didn't answer. Names of ministers weren't available in the directory. Still without knowing where I'd stay that night, I prepared to go.

A reporter from the *Christian Science Monitor* arrived at the house at 9:30 for a prearranged interview. We talked until about 10:00, after which we began the day's walk. Joining us for a short distance were Norma Rae's neighbor and daughter, as well as Norma Rae. We met up with Lani and Rebecca who took over walking with me from that point. The three of us walked on through Milford, a charming big-little town. The sun was bright. The weather was so warm we opened our coats. We passed stone walls hung with ice sheaths sparkling in the sun. We could lift them off, hold them up to the light, see through them, and then watch them crumble.

We had been told by a reporter to stop in at the newspaper in Milford. We did, and when they found out who we were they said, with extra energy in their voices, that we should sit down. They reacted to us as if they had just captured a bird and didn't want it to escape. When the photographer finally arrived he said, "Where were you!! I've traveled 40 miles looking for you." We explained we had stopped at Papagino's for lunch. He said something about chaining me to the chair—I hoped all in good humor.

Accompanied by her daughter Rebecca, left, and a friend, Lani Nolan, Mrs. Louise Bruyn is shown on trek through Milford yesterday. (Daily News Photo by John Lemish)

'Right On" To Washington, D. C.

War Protest Mother Leaves
Mendon On 420-Mile Walkathon

We went outside and obliged him by walking toward the camera three or four times, coats open, feeling full of Spring even though it was only Feb. 19.

Becky had received instructions to go on ahead to Mendon and try to find a hotel or church…somewhere I could stay.

Meanwhile, at home the organizing had begun in earnest. Jessie Jones, who had been sitting next to me during Friends Meeting for Business when I had announced what I was about to do, became the linchpin in the effort. She came to our house back in Newton every day, and arranged for coordinators for each state who became responsible for finding host families for me while in that state. She and my husband sent out mailings to all hosts to ask them to pick me up at my ending location, allow me a bath or shower and some rest time, arrange for media coverage in the area if possible, feed me dinner, arrange for a possible meeting with friends—anything that could possibly extend the message, get me to bed, feed me breakfast in the morning, and take me back to the same place they had picked me up. My job was to phone each host when reaching my day's destination and to call home before going to bed at night. At that time I would be told my contact for the next day.

Jessie was a God-send. She and my daughters and husband answered the phone (he needed to put in a second line), answered letters, and in a thousand ways, made the walk work, made it go smoothly.

And this being only the third day, Rebecca was sent on to find me a host for that evening. A place materialized and I don't remember how. I was to stay with the Coopers. Sue Cooper was to meet me at Lowell's Ice Cream Parlor.

It had gotten colder and I was alone again. I walked on to the ice cream parlor. Before Sue Cooper came in I had a cup of hot coffee and as I sat in a booth, I heard a young man at the counter say to another something about "protesting the Indo-China War." I turned around and then he said, "Are you the woman walking to protest the war?"

"Yes," I said.

We exchanged a few words. He was against the war, too. He mentioned something about being drafted soon.

"Do you know about draft counseling?" I asked.

He didn't, but said, "I don't want to do anything that's against the law."

I told him that draft counseling was entirely legal; often there were things in the law that people didn't know about. He could find out what his options were if he saw a draft counselor.

He didn't know of one in the area, so I suggested the American Friends Service Committee in Cambridge (AFSC). Not content with that, I wrote the address on a sheet from my tiny notebook and passed it on to him.

A reporter from the Milford paper then came in looking for me. I could tell from his questioning that he was centering on my physical being, blisters, etc. In fact, it seemed like he was completely in the dark about my action and started from scratch. Did I have any children? What was I walking for? Where was I from? I could also sense that he was a "Nixon man." He responded very defensively. "We have to support our President."

"Where are you staying? Are you staying with the Coopers?" he asked.

"I can't say unless I clear with my hostess," I answered.

Just then Sue Cooper walked in, and gave her permission to be identified. I found it interesting that in this small town the Coopers were generally known to be the people who would most probably put me up.

As we planned for the next day, Sue asked if I were a purist and would I want to be dropped off in the morning back in Mendon, or would Uxbridge do. Her house was between those two towns. This would be a short-cut for me of two miles. I had a negative idea of what a "purist" was: someone who wanted to be good or perfect for shallow reasons. And under that was the sense that somehow Uxbridge would be easier for her and I didn't want to put her out. Therefore, my initial reaction was, "Uxbridge would be fine. No, I'm not a purist."

Later in the afternoon when I called Sev, I told him what I had agreed to and didn't feel good about. We talked it over; he advised me to be firm on taking no shortcut rides. I was glad for his advice. It clarified my thinking. I knew I was involved in an inner discipline. If I had wanted to ride, I could have hitchhiked. I could even have flown, and would have made it much faster, at much less effort to myself. And where would my commitment to this action have been? I was involved in something deeper than just getting myself from one point to another. I would abide by the discipline of the task. Sue agreed to drive me back to Mendon in the morning. (Miles down the road I would face other times when people offered me rides, and their finding it hard to understand why I wouldn't accept their offers, but I never wavered again.)

Sue Cooper had made arrangements with a photographer to take pictures before we got to her home. We stopped at the highway sign in Uxbridge that pointed the way to the next town and posed with Sue helping me on with the pack. After the pictures were taken we went to her house.

While there I had a long interview with a reporter from the *Woonsocket Call*. He was a friend of the Coopers. He was very responsive to my whole action and did a beautiful job putting in all the information I asked him to. I told him how important it was to report the reasons for my walk, the napalm burning of villagers, old and young, the birth defects caused by defoliation chemicals, the percentage of arable land now sprayed with defoliants or pocked with bomb craters, the number of dead, wounded.

Henry Cooper, Sue's husband, walked in—tall, warm, gracious. Sue introduced us. He was welcoming. Then Sue explained who I was and what I was doing. His face brightened and he hugged me. He was delighted. He said he had heard about me but hadn't realized that I would be staying with them.

While walking during the last few days, I realized I needed more factual information. With the number of interviews that had already taken place, I knew I had a tremendous opportunity to get information to the public about our actions in Vietnam. In my nightly calls home I asked for information to be sent to me. Among the materials which I had received was a booklet written by the Stanford Biology Study Group (an ad hoc organization of some members of the Department of Biological Sciences at Stanford University). I had just read the paragraph about the circular reasoning of our government:

> American troops were sent to Southeast Asia...to protect the interests of the Vietnamese people. The destruction of the Vietnamese and their environment is unfortunate...but necessary to protect the lives of American troops in wartime.[1]

Then the phone rang. It was a radio talk show MC wanting to tape an interview for his station. I was fortified with my new information. I had the book right there, paraphrasing, as we discussed facts about the war, such as these:

> The U.S. Army admits to having sprayed defoliants over 500,000 acres of South Vietnamese crops through 1969. (The Japan Science Council claimed 3,800,000 acres of arable acres ruined.)

---

1 Stanford Biology Study Group, *The Destruction of Indochina; A Legacy of our Presence*, Stanford, California, 94305, copyright 1970, p.8.

The "resource denial" program (agricultural and ecological destruction in Vietnam) which the U.S. Army justifies, denies food to civilians and soldiers in "Viet Cong-held areas." This policy of deliberate starvation, which is hardest on children, the elderly, and pregnant and lactating women, is against the Nuremberg Principles which the United States helped establish and has formally accepted. 2,4,5-T, (comprising 50 percent of Agent Orange) had never been tested for birth-defect effects. In 1967, Saigon newspapers reported on increasingly common birth defects. The papers that questioned whether defoliation caused this were closed by the Thieu government.

The U.S. has dropped far more bombs in Vietnam than were dropped by the Allied Forces in World War II. In 1967–1968, more than 3,500,000 bombs (500–750 pounds each) were dropped in Vietnam. Were these craters (45 feet across and 30 feet deep) placed end to end, they would form a ditch 30,000 miles long—a distance greater than the circumference of the earth.[2]

The interviews over, I was able to bathe and rest before dinner. The moleskin did not cling too well after the third day. My body was weary and my feet were tender.

The Coopers had invited guests to come in that evening. Sue prepared a tray of peanuts and sherry and it felt like we were having a party, except that I was still dressed in my jeans and the guests didn't come. No matter. We had time to talk about important things, and got to know each other a bit better.

I wrote in my journal that this was the hardest day.

It was the 3rd day of strenuous walking and my muscles ached. I felt a deep exhaustion, but not much different than after the 3rd day of strenuous dance classes. The thing that still bugs me is waking up in the morning about 7:00 and beginning to think. Then my heart begins to beat like a trip hammer. It's been helpful to have learned the principles of relaxation in my earlier days, because I can almost relax all my muscles, such as when I have just arrived somewhere, have taken a hot bath, and am lying down. I completely let each muscle go—until I get to my heart—and then I think "it's going to stop." I say to myself, "It's going to stop. That's it. I've had it. I'm going to die right in this bed." But the fool thing keeps tripping away and

---

2 Ibid; pp.4, 5, 6.

sure enough I am able to get up off the bed to either eat dinner or breakfast. Evenings are better than mornings. I feel safe. Harbored for the night.

It was as I was walking on Friday that an image kept appearing far in the back of my mind. When I realized that the image kept returning, I looked at it full-square. It was that of a housewife using wooden clothespins to hang clothes on an electric high-tension wire. That's all it was. But when I looked at it head-on I could see what it was telling me. I became aware of the internal tension and the external danger. Here I was, "Newton housewife, mother of three teenagers" (my media tag), having the gall to walk to the seat of my government and tell my representatives and everyone on the way of my deep distress concerning our foreign policy. I knew the inherent danger, and the inner tension I had to accept. The only thing I became more aware of was that I couldn't let the internal and external tension get in the way of what I had to do. It must not bottle me up or exhaust me.

I heard through my phone call home that Susan, my daughter, had received an obscene phone call. She didn't want to talk about it. And I couldn't help her from a distance.

Senator Mike Mansfield, the Senate Democratic leader, said today that South Vietnam's operation in Laos represented a "military gamble" that could lead to an extended, broadened war in Indochina.

—*New York Times, Saturday, February 20, 1971*

Mendon to East Douglas, Massachusetts 4

Henry Cooper had worked as hard as he could to soften my boots. He rubbed them with saddle soap and worked the heels back and forth. I knew that would be a rainy day, and figured I'd need them, especially if it got very cold.

Sue Cooper drove me back to Mendon to Lowell's Ice-cream Parlor. Being Saturday, that would be the day Pat Simon, my friend from Brookline, would walk with me. She taught school all week and was only able to get away on the weekends. Sure enough she arrived at the ice-cream parlor around 9:30 and we started off.

Pat had three daughters, and her firstborn was a son. Pat's son, David, had joined the army in late 1966. He was sent to Vietnam, and in January of 1968, three weeks after he arrived, he was killed, two days before his 19th birthday. Pat felt that she had to find a way to counter such violence, such waste of precious life. She had been active against the war since 1966, had tried to find a way for David to become a conscientious objector, but, too late. He was shipped out ahead of schedule due to heavy American loss. One of the arguments used to continue the war was, what would you tell the parents of a son killed in the war that their son had died in vain? Pat felt that the only response that made sense was to acknowledge that we Americans had been misinformed about the war, and that we must work to end it as soon as possible, giving meaning to their deaths.

45

As we walked together in the cold and the drizzle, we talked about this issue, and her conviction grew that she needed to speak out as a Gold Star Mother, with the unique perspective of one who had experienced the painful loss, but who was against the continuation of the war.

Henry joined us a little later down the road. He wanted to introduce me to the "gas station-man" along Route 16. As we stopped there, about 10:30, a man driving in the opposite direction from that in which we had been walking, screeched to a halt and shouted, "Hey, do you want a cup of coffee?" It was the same man who had called to me from the ice-cream store the day before. Henry, Pat, and I looked at each other, at our watches, and called back, "Sure. Sounds great!" At that the man put the car in reverse, driving backward into oncoming traffic, which swerved to avoid hitting him. I held my head and shouted "Jesus!" A second later he was driving forward up a little driveway to a Ford Motor tractor sales place. We brought ourselves out of shock and ran across the road to join him in the sales room where he hosted us for a charming kaffee-klatch including the salesmen and parts-department men. Our host was most gracious. The coffee—excellent, just what we needed on this cold, damp day. (The Reverend Henry Cooper commented that the driving of our host had caused me to pray.)

These men seemed to be Nixon backers. I think they were more taken with the aura of publicity that surrounded my action than with the need for the action itself. My main message to these gentlemen was that if they had elected Nixon with the idea that he would bring peace—a platform on which he ran—and he was expanding the war instead, then they needed to write to him to tell him they expected more from him.

This had been perplexing to me—how to reach everybody. My rational side knew this was impossible. But my idealistic side said that everybody could be reached. No one was hopeless (though they might be without hope). Everyone had within him or herself the power to discern right from wrong, good from evil. Everyone agreed that murder is wrong, and if some action is proved to be murder, one could assume that people would be against that action. Here was the hitch. It was hard to convince some people that our action in Indo-China was like murder. Thinking got clouded over with defensiveness involving "patriotism" and with fear of "Communism." Secondly, if people were convinced that our action in Indo-China was equivalent to murder, they still might not take action to stop it. What to do, what to do. I could only proceed on the principle of "speaking to that of God in every one."

Our kaffee-klatch over, we strode on. What started to be a drizzle turned out to be a steady rain. We avoided as many puddles as possible. It was lucky that we had to go through Uxbridge again. The Cooper's house was available for lunch and drying out our clothes. I stripped down to the nub so that the dryer could take away the dampness of my rain-soaked clothing. I found out for the first time that my orange windbreaker was just that—a windbreaker and nothing else. It didn't repel rain. By myself for the rest of the day's walk, I wore my poncho, but by then the rain became a drizzle again and finally dissipated completely, just remaining cold, damp, and ugly.

When I reached a pharmacy in East Douglas, I called the Majeaus, my next hosts. Del Majeau came to pick me up. We had a ten-minute drive on a woodsy road through some snow until we reached a lovely cabin on the edge of a lake, the last cabin on the road. It was a winterized cottage, once having many rooms, but now spacious with living areas defined by rugs or furniture arrangements and exposed stairs descending into the main living area. It had a huge stone hearth, a modern kitchen area, and warm colonial furnishings. The view through three large windows was of an ice-covered lake, slightly misted over, and a large pine tree close to the house. What a joy it had to be to call this place "home."

Del showed me to the newly remodeled bathroom on the second floor where I relaxed again in a tub of hot, hot water, soaking the ache out of my feet. I rested a few minutes on the bed and then went about my business of calling home, calling ahead, and preparing to call Howard Nelson at WEEI at a Boston radio station with whom I had a Saturday night "date."

I called Howard at 7 p.m. so he would know what number to call when he called me at 7:30. He was very warm and supportive. This was the first talk show I had ever been on. I spent half an hour, 7:30–8:00, responding to questions.

A twelve-year-old called in and said, "I don't understand. How are you going to walk to Washington?" I told him that you just put one foot in front of the other.

A man asked about our commitment to South Vietnam. "We have to stand by our commitments to other nations." I asked him if he believed in democracy. If so, why were we fighting a war based on our commitment to a government that had the support of only 20% of the population at the time and that government had since fallen? His whole argument was based on the domino theory and the need to stand by our commitments.

An 84-year-old woman, with a grand Boston accent, called to praise my action and to suggest that every woman in the United States ought to write the President and ask him to see me. I agreed. (A beautiful idea!)

One woman called in but the only word I heard was "Stupid..." and she hung up. Howard Nelson identified her as a "Hit and run."

Another woman with a heavy accent spoke of our need to work through the United Nations.

As I waited during commercials or while listening to questions I would go into a state of complete shakes...not just my hands and extremities, but my whole body. As I spoke, in a voice that belied my inner state, my shaking would stop. After a half hour of this, finally signing off, I threw myself onto the couch and sobbed and sobbed. I could not get over the sense of responsibility I felt, the extension of power that was a result of my singular action. It was frightening. And I felt so vulnerable.

After about ten minutes of letting the emotion go, of unwinding the cables of tension that had tied me in knots, I was finally ready to sit down to supper with the family. Joe and Del and their young bearded son were so warm, kind, understanding; I felt like such a fool for having cried.

During dinner, a friend of theirs called and wanted to talk to me. He was a minister, Rev. Jack Daniels from Franklin. We had a lovely conversation. He was very supportive. Five minutes after we hung up he called back. He said, "You know, I've always had in mind that this war was going to have an O. Henry ending."

"What do you mean?" I asked.

He responded, "Unusual, unexpected. I was just thinking. Maybe your walk is it!"

Wouldn't that be great, I thought. I knew at the time it was not likely to be so, but how we will grasp at a straw. How we continue to work and to hope.

A "human error" yesterday put Americans on an emergency alert of the type that would be used in a nuclear attack. It was 40 minutes before the error was cleared up. The message contained the code word "hatefulness," which was to be used only in the event of a real alert...

The error occurred when a civilian operator at the center put on the wire a tape for a real alert instead of a test tape.

—*New York Times, Sunday, February 21, 1971*

East Douglas to Webster, Massachusetts

Day

5

Sun, Feb 21

That day felt like a party and a picnic rolled into one. In East Douglas I was met by Valerie, her friend Pete Kelsey and others. Chuck Woodbury arrived with his dog Tyson. He brought with him a poem from his wife Betty:

Dear Louise, We're with you in thought and loving you through the rain—hoping you'll feel sometimes like ignoring a "made" itinerary and doing your own when you don't want to walk two or four hours in the rain. Here's a Hindu poem I once sent Phil and would like you to know.

Sometimes naked
Sometimes mad,
Now as a scholar,
Now as a fool,
Thus they appear
on earth—
The free men!

Betty Woodbury

I carried the pack for about four-and-one-half blocks leaving East Douglas and after that, friends carried it for me until the very end when we reached Webster. A total of 18 people and one dog walked with me this Sunday. The road was clear, though a light snow drifted down later, just enough to make tracks. It was cold. And kept getting colder. I pulled the edge of my blue woolen cap down over my face and neck and tucked the bottom edge into my jacket neck. The black leather gloves, lined with wool, were not enough to keep my hands warm, but when I pulled an extra set of heavy wool socks over them I could feel the warmth radiating back into my fingers and palms. I wore my boots, plus two pair of wool socks on my feet. As long as I kept walking, I was warm. The road ran through a woodsy setting. The trees were bare with some snow still caught in the branches.

Someone expressed the concern that I might be feeling pressured by all the people along with me. It's true that I felt like a hostess, like it was a party at our house. I wanted people to meet each other, and wanted to spend some time with each person who had devoted that day to walk with me. I knew it was the idea, the war protest, they were walking for, not me as a person, but still felt personally responsible for them, checking to see that we weren't losing anyone, apologizing if I stopped to adjust my boot laces, or for walking too far ahead.

Photo by Henry Baker

A party and a picnic! Del Majeau, Pete Kelsey, Valerie Kreutzer, Louise and friend.

About noon we stopped in the woods, dusted the snow off rocks and pieces of wood, and sat down to eat our lunch. It was at this point that I got *really* cold, and my fingers felt like they would have become frost-bitten had I stopped by myself for that lunch in the woods. Del Majeau drove up with some hot coffee for all, a real treat, and I climbed in the car to thaw out. The cup of hot coffee was welcome not only to my innards, but to my fingers. After about a thirty-minute stop we trudged on again, happy to all be together.

We talked about the war, and what we all could do. I also remember that many people expressed the sense that they were gaining a new perspective, just through the process of walking. We all saw brooks, branches, birds, that we never would have seen had we been traveling any other way. The process of walking itself made us feel more human.

Ritchie Lowry, a colleague of Sev's at Boston College, drove up with his son and daughter, Peter and Robin. He had heard the radio talk show of the night before and felt that at one point I became ensnared in a fruitless argument. It was about our government's "commitment." I asked him for help in this kind of task I had ahead of me. "How could I better handle situations like that?"

"Ask a person to define his terms," he said. "Ask him what he means by 'commitment.' Often a person uses terms without knowing what they mean and to put a question to a person makes him think more."

It was good advice. I tried to use it in future encounters.

The entourage finally arrived in Webster. We stood for a few minutes saying farewell on the main street just before the turn-off where I was to walk up to the house of my next host. By a system of some drivers driving ahead and others leaving their cars behind, the walkers were able to be driven back to their cars.

It was during this wonderful day of walking together, experiencing anew what made us feel more human, that a chilling message had gone out over the news wires: "Hatefulness/hatefulness." It was the coded alert to signify a nuclear attack on our country. That code shut down radio stations around the country and people waited for further instructions. I learned later that there was chaos among the radio stations for about 45 minutes until another message finally came on with the appropriate code to tell folks that the "hatefulness/hatefulness" message was really false. Someone had put into the testing device the wrong pre-punched tape. It was human error. Human error and nuclear weapons were a terrifying combination.

A man came up to our group as it was dispersing and said, "You know, I don't think Webster is exactly on the direct route to Washington."

I assured him that it was, at least the most direct we could figure out using the yo-yo string. I got the pack back on my back and he accompanied me for about a block. We talked about the need for letting one's government know when we don't agree with its policy. "This is the responsibility of a people in a democracy," I said.

He left, somewhat confused, I felt. He had been friendly, but felt concerned that we "support our leader." My thinking became more and more clear that this expression, "We must support our leader," was the ideal foothold for the beginnings of fascism. The totalitarian state is built on loyalty to a leader. It is built on trust of a "father figure." Democracy, however, puts responsibility for making choices on the people. It is true that we have a *representative* democracy, but when our elected leaders make choices that are so far afield from the desires of the people, then the people must speak out; they must be heard. This is the strength of our country.

Mrs. Howland, my new host, greeted me with great warmth and I felt welcome. My feet were exceedingly tender. The boots had made my foot sore in a way I had not expected. It was not just blisters, which occurred in spite of all the Band-Aids, moleskin, and lambs wool I had used. It was my left metatarsal arch and joint of the little toe that were sore in a bone kind of way. I had the feeling then that if I had to wear the boots for a long time, I would do permanent damage to my feet.

I took a hot shower as usual and rested for about half an hour. Then we had a beautiful dinner with Reverend and Mrs. Howland and myself, and left about 7:00 for the church, where a meeting had been planned.

That meeting was an initiation. For me. From 7:30–8:00 I talked with a youth group. There were seven young people there and the leader. The teenagers didn't know much about the war. They didn't really know why I was walking, or if they did, they wanted to know "what good it would do." I explained the best way I could. I told them what I knew about the war; I shared the facts I had with me.

One of the teenage girls had really been thinking about the war. She was against it and also mentioned that she and her family could discuss anything. She said she was not satisfied with the answers people gave concerning the war or concerning Communism. She sounded to me like a very open-minded young girl, but one who needed real answers. She talked about how last year they used to have rap sessions at their school. I suggested that they might start them again this year, but have everyone ask questions together and then look for the answers for future sessions. (This idea might be a good one for any group of people who feel concerned about an issue, but feel they don't know enough to make judgments. It takes devoting time to formulating the questions and discipline in searching for the answers. But that is education. One does not need a teacher to learn.)

Two boys in the group had thought more about the war than the girls, and it was clear why. They had to face the draft in a year or so. I urged them to seek draft counseling.

Pretty soon the youth leader began to speak up and to question all that I had said. He felt we had to stop Communism somewhere. He said something about war being the Asian way to keep the population down, that Asians think differently, that they don't value life in the same way we do, etc. Later when the adults came in to the room and a few of the young people left, I heard more of the same.

Finally, a minister spoke. He was tall, handsome, warm brown eyes, white hair in a brush cut, looking like a loving teddy bear. He said, "We've got to stop Communism before it comes to the shores of America."

I said, "It seems to me that the way you stop Communism from taking over here is by taking care of the problems we have—eliminating hunger, illiteracy and poverty."

He said, "Why, we don't have any poverty in America. Doesn't everyone in America live like us? Aren't we the typical Americans?"

I looked at him. I said, "You're putting me on. You're just saying that."

"No," he said, "doesn't everyone live like we do here in Webster?"

I asked him, "When was the last time you visited a ghetto? What about the people in Appalachia? What about the tenant farmers in the South?"

"Well," he said, "Communism is going to start a lot of little brush fires around the world and we have to put them out."

"How do you propose to do that?" I asked.

"Well, you know how a fireman puts out a fire…"

I interrupted and said I didn't accept his analogy. "We are talking about people. What would you do if *people* wanted Communism. If people rioted because of poor conditions in their country, what would you do, shoot them?"

He nodded. "Yes," he said, "yes, I would."

My heart sank in the knowledge that there were thousands who believed as he did. I suddenly felt that all over the country there were ministers willing to kill other people if those people wanted a form of government or a kind of economy different from ours.

Another man in the group made a comment worth noting. He felt that the young men in the country owed the country their service. Angrily I suggested that if the older men in the country felt the war was worth fighting that *they* should fight it.

"Don't be silly," he said. "You know we can't do it. It's the young men who are strong and healthy," and he raised his arms, flexing his biceps.

I said, "Yes, and they come back home broken, maimed, blind, or they don't come home at all."

His arms drooped. He said, "Yes, you're right." It was a moment of communication.

A woman from Russia was in the group. She spoke with great energy. I am not clear where she stood in relation to this war, but I do remember one comment. She felt that a person in society was responsible to other members of that society. She said that if they did anything wrong, they had no right to live, and she made a slicing motion at her neck. I asked what she thought of due process of law, of individual rights. It didn't make any difference. They had no right to live.

This encounter tonight, with all these different comments and reactions, made me aware of the depth of fear that can exist in so many human hearts. It was so clothed in the appearance of civility and rationalizations that got expressed in violence as the solution to problems. It was a challenge for all of us to examine our reaction to fear. How might we, personally and nationally, find our way out of a reliance on violence, and transform that fear and anger to love? Now there is something to work on!

After we had coffee and cookies, and conversation had broken up into small groups, I noticed that an older woman and her husband were waiting to speak to me. She was small, soft-spoken. Finally, as we were going out the door, she said, "I want to ask you a question. The Friends send people to both North Vietnam and South Vietnam. Is it true that they might have information that we don't have?"

I said, "Yes," and mentioned Russell Johnson, a staff member of AFSC, who had brought back so much information for us.

She seemed satisfied. Then she said they had lost a nephew in the war. She was so sweet. She wished me well. I sensed that here was the soft voice of love. In the aggressive dialogue of the evening, with the loud voices, we had not listened to the quiet ones present. I made a mental note to hear those who were not as prone to lay their ideas out before the group, perhaps out of fear of disapproval.

Postscript: the minister with whom I had had the somewhat combative dialogue asked me who was financing my trip. I told him that we were, my family was. He wondered where I was getting the money to eat. I said that I was being housed by friends along the way who were giving me dinner and breakfast, and sometimes packing my lunch, and that transportation was costing me nothing except for the price of the boots. However, I said, our expenses would be measured in telephone calls, because in order to keep in touch with the family I was calling home collect every night, and I knew my husband and friends were doing what they could to contact news media by telephone to make sure that they knew about my mission. When I got out to the car, he pressed two dollars into my hand, "to buy a lunch along the way. From my wife," he said. I kissed him on the cheek and thanked him.

Reverend Howland, my host, had been a very helpful during this meeting. He had spoken about the economic connections between the head of government in South Vietnam and rich landowners, prostitution, and heroin. He sounded like he had done his homework.

The next morning, before I left the church to begin the walk again, he said, "Thanks for shaking us up. We needed it."

Day

Webster to West Woodstock, Connecticut 6

Mon, Feb 22

The morning was cold, but fairly sunny as I recall it. After buying a fresh batch of Band-Aids I started another day of walking, this time all by myself.

I was walking past one of the stores in town and a gray-haired, strong, outdoor type of man said, "Hey, aren't you the lady walking to Washington? Didn't I just see you on TV?"

I said, "Yes. That's me."

He said, "I want to shake your hand." And he told me what a great thing he thought it was. We parted and I had only gotten a few feet further when he called out, "Say, lady, would you like a cup of coffee and a doughnut?"

I thought about it, but said, "No thanks. Since I just started, I feel I should keep going. But why don't you walk with me for a block or a mile?"

He reached for my hand again, squeezing it, and laughed, looking in the direction we would be going, a twinkle in his eye, and said, "I'd like to go all the way."

At that *I* laughed, shook my head and said no, told him good-bye again and went on. I laughed for the next couple of blocks.

I had gotten as far as the outside edge of Webster, was about to take a rest break at a gas station when a man called to me from a car and then got out. He introduced himself as Mike, a sales manager from a radio station in Southbridge. He wondered if I would consider coming to Southbridge with him so they could tape an interview. It's funny, I didn't even question if that were the truth. He pulled out identification so that I could be sure he was who he said he was, but it really hadn't occurred to me to not trust him. I said I would be happy to go with him providing it would take no more than an hour and that he would drive me right back to where he picked me up. Agreeing, he and I drove off to Southbridge.

We arrived at the station in about twenty minutes. I left my pack in the car and up we went to the second floor of the little building. After my rest break there (instead of at the gas station), the interview began almost immediately. Mike asked me about the whys and hows of the walk and was most cordial. I tried to be as clear as possible about the reasons for the walk, and my intense sense about the need for everyone to take some kind of action to bring the war to a close.

After the interview, another man in the studio began asking me some questions, but there was an edge to his voice.

"Are you a leftist or a rightist?" he asked.

I said, "Neither one. I am a human being and I object to the slaughter of the Vietnamese people as well as the loss of our young men."

"Well, we need to protect people from the spread of Communism," he said.

I countered with, "I would hate to be saved from Communism in the same way that we are saving the Vietnamese from Communism— through starvation, bombing, strafing, burning, relocation, defoliation of the countryside. Besides," I said, "the people probably would have voted for Communism in 1954 under Ho Chi Minh, but we cooperated with the Diem regime in not allowing those elections to take place."

"Aha," he said, as though he had caught me. "You *are* a leftist!"

"No," I said, "I'm not. I do not believe that Communism should be our system in the United States, but I don't think that we should make the choices for people in other countries."

When I had entered the radio station, I had heard voices raised between Mike, the man who had driven me there, and this other man. Now that I was through with the taping and walked into the lobby, I saw Mike bringing my pack up from the car. He said something like, it was nice to have met me.

I said, "Wait a minute, aren't you driving me back to Webster?"

He looked around, as if looking for someone else who would have to do that. I said, "I wouldn't have come with you if I hadn't believed that you would drive me back." I was adamant. I couldn't believe that he would go back on his word. Something about him looked trapped. When I pressed him further, he agreed again to drive me back, but I had such a sense of having been let down.

On the return trip, I asked him what the raised voices behind the closed door were about. He said, "Oh, that. They were just accusing me of picking up a strange woman on the highway and said they would tell my wife."

Somehow I felt it was different than that. It bothered me for quite awhile. I was deposited back at the gas station about an hour from when I left, thanked him for the opportunity to speak over his station, and started my walk again.

It was close to noon and time to eat the sandwich that my hostess in Webster had made for me. I was looking for a place to get a cup of coffee. Soon I came to the intersection of highway 197 and 131 where there was a little store, a gas station, a motel, and a few other places of business, but no obvious place to get a cup of coffee.

As I thought of going into the store to ask whether such a place were near, I saw a woman looking at me through the front window of the store. She was about my age, wearing a cardigan over an apron. Her face was expressionless. I could read no feelings behind it, unless it was wariness. I went in to ask my question. She replied that there was no place nearby. I saw an old wooden chair by the doorway and asked if she would mind if I sat down there and rested for a few minutes before going on. She said it would be fine with her. A man was also in the store, looking over newspapers.

I sat down, took off the pack, unzipped the pocket of the pack that held my plastic water bottle and refreshed myself with a drink of cold water. The man began a conversation with me. I could see from what he said that he knew who I was, and what I was doing. We began to talk about my walk, and the war. He had six sons, some of whom were already in the service. He, too, felt that this was a senseless war, and deplored the killing. I spoke about my feelings that it was important for each person to make his or her opinion known so that the government would have to become accountable to the people. I spoke of ways to protest other than just writing letters, how as long as we continue to pay taxes we are responsible for what our government does with our money.

By this time I had unzipped my jacket and taken off my cap. I asked if I could eat my sandwich there. The woman nodded. After I finished, I went up to the candy counter to pick out some candy for energy later on the road. I chose some chocolate covered raisins, laid down my dime, and the woman pushed the dime back toward me. She said she wanted to give them to me. Then she asked if I wanted a cup of tea. It sounded great. She disappeared into a back room and after a few minutes brought forth not only tea in a china cup but also a plateful of delectable confectioner-sugar-dusted cookies and a fancy paper napkin.

Instead of feeling like an intruder, as I had when I first came in, I now felt like an honored guest in her home. She told me then that a friend had called ahead and told her I was passing by. She had been looking for me. We talked now about herself, how she was the sole owner of this store, how her parents had died in this past year, and that her brother visits her every now and then. It was not a long conversation. There was a wistfulness about her.

I finished the tea, but could not finish the cookies. She insisted I take them with me and wrapped them in the paper napkin. I tucked them gently into my pocket, zipped up my jacket, pulled on my cap, slipped my arms back into the nylon straps of the pack, fastened the belt strap and stood up to go. I thanked her for her hospitality. She wished me well and said she was with me. I said I would remember her for a long time. She said, "My name is Chris."

I walked out into the cold to continue the walk. After awhile a newsman from a local paper met me along the road and walked with me for about a mile, asking me questions along the way. A photographer followed in a car, and when the man had all the information he needed, we crossed over to the right side of the road so that the photographer could take some pictures. He wanted a picture with a story, so I pulled out a map and looked at it. I think it was the first picture with the map. They were both lovely young men, and we had a happy time. Soon they were off. I crossed back over and continued alone for the rest of the afternoon. It was the first day that I carried the pack all by myself.

I walked through North Woodstock, just a cluster of houses and a post office. Tired from walking, I went into the post office, looked around and saw that no one was there. I took off my pack and lay down on the floor for about 20 minutes, after which I felt refreshed. I'll never know if anyone saw me. If anyone did, I'm sure they thought this was some "crazy-lady-walking-with-pack-on-back and lying-on-post-office-floor-for-nap." I was too tired to care.

Not too far from this point I had to take a county road in order to cut through to West Woodstock. It was *really* deserted. Only a few cars passed me for the rest of the afternoon. One was driven by a white-haired postman. He stopped and said in a friendly manner, "Where are you going?"

I said, "I'm walking to Washington."

"Oh," he said. "Would you like an orange? I have some oranges in the car."

"No thanks," I said. "I have an apple with me and I don't want to carry too much. Thanks very much."

He went on. About twenty minutes later he drove past and stopped again and said, "Washington, Connecticut?"

I said, "No, Washington, D.C."

"Oh, my goodness!" he said.

From there on I told him what I was doing it for, and we exchanged views about the war. He agreed that the war was a terrible thing. He offered me housing at his house, including dinner. I assured him that I had housing for the night, but wanted to make sure I was on the correct road to West Woodstock. He confirmed my directions. I thanked him for his offer of hospitality and help. Later I found out that he had actually driven on ahead to tell the person with whom I was to stay that I was on my way, that he had talked with me.

It seemed like I would never reach West Woodstock. The road kept going on and on through farmland and woods. It was nearing four o'clock and the sky was getting gray and the temperature dropping. I began to feel anxious. A school-bus passed me and dropped off some children in the distance. Eventually I thought I had better stop in one of those houses and find out how far I was from my pick-up point.

I rang the bell of a house by the wayside. A woman answered and I asked if she would mind if I stopped for a few minutes to warm up and ask directions, and perhaps to make a phone call. She said, sure, and offered me a cup of coffee. I took off my pack, my jacket and hat and made my call. I found to my relief that I was only about an eighth of a mile from my destination. West Woodstock was an area, not a visible town, and just around the bend I would have reached the intersection that was my destination. So I asked my hostess for the evening if she would want to pick me up at the house where I had stopped. I described it to her and planned to wait there for her. I felt secure again.

I sat down at the kitchen table with my interim hostess to enjoy a cup of instant coffee. She made me feel very comfortable. Two children, a girl and a boy, both of junior high age, sort of hung around the edges. My hostess said, "Would you like to watch *Dark Shadows?*"

I said, "No thanks, this is just fine."

We talked for a few moments about kitchens and kids, and then she said again, "Are you *sure* you don't want to watch *Dark Shadows?*"

I looked at her and became aware. "*You* want to watch *Dark Shadows*. Of course, let's go in and watch it." And we both laughed and went in to watch.

During a commercial, we talked a bit about the war, how awful I felt it was, and how we all needed to do what we could to stop it. She referred about three times to a cousin or nephew of hers who had been over in Vietnam, how awful the fighting was and how bad the Communists were. She said he would go over again if he had to.

During another commercial, her daughter mentioned something about monsters. And the mother said, "You hear about the monsters they're looking for in California?"

"No, I haven't," I said.

"Yes," the daughter chimed in, "they're supposed to be eight feet tall and hairy."

"You know," said the mother, "I think it's the earthquakes."

"What do you mean?" I asked.

"Well, what do you call those old prehistoric animals..." and she held her forearm up at an angle using the hand to form a head.

"I said, "Do you mean dinosaurs?"

She said, "Yeah. I think when there are earthquakes the ground opens up and these dinosaurs just come right out." I looked at her. I decided not to say any more about the war. She continued to watch *Dark Shadows*.

Before I left, she told me that her son had been on the school bus that passed me on the road. When he reached his mom, he had said, "That's the woman walking to Washington." His mom had just said, "You're a liar." She laughed when she told me this. It was a great joke on herself. The son came forward then with a sheet of paper and a pen and asked if I would sign it for him. He said the kids at school would never believe him unless he had my signature. I happily signed and by then my ride had arrived. I put on my jacket and hat, thanked the family and left, carrying the pack to the car.

Polly Rabinowitz, my host for the evening, picked me up and, in the company of a local reporter, whisked me off to their beautiful Victorian home, owned by an historical society. Not too long after I arrived, Marj and Bob Swann, my helpful friends from Voluntown, came to the house. They had looked for me along the way, intending to walk with me. How exciting it was to see them, but it was so disappointing to know they couldn't find me. Evidently there was some confusion about where I would be that day. Certainly it wasn't on the itinerary that I would be lying down on a post office floor, or having coffee at a local home.

When I called home, which I did every night, I got the message that I was to call Channel 4 in Boston. I did, and we made arrangements to meet somewhere along the road about 11:00 on Wednesday morning. That day would mark the beginning of the second week of walking and they wanted to have a news team out there to meet me. Walt Sanders was to be part of the crew.

That evening I had another radio interview, followed by an elegant dinner. The setting, in that small room with the Wedgwood blue and white wallpaper and maple antiques, was as if we were in another period. How I ached for what I could imagine as the peace of another era. I longed for a simpler time, when the horrors of a technological war did not impinge on our consciousness.

I fell into bed early that night, without even taking the bath I had promised myself. The next morning would be soon enough to be clean. It was more important to sleep.

...at an antiwar teach-in at Yale University tonight... Repeatedly the speakers deplored the increase of air operations in Southeast Asia as American troops are being withdrawn...

With heavy enemy fighting continuing, the South Vietnamese drive against Communist supply trails and bases in southern Laos was reported stalled today for the 5th consecutive day.

—New York Times, Tuesday, February 23, 1971

Day

W. Woodstock to Warrenville, Connecticut   7

Tues, Feb 23

The weather that morning looked truly rotten! I wondered whether this would be one of those days that I would have to sit out somewhere. There was a light sleet. The trees and bushes were shiny with ice and the pavement as we walked to the car was pebbly with the slippery stuff. I was driven, very carefully so as not to skid, to the intersection in West Woodstock where we met Nancy Fleagle. That time I was fully prepared for the weather and put on the poncho before my jacket got wet. Starting off, Nancy and I walked on through the light rain, sharing experiences, thoughts.

The actual process of walking through the countryside became one of great beauty. As I relaxed about the possibility that it would keep me from going forward on my journey, I found in it an exquisite rarity. That was the kind of weather from which we ordinarily shielded ourselves. We thought of mist, rain, sleet, and ice as unfit for humans. Instead, on that day, I was reminded of my childhood, the joy of being out in the elements, experiencing the wet face, cold nose, the sound of squeaking as the wind rocked the ice clad branches back and forth. Shapes in the distance were softened by the mist that formed in the hollows, and the clusters of trees on the hilltops sparkled. The remains of ice-sheathes that had covered the telephone lines dropped to our feet as we passed (luckily not hitting us). Some branches were down. But except for the squeaking and the sound of our own voices it was like walking through an acoustically insulated sound chamber. Nancy's face was rosy from the cold. Probably my face was the same. But we were warm on the inside from the exertion. It was a happy day.

We passed a little store and post office as we went through West Stockbridge and heard a knocking on the window. We looked up and saw a figure motioning us in. We obeyed and walked into the tiny post office whereupon a woman said to me, smiling, "Are you the lady walking to Washington?"

"Yes," I said, "that's me."

"Well, I have a message for you."

I couldn't believe it. There, in that rural setting, by a method of communication as old as humanity itself, someone had been watching for me to go by in order to pass on a message. The message was from some friends of my brother who wanted me to contact them when I got to Storrs. I thanked the woman for stopping me, took the written message with me and Nancy and I walked on.

About 11:30 we stopped at the General Lyon Inn. We were dripping wet and cold, but inside the inn was warm and cozy, not just with temperature but with a visible hospitality written into its aged structure. For a hundred years or more it had been standing by this road, ready to give rest and food and warmth to passersby, but I thought I appreciated what it was offering in a way people for the most part have forgotten. We had not been driving somewhere in a car, happy to get out and stretch our legs; we had been traveling by our own effort and to us the most heavenly thing we could do was to sit down to rest our backs and legs. Even though I was wearing a poncho, it clung to me with the dampness, and my jean legs had gotten completely soaked, right through the thermal underwear.

The dining room sparkled with elegance—china dishes, glass glasses, linen table coverings, a flower on each table. Nancy and I sat down for a cup of coffee and sweet roll and talked intently about the purposes of the walk and the need for the news media to report the facts about the war to the people, even in small town newspapers—perhaps even *especially* in small town newspapers. For some people the newspaper was their *only* contact with the outside world.

After awhile, an elderly woman in a white uniform asked if I were "the lady walking to Washington." When I told her "yes," she wanted to give us all lunch on the house. It was Mrs. Kennedy, the woman who had run this inn and the kitchen for years. She was so gracious and sweet. While we had been talking, her house guests had filtered down into the dining room for the mid-day meal. There were about seven of them, each one well over 60. Mrs. Kennedy introduced me around. She said, "This is the lady who is walking for peace. She's walking 450 miles to Washington, D.C."

One elderly woman responded with "Isn't that nice," (in a manner similar to "Isn't the weather lovely today").

A gentleman, hunched over by his years, said, without explaining, "I once walked 210 miles in seven days." It made my endeavor pale by comparison.

"You must have run," I suggested.

He laughed and said, "That walk is why I look like I do now!"

It was time for us to go. Mrs. Kennedy insisted we sign the guest register, after which we put all the paraphernalia back on and headed out into the cold again.

We had not gone 50 yards but there was Emily Sander, our friend from Cambridge Friends Meeting! She had driven out all this distance to give me companionship and hot coffee. And then she had had trouble finding me! Here we had been sitting in the General Lyon Inn, practically across the street, while Emily had been sitting outside in her car, waiting for us to pass on the road. It was beautiful to see her, and to know the caring that was involved in her giving up a day from her busy schedule to come minister to me. She had a thermos of hot coffee and snacks. Gratefully, we indulged again in the coffee, and she loaned me some mittens to put on over my gloves to keep my hands warmer and dryer. The wool socks on my hands were, after all, a bit clumsy. Emily walked with us for a ways and then headed back to the car.

Nancy stayed with me until we reached Warrenville. We had talked a lot during the earlier part of the day, but as we got closer to our destination we fell into longer periods of comfortable silence. By the time we arrived at the country store in Warrenville, she admitted to aching legs and feet, but a happiness at being able to finish at least one day's walk.

I was grateful for having had her lovely spirit accompany me. I phoned my previous host, who was to pick me up at the store and keep me until my next hostess returned from school teaching, and Nancy phoned to arrange her ride home. When my ride arrived I left her in the store, a young new friend.

As planned, Polly, my previous host, picked me up and took me back to her house where we spent about an hour sipping tea and discussing alternatives to our present life.

I heard during this discussion about some people who had limited their income to not exceed the poverty level; that way they could live without paying taxes that went toward the defense budget. They bought land in New Hampshire or Vermont and by disciplined, frugal living, managed to work the land, and still had time for writing, music, and peace activities. How tempting this sounded. It was so refreshing to think one could forge one's own way, according to one's own moral convictions, to live in a style that was in tune with the interdependence of humans and the earth. And yet for us it would be too big a wrench from our present life styles. But how freeing to our spirit to live without paying for this war!

My ride soon came to connect me with my host family. It was Mark, the son of Wendell and Allison Davis, a college graduate soon to do alternative service as a conscientious objector. Off we went to his house, some ten miles in the other direction, through what had now become a heavy snow.

We arrived at his 1750's home, in a rustic setting, where trees in the countryside and the shrubbery around the house were beginning to turn white from the large fluff-balls dropping from the sky. My eye could appreciate the beauty; my heart was anxious for my welfare. If too much of it collected I would have trouble traveling the next day. Meanwhile, I could be grateful that I was safe in a home for the evening.

A collection of cats greeted us at the doorway before we walked in. Entering the Davis's house was like stepping back in time. This kind of house touched that part of me that longed for a connection with the past. What was it that happened? I supposed the feeling was a time link with humanity. When we could pass the barrier of time and space we entered a unity with all people, with all creation.

The house was built to another scale. The doors were smaller, the ceiling lower, the granite fireplace larger, filling almost an entire wall. In the large dining room-kitchen area, the first we entered, the plaster was painted white, the woodwork blue. A long trestle table stretched to welcome many guests, or a family that had once been large. In its center was a large bouquet of dried flowers.

Allison greeted us with warmth. She was back home from teaching her kindergarten pupils. A large potful of vegetable beef stew was cooking on the stove, and from the oven came the scent of home-made bread. Allison showed me to my room, which was up a narrow flight of stairs boxed in by walls almost close enough to touch with both elbows at once. The door stayed shut by turning a small wooden square to fit a latch. The room held a bed, a chest, and a small loom. The room itself seemed not much bigger than double the size of the twin size bed. The air was chill. A charming small bathroom across the hall contained a space heater, so that shower time was quite comfortable. I took my shower, rested and then called home.

I met Elizabeth Brown, Allison's mother, Mark's grandmother. To me she represented all that was admirable in the older generation. Ample of build, gray hair, she was her age, whatever it was. She was not trying to be something other than herself. She could converse with any age, because she listened and responded. I felt her inner peace and maturity.

We all watched the news, wondering what the latest Vietnam War news would be. It was all so horrible, and always reported so matter of factly, so dispassionately. How much damage can one people do to another before they are repulsed by their own barbarism? That was also a time when the population around Boston was so concerned about the people still trapped under the Commonwealth Avenue building that had collapsed during the week before I left on my walk. The bodies had still not been found. Surely that event would help people understand what war was like.

The evening we spent in front of the fireplace in the sitting room, reading some of the material I had in my packet, reading the newspapers which were reporting the Yale and Harvard teach-ins and discussing the anti-war movement, the ecology movement, and life in Connecticut in general. It was a beautiful evening, filled with the snapping of the fire, the click of Elizabeth Brown's knitting needles and the creaking of her rocking chair on the wide board floor. Peace—exquisite, unreal.

At bedtime I was concerned that I might get a sore throat by sleeping in a cold room. Sickness I did not need. Ordinarily I wouldn't have thought of it. Allison offered that marvelous old remedy, a hot water bottle between the sheets. We took some of the chill out of the air with the transplanted space heater, I donned my orange mohair sweater over my night gown, pulled on my warm cap, and slipped under the covers. It was a delicious sleep.

Week Two

Lieutenant Calley said that during the enemy's Tet offensive of early 1968 the American commanders in Vietnam were demanding reports of victories, reports often bolstered by inflated body counts of enemy dead.

"It was very important we tell the people back home we were killing more of the enemy than they were killing us," Lieutenant Calley said. "You just made a body count off the top of your head. Anything went into the body count: V.C., buffalo, pigs, cows. Something was dead, you put it in your body count, sir."

—New York Times, Wednesday, February 24, 1971

Day

Warrenville to Storrs, Connecticut 8

Wed, Feb 24

At 8:00 in the morning I called Channel 4 in Boston to confirm the appointment we had made for 11:00 a.m., "somewhere along the road." Walt Sanders would be out there for sure, I was told.

Mark drove me to the beginning point, Warrenville, where I had stopped walking the day before, 10 miles from their house. How little 10 miles seems in a car. Yet walking that far is, for me, at least half a day's effort.

Waiting for me were four young people who had driven all the way from Newton North High School to interview me for their newspaper. We all started walking together.

That was Wednesday morning, one week after I had left home. I was now, judging from the approximate planning we had done, about 70 miles from Newton. And already I had had a wealth of experiences. And I still had five more weeks of walking ahead of me. One week's walking and I was only in Connecticut. But I was in Connecticut, no longer in Massachusetts. I had made it that far.

Lo and behold, around 11:00 in the morning, there was Ginny Hutchison from Friends Meeting. She had driven all the way out to ply me with coffee, sandwiches and snacks called "Space Sticks." As I was rejoicing in her company, the two of us perched on the back end of Ginny's station wagon, along came the TV crew from Channel 4.

Before taking any footage, Walt Sanders told me the questions he

71

would be asking me, such as "How has the weather been? Have you had any second thoughts since you left home about continuing the journey?" I tried to prepare for those minutes I knew would come. The crew discussed whether they could take walking footage on the main road, and instead decided to take the footage along a side road (going in a different direction, of course. I asked them if they would then print "Simulated Walk" on the screen during the broadcast, remembering recent coverage of putting a man on the moon). I knew how hard it had been for me to keep talking and walking at the same time, how out of breath I became when talking to him a week ago, so I suggested that we only stand for the interview. He was happy to comply.

In response to the question about the weather I found myself going on and on about how weather could be "bad" but still beautiful, how the trees sparkled, etc. No, I did not feel any less desire to keep walking. Felt stronger, physically and spiritually. "What do you hope to accomplish by this walk?" Perhaps it would stir a few others to take action that was for *them* the strongest they could take, etc. Before I knew it, the interview was over and the crew got a few shots of us walking along the road together. Immediately after the group shots, the Newton young people headed back home, later than they should have since we had waited so long for the TV crew. Walt said they would meet us farther up the road when we arrived at the University of Connecticut.

The more I walked, the more depressed I got. I had not used the time on TV well. I became madder and madder that I had let him formulate the questions. I had spent so much time talking about the weather. If that would be the choice they'd make of what part of the interview to show, the effort would be completely wasted. I was not on this walk to talk about weather and blisters. I wanted to speak of the horrors of the war, the insensitivity of us as a people to have allowed it to go on this long, the need for each person to feel responsible in order to take the necessary action.

About 2:15 we arrived at the big sign that said, "University of Connecticut." They were waiting there. I went up to Walt with my concern, asking if he couldn't film a few more feet of interview. I wanted to speak of the feeling people would have in Newton or Charlestown if the government said to them that they would have to move out, they couldn't stay in their homes. They'd have to move to Alabama or Tennessee. Then, when all the people had left, all the homes would be burned, all the possessions cherished by families, but unable to be carried, would be left behind and destroyed. This is called "relocation." I wanted to speak of the great feeling people in Boston had for the men trapped in the building that had collapsed on Commonwealth Avenue. Yet daily, people were being trapped in buildings, caves, trenches due to intentional bombing. If people could just feel the same immediacy and compassion, surely they would move to bring an end to the war.

Walt said he might be able to tack on a comment of that type but he couldn't film any more. He was most kind and understanding. To him I underlined the importance of the news media in educating the public. I had, in the walk, become more aware of the tremendous responsibility of the media. I pointed to the camera and said, "That is one of the most powerful tools there is." He agreed.

We waved goodbye, and I walked the remainder of the way to Storrs and the home of the Planks, my next host family.

Eleanor and John Plank, daughter Margaret, and sons David and Geoffrey somehow seemed like old friends the moment I met them. This night I was to speak to a group gathered at the University. It was to be my first more or less formal meeting.

I was very eager to watch the news that night. Sure enough, on the 6:00 news, Channel 4, Melvin Laird, Secretary of Defense, was explaining the latest moves in Laos, defending the government's actions. The next item of news was "Newton housewife, mother of three, is still on her way to Washington to protest the war in Indochina." Following were excerpts from the interview. True to his word Walt had not spent too much time on the weather, but it was there. Though nothing was included about the Commonwealth Avenue building, my main reaction was one of amazement. My God, I'm the only available protest. The news media had put me right up next to Laird!

The meeting at the University had about 40 people present. About half were students, about half were members of the Friends Meeting at Storrs. And also present was the friend of my brother Edgar, whose message had reached me via the rural post office. I began with a statement about what had prompted me to walk, and what the facts were about the war as I knew them, gleaned from sources sent to me from the home front. I spoke for about 20 minutes, maybe even longer. I had never given a talk like this before.

Following my talk, I suggested that people break into buzz sessions of 8 or so people, agree on one person as leader and another as recorder and ask themselves the following questions:

1. What "peace actions" have you taken in the past?

2. How many in the group are still debating the rightness or morality of the war? If any, on what grounds? Commitment? Communism? Economic collapse? Racism? Our leader knows best?

3. What protest actions are you willing to take part in?

4. Have you new ideas for action not mentioned yet?

In the five groups, only one got involved with the second question. Apparently everyone else felt certain that the war was wrong. In the group that discussed #2 at length, the young woman who was still uncertain was just beginning to see the economic reasons for continuing the war and in the process of exploring them, the group began looking for economic means of stopping the war, such as boycotts.

Everyone there reflected the discouragement about taking new actions. They spoke of apathy. It was not that people didn't care. They were tired. No action seemed to matter, and they cited the previous year's flurry of activity with no visible results. But in discussing possible directions they could go, they mentioned a display in the library that would attract more student attention. It could be a focal point for new information concerning the war. I suggested that later in the spring they might let me know what course they followed.

Due to the excellent planning of Howard Reed, a professor at the university, the evening had been maximized. In whatever way outreach was possible, it had happened in Storrs. Had I stayed home in Newton and only *thought* about walking, I wouldn't have reached anybody. The group of 40 to whom I spoke this evening was a tremendous step forward for me.

Mark Davis, who had tried to find time to meet me earlier along the road but didn't, had made it to the meeting at the University. When I said goodnight to him he handed me this note, the words of the song he had tried to remember the day before:

Step by step
the longest march
can be won, can be won.
Many stones can
form an arch –
singly none, singly none.
And by union what
we will
shall be accomplished still.
Drops of water
turn a mill –
singly none, singly none.

— *Traditional*

...a 76 page report [was presented to a Senate subcommittee today] on the Army's domestic intelligence project known as Conus Intel, or Continental United States Intelligence.

Mr. Pyle [one of 5 former military intelligence agents] testified, "The United States today possesses the intelligence apparatus of a police state. ...it exists today as a loose coalition of Federal, state, municipal and military agencies."

—*New York Times, Thursday, February 25, 1971*

Day

9

Storrs to Columbia, Connecticut

Thur, Feb 25

In between breakfast and the time I was to begin walking at 9:30 on that Thursday morning, I was able to write a few more notes. Geoffrey did so want to walk with us for a ways. He was only 10, and Eleanor felt that it was more important for him to go to school. I could sympathize with her dilemma. Which process is more educating—going to school for the day, facing the necessity for each of us to do the best we can in our own area, or breaking the routine in a walk of this kind? She stood firm that for him the most important thing was to go to school. His yearning was agonizing. But go to school he did. Margaret, the high school daughter, planned to take the day to walk with us. Older son David would also go with us.

A contingent of 14 people had gathered at the post office in Storrs to walk with me for a ways. We felt a gay procession trudging out of Storrs together. The weather was brisk, but the sun was shining, and the air had a light feeling to it. Maybe it was just my spirits.

We had gotten about a mile from the University when a young man pulled up in a car, got out and ran over to me. He said, "I just had to come and tell you. Today I'm dropping out of school to go to New York and work full time with the Vietnam Veterans Against the War." He'd been over in Vietnam and had returned to school. I don't know whether my walk was what made him decide that day to leave school, or if it was just a coincidence. The point was that for him it mattered that he tell me. It certainly supported the sense I had of the urgency of our protest and gave me hope that others too felt the immediacy. Our conversation was brief and beautiful. It had that sense of spirit touching spirit. It was like a flame burning brighter because two individual flames had joined. Within five minutes he was off.

We arrived at the intersection of Rtes. 32 and 275 about 10:30 A.M. and sat down on some steps in front of a church, ate apples, drank water, and gathered a bit of energy to continue down Route 32. About half an hour later we were joined by Betty Woodbury and her dog Tyson (the same one who had walked with me on Sunday) and not too long after that, Olivia Hoblitzelle and Sharon Satterthwaite drove up in Sharon's VW bus. They were filled with an exciting plan, and wanted to check with me before proceeding.

"Louise, what would be your response to having other people join you as you walk into Washington, D.C.? If it would feel right, we would like to organize it. Would you really want that?"

I said, "Oh, my, that would be beautiful." I had given some thought to how I wanted to end the walk and passed on my picture of it. "If others were to join me, I would prefer that no one carry signs or banners. At this point I want to walk in silence on the last day, and so I would hope that anyone joining the walk would also keep silence." I'm not sure when it seemed to me right that I walk in silence. As far as having others join me on that final day, I knew there was a call for thousands to appear in Washington on April 24th. If people had to make a choice, and could not go both times, then they should be in D.C. on April 24th. If they could use their time better by organizing something at home, then they should do that. I felt that this walk was one action that depended not on numbers, but intensity. I was not yet clear on how to respond to their idea, but continued to think about it.

Olivia and Sharon were so keenly sensitive, wanting to sound out my true feelings, not wanting to create anything that would dilute my action or frustrate my purposes or cloud the message. In this week since I had left they had been talking among themselves at the Wednesday morning mothers' group at the Friends Meeting and felt that there must be some way that they could lend weight to my walk. They were looking for a way that would make it reach beyond the local area. Our conversation was a beginning. Our minutes were limited. I had to leave by 11:45 in order to make it to Willimantic by 12:15. I was to appear there on the local radio talk show from 12:30–1:00.

Along the way our ride came; someone whisked me into a car together with a few other walkers who wanted to go with us to the station.

At 12:30 I was in the radio studio with about four others. That was one of the most comfortable interviews I had; I'm sure it was because of the sympathetic attitude and understanding of the man who was questioning me. He questioned me in a friendly manner for about 10 minutes as to my motives, method and goals. I sat in front of my own mike at a table on which I could spread out all my materials, from which I could get immediate access to facts and their sources. I could then answer any questions that might come in. During the period before the broadcast and during commercials, I did stretching exercises, running in place, shakes and bounces in order to dispel the nervousness that invariably led to great muscular tension and tremors. Even though I know it looked silly, it was a great help in allowing me to talk with clarity and keep my mind focused on the message.

I had been warned that probably the first caller would be a certain man who called in regularly to speak against Communism. Sure enough, he was right there, defending our actions in Indo-China. It ran along the lines that maybe we shouldn't have gotten into the war in the first place, but now that we were there, we had to finish the job. I mentioned the possibility that we were there for other than heroic reasons. Perhaps oil was an incentive, I said, a possibility that had been posed by many.

A woman called in saying she thought I was aiding the Communists.

Two of the five or so calls were supportive. I did my best to speak to the doubts the others had about my motives or principles. It was harrowing, in one respect, but entirely understandable in terms of where many people were.

When we were all through and about to leave, I got a number of phone calls that came in to the receptionist in the office. They were all highly in favor of my action and wanted me not to be discouraged by what had greeted me on the air. I thanked each for calling and my heart felt open and vulnerable and grateful for the caring of those who called in.

From the studio I called a sister station in Southington which had expressed an interest in doing an interview when I got closer to Middletown.

Betty had waited at the small store for our return and she and Tyson greeted us and then left. We walked on. By now it was almost 1:45. We had a long way to go yet before reaching Columbia, my destination for that day. There was much trading around with my pack, so I really didn't carry it very far that day. About 3:00 who should pull up but Eleanor Plank with Geoffrey. School was out and now he could walk with us. He was delighted, as was I.

We walked on together for quite a time, heading into traffic as usual, keeping on the outside of the white line, but just barely. There was talk about shifting the pack again. This time Geoffrey wanted to carry my pack, so David, big brother David, strapped the pack on little Geoffrey. It extended far above his head. We walked on for about 50 feet and Geoffrey must have needed to bend over slightly when the entire pack began to tip forward over his head, knocking him off balance. There was a sudden scramble to keep him from falling down, and he was safely caught, but we all became aware of how near tragedy we had come, because he could have been thrown into the path of an oncoming car.

That day would end with the hardest part of the walk. About 4:00 we began climbing the hill that led to Columbia, and we climbed and we climbed. We stopped often to catch our breath, and turned to look at how far we had come and turned again to look at what we had yet to do. But one step at a time put the hill behind us. We had nearly reached the top when a car coming toward us pulled over on the side and stopped. A woman got out and came over to us. She introduced herself and said she had heard about my walk and thought it was terrific. Not only that, she wanted to know if she could offer her house for the night and would I have dinner with them.

I thanked her for her kind offer. It was the second time I had been offered overnight hospitality by a complete stranger. I was moved by the complete trust she had to do that. I told her I already had a home for the night. As she was finally convinced that I didn't need anything, she got back in the car and pulled out into traffic, more abruptly than felt comfortable to me, but she made it, no doubt more accustomed than I to the traffic on the hill.

We had gone not more than a block (approximate only, as this was a highway), finally cresting the hill, when another woman passing in a car called out greetings and asked if I needed a place to stay. "We have four clean beds. We'd love to have you." Again, I thanked the woman, but explained that my needs were taken care of. She smiled, waved and drove on.

This time we had gone about half a block and heard someone calling after me. It was the woman who had called at the radio station, who had said she would look for me as I walked past her house. And here she was. We had an enthusiastic conversation after which she asked if I would like to meet some of her friends. We crossed the highway and she ran up to two neighboring houses to bring out two other ladies who seemed very happy to meet us. These women had been ardent workers for peace, and now were so grateful to see some visible protest to our Indo-China policy. They offered coffee, but since the hour was late, it being almost 4:40, I felt I had to contact my next hostess. I had been walking through Columbia. It had proved so far to be the most friendly town I had passed through.

At the intersection of 287 and 6, Eleanor was waiting with the car to pick up all of us remaining walkers and take us to Howard and Martha Roberts in Andover, a drive of 5 or 6 miles. It was a fond farewell I said to Eleanor and Margaret and the kids. In such a short space of time I felt so close to them. They drove off.

Martha was very warm and welcoming, as were the Roberts two Newfoundlands, great giants which resembled bears more than dogs. And one was just a puppy! Again I was in a home built about 1780 with massive fireplaces, wide beamed floors and narrow steep stairs.

Martha wanted to hang up my jacket for me before showing me to my room, something most of my hosts tried to do, but I always found life easier if I kept everything together. My pockets served the same purpose as a purse, so it was much more convenient to keep it available in my bedroom. I hung the jacket on a chair in the room I had been offered, propped up my pack against the wall and took a shower.

The evening was to be devoted to an interview with Anna Frisina from the *Manchester Evening Herald*. A more aggressive interview I had not had! I felt I had to fight to get my message through. She dug deep, but her questions were loaded, had false assumptions, seemed to focus on things that for me were not the focus. She and her husband had evidently picked apart the five theses before she came over, and she wanted to know what my thinking was in relation to their questions. "How are you going to be sure that the North Vietnamese would abide by any agreement? Don't you think that if we pulled out a bloodbath would ensue? How do you propose to set up these international commissions? You want *immediate* withdrawal? Suppose we did withdraw. What government would take over?"

At this point I said I felt Hanoi would probably take over.

She looked at me. "Hanoi?"

I said, "The Saigon government does not have the support of the people. They would only last for a few months maybe and then most likely the Communists would take over."

Suddenly I heard what I was saying. I was saying it was all right for the enemy to win. I saw it from her viewpoint: how treasonous! Yet it made sense to me. The amount of destruction we were wreaking upon the Vietnamese was insane, inhuman, beastly, yet masked by the words "technological warfare." Somehow it was all right to "defend" the Vietnamese from the Communist North by flame throwers, phosphorescent bombs, napalm, anti-personnel weapons such as cluster bombs or needle bombs, razing of total villages to save them from the enemy, transporting entire populations of those villages to "strategic hamlets" no matter that they felt attached to the land of their forebears. So a few of the South Vietnamese, whom we were there to protect, get hurt in the process, like 1,100,000 dead, 2,200,000 wounded. Small price to pay. After all, we're saving them from Communism. I could no longer look at these fraught words as I used to: Communism, Domino theory. Instead I saw blood, broken bodies, anguish, and death of real people—real children, whose mothers and fathers loved them, real grandparents, beloved by their families, real brothers and sisters and cousins and aunts and sons…how many sons!…theirs and ours. That's how I saw the war.

I couldn't say all this at the time. Instead I tried to explain that it was not my job to figure out exactly how we would get out of the country, how exactly we would set up the international commissions to provide economic aid for development. We had people in this country who spe-cialized in that sort of thing. If I wanted to build a house I might not know exactly how one nails the thing together or plans for the wiring and plumbing and heating. That's what the architect and builders were for. But I could tell them whether I wanted my house built on sand or on rock, and what the general specifications were. I believed we had to build our world house on rock, on the firm foundation of international law, and put all our creative effort into making it work. And yes, beyond the concept of law, there had to be that element of caring, of concern for the people of other nations, as well as caring for those we knew person-ally. Some called this compassion. Some called it love.

I was not as clear with Anna as I could have been. In fact, I felt very threatened by her. My stomach was in a tight knot the whole time we were talking and stayed that way after she left. I was afraid I was shown up to be a fool. Knowing that I was not a Communist, yet fearing the label in light of my statements, I trembled for what others would think of me, that my statement would be blown all out of proportion. "Peace walker wants Hanoi to take over government." I wrestled with this fear most of the evening. I felt very depressed and subdued. Martha and Howard struggled with me, trying to measure Anna's understanding of my mission and her past reporting, trying to assure me that she was reading me right, but questioning even their own assurances. I finally decided that the only thing I could do was call her.

On the phone, about 10:45 that night, I re-explained my position con-cerning Hanoi, that it was not that I wanted them to take over, but with the lack of support the Saigon government had, it was probably what would happen, and was the lesser of two evils. She was most under-standing and said also that she would drop the article off at the house in the morning before she took it to the newspaper. My insecurities had made me paranoid. I breathed a sigh of relief and went to bed much happier.

...former military intelligence agents...testified before the Subcommittee on Constitutional Rights hearings on the pervasive collection of information on American citizens by their Government.

At times, the Fifth Division military intelligence staff worked closely with agents of the 113th military intelligence group...at other times, the two units competed with each other and with still more intelligence organizations.

(continued on page 91)

Day

Columbia to Marlboro, Connecticut

10

Fri, Feb 26

As it happened, the news article was quite thoughtful. It reported the walk from my perspective, quoting some of the "press packet" we had put together—my letter to our Christmas card list, my daughter's letter to *Life Magazine*. She included my comments regarding what would happen if we pull out by quoting me as saying, "It would be gratifying to see them come to terms (North and South Vietnam) and have peace, but even should they choose to fight each other, this is their war, not ours, and it is their decision to make..." And she included the Five Theses.

On Friday, Martha took me to the intersection of 6 and 287 and, with a fondness that went deep despite the short time of knowing one another, we parted.

That day I walked all by myself. Alone on the road, I sang to myself and even sang Happy Birthday to a daughter's friend, who couldn't hear me, of course. I was glad nobody else could either.

As the day wore on, I wore out. I felt every hill. I paused often to catch my breath, to sit on a guard rail, to lean against a post. At one point I spread out my orange poncho on a rise above the road, took off my pack and lay down for about 20 minutes, feeling guilty that I would worry passersby in cars, but being too tired to get up. I only got up when the cold of the ground began to seep through my clothes to my skin. My God, I was tired! Maybe there were just more hills than usual. I had thought somehow, naively, that they would cancel each other out. That

...in mid-September, 1969, rumors of a large demonstration outside the gate of Fort Carson had drawn agents from the Fifth Division, the 113th military intelligence group, the Air Force, law enforcement agencies, and "even two Navy intelligence officials from somewhere on the West Coast." "119 demonstrators participated in the protest," but of those "53 were intelligence gathering personnel or representatives of the press."

—New York Times, Friday, February 26, 1971

may happen when one is biking, pumping the bike up, then coasting down, but not walking. One walks up and then one walks down—over and over again. Eventually I reached Marlboro.

I reached the ubiquitous phone booth and placed my call to Sandy McFarland and in a few minutes, Sandy's friend, Wilma, was there with her car to whisk me off to Sandy's house.

The next day would be my daughter Becky's seventeenth birthday and the family would be driving out to walk with me, it being a Saturday. I wanted to have a birthday present for Beck, so after dinner I asked if there were someplace we could go where I could get her something. Sandy and Wilma suggested the Marlborough Country Barn, open until 9:00 p.m. and gathered me into the car. I was so happy. The Barn was one of those wonderful places one finds so often in the East, full of handcrafted items, colonial reproductions, soaps, candles, glassware, tin ware, furniture, etc.

It seemed strange to be shopping again. I had been so focused on this mission for over two weeks that I had forgotten the pleasures of nosing through a store. I seemed to have lots of energy again and chose a beautiful paperweight for Becky. It was something not based on need at all. I wanted to give her something of beauty, wanted her to know how much I loved her and how happy I was that she was now 17. I also found two corn-husk dolls, one for each daughter, just because the dolls had a special spirit to them. The one I chose for Sue was holding a bird high over her head on a stick. Freedom. Joy. For Beck there were actually two figures, arms around each other, singing and holding the same book. Love. Companionship. My shopping over, I climbed another set of stairs to look at some rugs, and suddenly felt absolutely drained of all energy.

I sat on a couch until I could catch my breath. Wilma and Sandy were aware of my exhaustion, and we got back to the car as soon as possible. In the back seat of the car, in the darkness of the night, I cried as quietly as I could. I didn't want my friends to hear me. I think Wilma saw my wet face, though, and surely when I got out of the car they saw my red eyes. I went to bed as quickly as I could, but even lying there I was so tired I couldn't get to sleep until past midnight, a most unusual condition for me.

February 26, 1971 CONGRESSIONAL RECORD — *Extensions of Remarks* E 1171

Posted on the following page in the *Congressional Record* was the Five Theses

WOMAN TO WALK FROM MASSACHUSETTS TO WASHINGTON, D.C.

HON. ROBERT F. DRINAN

OF MASSACHUSETTS

IN THE HOUSE OF REPRESENTATIVES

Thursday, February 25, 1971

Mr. DRINAN. Mr. Speaker, I present some documents about a very moving story of a woman from my congressional district in Newton, Mass., who has undertaken a heroic walk of 45 days from Massachusetts to Washington, D.C., in order to protest the continuation of the war.

I present first the letter of this wife and mother, Mrs. Louise (Severyn T.) Bruyn of Newton Centre, Mass.

Following Mrs. Bruyn's letter is an explanation by her husband of the reasons which led his wife to begin this 45-day pilgrimage to Washington.

Following her husband's letter is a very touching open letter by Mrs. Bruyn's daughter, Susan.

Finally there is a statement of the Five Theses on United States Foreign Policy which Mrs. Bruyn desires to bring to the attention of every Member of the Congress.

I commend these documents to every Member of this great body and here salute the leadership, initiative and enormous generosity of this housewife from Newton, Mass., who has undertaken a long and lonely journey in order that she may somehow call to the attention of the American people the indescribable brutality of the continuation of the war in Southeast Asia.

I insert the following items in the RECORD at this point:

NEWTON CENTRE, MASS.,
Feb. 14, 1971.

DEAR FRIENDS AND RELATIVES: I feel I must write each of you to tell you my plans. This Wednesday, February 17, I am leaving our house in Newton, Massachusetts and walking to Washington, D.C. It should take about 45 days to get there. I may arrive around April 2nd, providing I make it.

I am moved to do this because I can no longer sit in the comfort of our beautiful home, knowing the death and destruction we are causing in another land. I cannot separate myself from this though heaven knows I am well insulated. But I know it is my money supporting the war machine, my senators and representatives in Congress approving war measures. People feel so trapped. I felt that I must break my own routine in order to make my protest heard. For me, this is what my action means. I am speaking as strongly as I know how. It is my deep hope that others will be moved to take some action which for *them* is right—as strongly as I know how—to end the war.

None of you needs to have the horrors of the war described. I know of no one who feels the war should continue. Many of you are already engaged in a total commitment to work toward peace. I am trying to reach those who have become anaesthetized , and feel there is nothing one person can do. I am asking them to look for alternatives, to actively say "no" to the death machine which is war, in *their own way.*

In hope,

LOUISE.

———

Feb. 14, 1971.

To WHOM IT MAY CONCERN: My wife, Louise, has decided to walk from Newton, Massachusetts to Washington, D.C. as a protest against the spiraling effects of the war in Vietnam and against the war itself. She is a housewife, a dance instructor at the All Newton Music School, a mother of teenage children, a person whose home means a great deal to her. I believe her protest is noteworthy because she is willing to give up the comforts of her home, her family, her artistic involvements, in order to make an action statement against the war; furthermore, her protest is one which should be communicated to those who have felt it impossible to be articulate about the developing holocaust in Southeast Asia.

Her reasons are simple. They augur a change in the temper of protest. The war has developed into a system of such devastating proportions that there is no longer time to debate its morality. The time has come for a fundamental kind of action which will bring it to a halt. It is the kind of action in which ordinary people who lead ordinary lives—housewives, businessmen, teachers, mailmen, bus drivers—can stop their routines and say that the war has become a seven year massacre. It can no longer be tolerated by any measure of humanity. Debate has ended. This must be the year of citizen action. If nonviolent means of protest are not exercised quietly and firmly across the nation to end the war—by halting work, by ceasing to perform housely duties, in order to engage full time in protest—then surely action as violent as that which the administration is perpetrating on the people of Vietnam, will take place. Ordinary, conscientious people must begin to take the leadership to bring this war to a forceful halt. Soldiers have been in a row telling us about the many My Lais not open to public view. They have told us about the established practice of cutting ears and heads off Vietnamese by our own soldiers. The war is brutalizing American youth. Six million people have been forcibly relocated and close to a million people have been killed—according to our own Defense Department statistics. The massive air attacks on Laos, Cambodia, and Vietnam, the vast destruction of foliage and natural life with its horrendous radiation effects on the people and the genetic consequences to their children are morally indefensible. If China were moved troops into Canada in support of the Quebec Liberation Front, we would take extreme measures to protect this hemisphere from foreign invasion and ideology. Can China be expected to remain silent much longer? The American war in South-

east Asia must come to an end before extreme measures—a Chinese nuclear bomb with delivery power—enters into the framework of war or into negotiations. The German people did not do anything collectively and openly to resist their war and the atrocities perpetrated against the Jewish people. This inaction was condemned by the Nuremburg trials. In the United States, many people have debated and talked against the war but little direct action to stop the war has occurred except for the bombings of a radical few. These bombings have been called outrageous by the public when they are directed against buildings and the offenders are hunted down and sentenced. What a twist of morality!

The amount of bombings over Vietnam released by American airborne to kill, burn, and ravage the land of a foreign people averages 3½ Hiroshima bombs per month! The fact that the public should condemn rock throwing in store windows and at the same time support the administrative policy which brings massive human destruction is almost beyond belief! People then wonder why, after the futile attempts to change such morally outrageous war policies, youth turn to a rock or a bomb, or finally, violence against themselves with drugs. Where has the leadership of this nation gone?

My wife expects to leave next Wednesday, February 17th. We will miss her—but she goes with our full support and all our love. She will have the support of her friends in the area. She hopes that her walk will signal others to act nonviolently on a scale that will bring this monstrous policy of killing people in Southeast Asia to an end.

SEVERYN T. BRUYN.

NEWTON CENTRE, MASS.,
Feb. 14, 1971.

LIFE
*Rockefeller Center,
New York, New York.*

DEAR SIRS: I write this letter to inform you that my mother, protesting the war in Indo-China, is walking to Washington, D.C. from Newton, Massachusetts. The distance is 450 miles and she is going alone. I have often asked myself how I deserved a mother like this. She is a beautiful woman, strong in her beliefs, and full of love and understanding. Yet, this war, she cannot understand.

Thousands of people have died without knowing why and yet we continue to further the massacres and self destruction in Vietnam. All we have been able to accomplish is to destroy a good portion of that same population which we are trying to "save". To decrease casualties, you pull out or never enter the war instead of finding new borders to invade. Thousands of beautiful Vietnamese children have suffered so incredibly because their skin has melted into grotesque distortions from American napalm. They could have lived normal lives.

We have protested, leafletted, signed petitions, and cry for recognition—not for us—but for our country's mistakes. We are thrown in jails for getting exasperated enough to throw rocks, yet at the same time a soldier in Vietnam is being awarded a medal for killing innocent women and children. What has this country come to? Are we looking for a nuclear war with China? We must stop now in order to save the lives of husbands and sons who would have died in vain.

For these reasons my mother walks. What does she think it will accomplish? Perhaps nothing. But she wants people to realize that the war will not stop by itself.

My mother will leave February 17th from Newton and hopes to arrive in Washington, D.C. on April 2. She needs support. My love and prayers walk with her. I ask for your support to help her through this difficult journey.

Thank you.

SUSAN BRUYN.

Marlborough to Cobalt, Connecticut

Day

11

Sat, Feb 27

I awoke to a rainy morning. Saturday! Becky's birthday! What awful weather for them to have to walk in. Though I still felt depressed and weary, I knew I could keep going, but dear Wilma offered to walk with me, and having her there really lightened my load, both physically and mentally.

I began to realize that my exhaustion was probably partly due to the fact that my task remained constant. Each day I was traveling about the same distance, ten miles rain or shine. Ordinarily at home my energy level fluctuated so that one day I'd have a great deal of energy and could accomplish worlds of work, another day it would be low and I might not do anything needing physical exertion. Another fact was that the weather had become damp. When the humidity was high, I had more trouble breathing. My condition then was more akin to how I used to feel when I was about ten years old in fifth grade, and we lived on the third floor in a Chicago apartment. Each day after school, when I arrived at the top floor, I could hardly catch my breath, and would have to lie down. I was told that I had an enlarged heart. This feeling had often haunted me, this pressure on my chest, the sense that I can't get enough air. But doctors have told me over and over that my heart was fine except for mitral valve prolapse and that I was probably suffering more from nervous tension than anything else, and knowing how I had been able to dance in the years since, I believed them. So the third reason for my condition was no doubt tension, emotional exhaustion. Whatever it was, it wasn't severe, only enough to make me think through those reasons and respect my body and mind in this project.

Wilma walked with me for about two hours. The rain fell gently or hung in the air as fog. Soon my family would be coming along and I began to watch for them. I was afraid they'd miss me in the mist, so I was especially glad to have on my orange poncho. Wilma was finally picked up by her husband, and I had only walked about ten feet when another car stopped. It was a reporter and photographer from the *Middletown Press*. I did my best to get across to the reporter the importance of letting people know the facts about the war, and the reasons for my walking as well as the ways each person could take action to stop the war.

About ten minutes later two college students from Boston College, where my husband taught, arrived. They wanted to interview me for the *Heights*, the B.C. newspaper. The three of us walked on for a bit, and seeing it was now noon, I said I thought we should eat lunch.

I wondered how to attract my family's attention, since I wouldn't be walking alongside the road, but sitting on a wall. After hanging my orange poncho on a sign on the left side of the road and leaning my orange pack against the right side of the road, I climbed up onto the stone wall and we began to eat.

And there they were! My family! My kids! My husband! They had found me. They jumped out of the car and we threw our arms around each other. And Pat Simon had come, too, with her daughter Joy who was the same age as Susan. What a joyous reunion! What a happy, happy birthday. I wished Becky a happy birthday and brought the surprises out of the pack. Becky and Susan opened their presents with anticipation and seemed happy with what they found inside. We then *all* ate our lunches and from that point on, the rest of the walk seemed like a party.

Photo by David Blohm

"...we threw our arms around each other..."

Photo by David Blohm

They had found me! Joy Simon, me, Pat Simon, Becky, Sev, Susan

Sev had to drive our car ahead to Portland, Connecticut. As usual, our '62 VW bug needed fixing. Something was always going wrong. We planned to meet him when we got there.

We talked about all kinds of things as we walked. Susie told me her adventures during the week, Becky hers. For Beck, it was the surprise birthday party her friends had given her the night before. Both reaffirmed how great the kids at school had been. They told me how friends were bringing food in every night and how Jessie Jones was devoting hours of her time every day to answer the telephone, which was continually ringing.

Joy began picking up trash and dragging it in a box behind her. Beer cans, broken glass, paper...and I thought, "If everyone picked up just a little..."

Pat talked about how she would like to organize the Gold Star Mothers to take some action, to find some way to begin responding to the war as a group. (Days later she would go to the War Records Department to copy names of families who had lost sons. She followed that with writing a letter to the mothers, inviting them to participate in the week-long protest of vets in D.C. planned for April.)

It was a time of closeness even though no more than two could walk together at a time because of the narrowness of the shoulder of the road.

When we got to Cobalt, I called Florence Taylor to say we had arrived this far, but still had energy enough to walk further on toward Portland. At the gas station 50 yards away a man called out "Where are you going?"

"To Washington."

"What for?"

"To protest the war."

"What's the matter. Don't you like it?"

"No!" But I didn't have the heart to go over to him and begin the long conversation that I knew would ensue. And scolded myself later for missing an opportunity.

I did so want Martha and Howard to meet Sev, and remarkably we all converged at the same point just outside of Portland. We asked the Roberts, who had brought their three children, to join us for the surprise party that was planned for our arrival at Florence's. Unbeknownst to Becky, Pat had baked a cake for her (and so had Nancy Strong, our friend back home, who couldn't come). So we all went over to Florence's house, a beautiful hideaway off the main road out of Portland, built right next to a rushing waterfall that roared continually. The kids were ecstatic. We trooped in, the eleven of us, and while Becky was washing her hands, Pat set up the cakes and the paper plates and napkins she had brought and lit the candles just as Becky returned to the room to our singing "Happy Birthday." She seemed genuinely surprised and pleased. I'm sure this would be a birthday she would never forget.

Florence fixed coffee and a cool drink for the children, the cake was downed, and everyone had to go. Pat took the three girls with her, and the Roberts left with their lovely family. And now there was just Florence and Sev and me. It was wonderful for Sev to be able to stay the night. I felt much more secure.

And now just one more major thing faced me. It was Saturday night, and I had a phone date with Howard Nelson at WEEI in Boston. I placed the collect call at 7:00 to give Howard the number he should call at 7:30.

Howard was his jolly, reassuring self. I told him that my feet were fine, health good, that my family had been with me that day, etc. Then the calls came in.

That time, the callers were women filled with creative ideas on spreading the word to other states of the union. Some were in touch with Olivia and Sharon. Others talked about what they were doing for a rally in Boston. I had a sense that there was all this power out there, all ready to be unleashed, women who had suddenly found a way to express themselves against the war. One woman called in to suggest that the alumni of colleges ought to rally around the students to support their war protest actions. She was going to try to look into that as her effort. One young lady called in to say she didn't see what good my walk would do. I said it was one way for me to act. It was available, and in the face of the wanton destruction of the war, it was a small act, but the best I could do, and in the process I would be doing more than if I had sat at home. She warmed to the thought and commented that she would think about what she could do.

The conversations over, I hung up the phone and was present again to the cabin by the waterfall. Florence had a beautiful dinner ready; we ate eagerly, rejoicing in one another's presence and feeling at peace. Sev had brought me more material about the war, which I looked over and soon it was time for bed. I was tired, but happy and relaxed.

About 75 Bostonians demonstrated their opposition to the Indochina war this week by turning over their Federal telephone taxes to the farm workers' union rather than the Government.

The War Tax Resistance, which coordinates the efforts of tax resistance groups in Boston with those of similar groups in 174 other cities in the country, reports an increase in such activity.

—New York Times, Sunday, February 28, 1971

Cobalt to Durham, Connecticut

Day

12

Sun, Feb 28

Sunday morning. The sun was bright and so were our spirits. About 9:00, Sev and Florence drove me to the spot where we had stopped the day before. I began my walk. The two of them drove on to Durham, ten miles ahead, where Sev would leave his car and Florence would drive him back to meet me.

My God, the air was clear! Everything smelled so good! The bare trees in the distance were in sharp focus, the blue of the sky intense, the wind strong. A good day for flying kites. Though the temperature was nippy, I felt Spring was in the air.

After about 45 minutes, and my almost arriving at Portland, Florence pulled up with Sev. Now we were to go to Meeting for Worship at the Middletown Friends Meeting. We arrived in time for Forum, a time when the meeting discusses topics of interest. They had set aside their planned topic of the day, the Near-East Crisis, and we talked instead of the Indo-China Crisis.

The deep silence of the Meeting for Worship was balm to my spirit. It lifted me again to awareness of my leading.

David MacAllister read the Minute sent with me from the Cambridge Meeting. (A minute is a statement of belief, or decision made, recorded in the Quaker Business Meeting, often one of support when carried by an individual.) In our discussion when we were looking for new ideas, he thought of asking the question, "Are we leaving the morality of the war up to our children?" He thought of writing this in letters to the editor and ads. It seemed a good springboard for getting other people to think.

I had promised last night to call Mary Lou Shields by noon Sunday. After Meeting, I placed a call to Cambridge, Massachusetts, only to find Mary Lou and Peg were about to be interviewed by the *Boston Globe* concerning their plans for protest in Boston.

David MacAllister put us back on the road and soon just Sev and I were striding along, with Sev carrying my pack. It was so much easier to walk that way, at least for me. The wind was extremely strong, blowing in great gusts.

We were about to cross the Connecticut River over the huge bridge when we met up with Mike and Chuck Fager. Chuck we knew from Cambridge Friends Meeting. He had come to do an article for the *National Catholic Reporter* and *American Report* if they would take it. His brother Mike was doing the photography. They stayed with us for a long time, Chuck asking searching questions, Mike running across the street to get long shots, or framing them with significant things as we passed.

Sev and I continued on, with him still carrying my pack, buffeted by the wind. By the time we arrived at the Gateway Restaurant in Durham, where he had parked his car, he was exhausted, saying more than once, "We've got to find somebody to carry this pack for you. It's too much for you to carry!" I appreciated his concern, but knew I had already come that far with it, and could most likely go the rest of the way. I was extremely grateful for his carrying it that particular day. I was tired without having carried it. It would have been a real challenge to my stamina to have carried it in the wind.

Our host for the night, Walter Morris, met us at the Gateway and we followed him to his house in our car.

Soon it was time for Sev to leave. I knew I wouldn't see him again until New York City, a week and a half away, and a hundred adventures later. Without too much lingering, he was up and away, and I had a sort of hollow feeling in the pit of my stomach. Again I was on my own, though I knew his support enveloped me and held me up from wherever he would be. Though he would not be physically present, he was with me.

The number of American helicopter missions in Laos continued to be high with 1,100 reported for the day. This brought the number since February 8 to 18,000. B-52 bombers were also in action.

—New York Times, Monday, March 1, 1971

Durham to Northford, Connecticut

Good morning! It was March! February was over! I now had only one more month of walking.

After a delicious breakfast fixed by Mona Morris, I placed my call to Bob Gregory at WNTY in Southington and we made plans for him to meet me around 11:00 on Highway 17. The only way I could make plans to meet anyone in such a vague way was to just assure them that I would be walking or sitting along the road about a half hour before and half hour after our meeting time. Sometimes I would go into diners for coffee or a gas station for a rest break, but if I knew someone would be meeting me I would be sure to stay along the road during that time frame.

Mona drove me back to the Gateway Restaurant and I began my walk again. I had lost my favorite red Paper Mate pen a day or two before, so I stopped in a store to buy another. For some reason red had become an important color for me. There are those who might connect that with a political persuasion, but for me I think it had been a more aggressive nature coming forth. I was always a powder blue or aqua or brown person. Lately it had been red, which I never used to like. With my red pen tucked into my right hand jacket pocket, next to the little red notebook in which I wrote pertinent data, such as names of people who walked with me, or appointments (Bob Gregory, 11:00 a.m.), I felt happy and complete.

My pace started a little creakily. Daily, I noticed beginning the walk was always slow for about a block or two. My rusty body didn't want to go forward, but after a while the joints would feel better oiled and a more buoyant pace followed. Always in the morning, as I was set upon the road and I put on my backpack, my hands would feel sweaty. Uncertain adventures lay ahead. Daily, I was parting with the known.

It was another beautiful morning. The sun was bright, the air nippy, and the wind was down from the day before. It seemed like it would be a quite manageable day.

About 11:00 I had just taken off my pack to rest by sitting on a cable guard rail when Bob Gregory of WNTY arrived in a station wagon. I leaned my pack against his car and got in for a taped interview. We talked for about 20 minutes. He asked the usual questions about "what I hoped to accomplish" and how had I prepared for this walk, how my feet were holding out, what was in my pack, how do I eat and sleep along the way. But we soon were talking about the devastation of the war, the loss of lives, both Americans and Vietnamese and now Laotians and Cambodians. We talked about the need to set a date for withdrawal and how I felt each person in a democracy needed to make his or her voice heard. We spoke of the protest actions that were available and necessary when one's government was pursuing a course so obviously counter to our country's ideals, let alone international law. I didn't know what part of the interview was aired, but I felt good about having said what I felt and thought.

Two friends from Sudbury, Massachusetts, had driven down especially to walk with me for several hours. We finished the walk fairly early, arriving in Northford by 2:30. Because the town was so tiny, we could walk right up to the house at which I was to stay, that of Rev. Lester and Ruth Gallihue. Ruth met us at the door with her beautiful toddler son Joel, rosy from sleep, in her arms. She made us feel most welcome. I didn't stay but for a few minutes at that time because someone whisked me off to the *Wallingford Post* in Wallingford, about ten miles from Northford, where I had an interview with Neil Hogan.

After the interview, a few of us sat around discussing peaceful protest and the unconscionable aspects of this war. A man named Gilbert said, "You know, we have wasted so much money trying to elect peace candidates!! It seems to me what we ought to do is put all our money together and get some advertising firm to 'package Peace'. We've been sold soaps and cigarettes by this method, and now we are being unsold cigarettes by this method. Why not do the same with Peace?"

We all agreed it sounded like a great idea. The question was "How?" Would advertising reach down to such basic attitude formation that it would lead us to peace? Certainly the media fostered our readiness to accept war by what it reported and the way things were said. Words could whip up emotions or soothe them. It seemed to me that if one were to try this method, it would be most important to adhere strictly to truth. There must be no thought of trying to sell the public a "bill of goods," or manipulating them through falsehoods. There must be a means for making the apathetic or powerless or hopeless Americans more aware of their responsibility, their power. Through energizing them they might become engaged in actions to stop the war. The discussion ended, but we were all stimulated by the new ideas expressed in our conversation.

At the Gallihue's once more, I met their seven-year-old son, Mark, a boy of winning openness, self-confidence, directness. He fairly rang like a bell. He asked me searching questions about why I was walking, and how much did my pack weigh, and how much did I weigh. Then he took me outside to look at the fort he had built with his friends. It was great to see children using scraps and cast-offs and nature's gifts of trees and bushes and hollows for their play.

Ruth was one of those mothers who was so well organized and gentle and firm. Raising her children and taking care of the house was a no-nonsense job, and she managed it with a grace that was a delight to see.

At dinner, hands were held around the table, including Ian, the 6-year-old (not as verbal as Mark), and grace was sung, not in any way I had ever heard before, but freshly. The words were "Thank you God for this food," sung four times to the tune of "Happy Birthday to you." They told me the children had helped to make it up around Christmas time when they realized it was Jesus' birthday.

That evening we got into a conversation in the living room. Rev. Lester Gallihue wanted me to know that the solution I was advocating in

Vietnam was not as simple as I was making out. He had been to the East European countries and witnessed the presence of an armed militia everywhere. Red Chinese communism, he said, was an especially virulent form of Communism. He thought I was underestimating the belligerence and cunning of the enemy.

My answer was that nothing could possibly be as bad as the death and destruction we were causing by our presence there.

He felt our presence there was necessary to keep the other countries from becoming Communists. He agreed that we shouldn't have been there in the first place, but felt that it was now very difficult to pull out. I knew he had spoken out against the war from the pulpit. He had had a Peace Church Service once that he told me about.

At one point he said, "Above all else, I consider myself an American," and went on to explain what he meant by being an American.

I then said, "When I think of what I am, and perhaps you meant this, too, but just didn't say it, I consider myself first a human being."

He said, "No, I don't. However, if you had said you considered yourself first a Christian, then I could have accepted that because Christ transcended nationality."

I hadn't formulated my thoughts at that time into the following words, but underneath I was conscious that even to define oneself first as a Christian became divisive. It separated people into religious categories, such as Jew or Buddhist or Hindu, and I didn't want to separate myself from anyone in that way. I didn't think Jesus meant for us to do that either. It was only later that people called themselves Christians. While he walked among us, he spoke of loving the Lord thy God with all thy heart and loving thy neighbor as thyself.

Ruth tried to help us both to common ground, saying that of course we were products of the culture around us.

There was a phrase he used that implied that my approach assumed a certain arrogance, of believing I was right, a lack of humility. Perhaps that is why the conversation hurt so much. That evening as I was getting ready for bed, I wanted to run away. I wanted to pack my backpack and slip out into the night and push on to the next stop. Why, why was I so uncomfortable? I wanted to cry.

I think now I couldn't face my own inconsistency. I could not love

Lester. I spoke of loving thy neighbor, and because he didn't agree with me, I was deeply angry inside and hurt at the thought that he would think I was arrogant. It was as though something must be wrong with me, or something wrong with him. That to me was the most difficult thing to do, to disagree with someone heartily and still sincerely love him or her. Perhaps the only way to achieve that is to leave the resolution of the disagreement up to the God-power. In this way one could proceed on the basis of faith, and not let one's ego become personally threatened.

A bomb, apparently planted by a group or person protesting against the Vietnam war, exploded early this morning [Mar. 1] in the Senate wing of the Capitol, causing extensive damage but no injuries. The powerful explosion occurred in an unmarked out-of-the-way men's lavatory on the ground floor of the building. It damaged seven rooms...The explosion took place at 1:32 a.m. A half hour earlier a telephone caller warned an operator on the Capitol switchboard that a bomb would go off in protest against the Laotian operation.

—*New York Times, Tuesday, March 2, 1971*

Northford to New Haven, Connecticut

Day

14

Tues, Mar 2

Another sunny morning. A bright Tuesday. About 9:30 a.m., with my pack on my back, I began to walk away from the house, only to find that some of my friends from the day before had been waiting for me across the road in a car in order to walk with me. It was great to have company. They walked with me for an hour or more. It was warm enough for me to take off my hat.

We passed an electric line crew, three men working on some lines by the side of the road. We stopped to talk for a few minutes. One of the men recognized me from the paper or from television. He was gray haired, and had two younger men working with him. He was so courteous, gentlemanly. He was in agreement with me, with the purposes of the walk, and thought the war was terrible. But among other things he said was "What can we tell all those mothers who have lost their sons?"

My response was thoughtful, remembering my friend Pat. "Well, it doesn't help to have more mothers to have to explain it to...the death of more sons would not be an answer...perhaps the deaths would have value if we learned something from them."

His question haunted me. I felt it was a key to the feelings of the American people. What could we tell all those mothers? How could we explain that it was a mistake, that we tried but failed? How could we explain defeat? I kept the question close to my heart.

Marion McDonald from the *New Haven Register* met us along the road. She walked with us for a short bit, interviewing as we went. More than once in her questioning she asked what I thought the "other side," meaning North Vietnam, should do, and how can a Newton housewife judge the Indo-China situation. What are her qualifications? Though her questions sounded challenging, the outcome in the *Register* the next day was thoughtful and fair. She printed the gist of the Five Theses and ended with the poem "Atlas."

My destination that day was New Haven and then I would get one day of blessed rest. I would be staying with friends, Jay and Ruby Nolan, who had been our neighbors in Newton. I was really looking forward to it. Before noon the friends walking with me had to go so they were picked up and I walked on alone. I decided to press on without lunch because it wasn't too much further.

About one o'clock I reached the outskirts of New Haven, where one has to be careful to take the correct turn or else one might be walking on an expressway. That I didn't need. I stopped in at a gas station to ask directions.

The first response was direct. I should take thus and such a turn. Then the man, who spoke with a heavy Slavic or Hungarian accent, looked at my armband and said, "What are you wearing that for? Did someone you know die?"

I explained that it was a symbol of mourning for me for all the deaths in Vietnam, that I was protesting the war by walking to Washington, D.C.

He looked at my pack and my jacket (both orange). "Are you wearing those colors because you are a Communist? A Red? How come you are protesting fighting Communists? How come you didn't protest when Russia invaded Hungary and Czechoslovakia? Where were you then? My brother and I have lived under the Communists. We have lived in slave labor camps. You don't know what Communism is. You have no freedoms. We came to this country with nothing, didn't even know the language. Now we own this gas station and we've brought over our whole family and our people have built a church here. You don't know how good things are in this country." His tirade went on and on. When he asked a question he didn't wait for an answer.

I tried to explain why I was doing what I was doing, that I felt it was our democratic responsibility to protest a policy we felt was wrong...

that this action was not subversive…that I was not a Communist, but believed that people had to stay informed in order to meet the responsibility of citizenship.

He went on to describe, with anger and disgust, all protesters, their long hair, and the way they made "V" signs with their fingers. (He looked at my short hair but couldn't say anything.) He never let them in his bathrooms, saying if they wanted to protest their government they could go out in the woods. He made one concession to me. He said, "At least you are standing here talking to me. The others never do."

He said, "You know what I would do if I were the leader of this country? I would make everyone carry an ID card and if I found anyone who didn't belong here in this country or who was an agitator I would send him out, get rid of him."

I said, "But that's what one does in a totalitarian state! You would get what you ran away from."

"No," he said, "everyone would be paid $100 a week and they would have to put some of their money in a bank." He went on and on.

It was getting colder, and I asked him if he minded if I stepped inside his station to put on my sweater under my jacket. He allowed me to. Inside the station, he and his brother went on to tell me more of the hard life they had led. Their diatribe continued against all those who were on welfare and who didn't work. They had worked hard, against tremendous obstacles, and they would give no slack to anyone who could not do the same.

I had slipped off the pack to take out my sweater, remove my jacket and don the extra warmth. Pulling my jacket over the sweater, I now wanted to put the pack on again. I needed to set my pack on a support in order to slip my arms through the straps. They had spoken of not expecting anything from anybody and they didn't want anybody to take anything from them, so I said, "May I set my pack on your desk in order to put my pack back on? I don't want to take anything you don't want to give me." I was smiling.

Reluctantly, but not unkindly, he said, "Yes, go ahead." So I got myself strapped back into the thing.

The parting comment came from the brother. He said, "You know, I have the solution for this war. We should just drop one bomb on Hanoi. An atomic bomb!"

"Yes," I said, going out the door, "That would be the final solution. For them and the rest of the world." And I walked out into the chilling air.

The walk into New Haven was the first time I felt the eyes of suspicion on me. It was the first time I felt hostility from strangers, from windows, from doorways. My faith had been threatened. It was threatened on this basis: These men had suffered under Communism. Their view of reality was so different from my view of reality. It blew my mind. Why could we not see reality from the same perspective? Why could the two views not be reconciled? How could I speak to them from my experience? I had not suffered. How could I convince them I was right? My view was right? How did I have the audacity to say that? These self-doubts stayed with me all the way into the city. I deeply yearned for truth, the ultimate truth which everyone could agree was truth. Where was it? If it were truth, wouldn't everyone be able to see it?

I had been told to call Channel 8 and talk to Ken Venit, whom I had previously informed that I'd be arriving about 3:00; now he said it was too late to do anything that day. So I proceeded to finish the walk. I got to the New Haven Green about 2:30 and stopped in a luncheonette to have a sandwich, a rather delayed lunch.

It came to my mind as I was having lunch that New Haven was where Rev. William Sloane Coffin was. He was the chaplain at Yale. I had admired him highly during those years for his outspoken statements and actions for civil rights and against the war. He had put his body on the line by risking arrest to support draft resisters. We had met only briefly in Newton during the October Moratorium in 1969. Now I needed to see him. I needed to talk to someone who could set me back on center. I called his office and was told he was out of town, but would be back Wednesday night. This was Tuesday. Thank goodness I had a rest day here. I might still be able to see him.

About 3:30 I was crossing the street on the way to the middle church on the Green where I was to meet Ruby, and was confronted with a tooting horn, a swerving car with Channel 8 written across its side and a shouting man. I finished crossing the street while the car pulled over to the curb way on the other side. I wasn't sure this concerned me or someone else. I kept looking around to see if he meant me. The man ran across the street, camera around his neck. "Where *were* you! I've been looking all over for you!!"

Stunned, I said, "I've been in there," pointing to the luncheonette.

He said, "But you said you'd be here at 3:00."

I retorted, "I *was* here at 3:00. I was even here at 2:30, but I was told you wouldn't be covering me." (His anger reminded me of the White Rabbit in *Alice in Wonderland*. But in reverse: "You're late. You're late.")

He told me how he had been driving around the block several times, had driven back along the road to look for me, then back again, and had waited at the corner of State and Elm. I explained what had been told me on the phone. Obviously the TV people had changed their minds, and at this point he said all he could take was just a little walking footage. So we recrossed the street together and I retreated one of the blocks I had already walked and walked it again, this time for the camera.

That ordeal over, I continued to the First Church of Christ to watch for Ruby. She arrived shortly in their red VW bus, and we had a lovely reunion full of talk about her family, my family, and what a weird way this was to meet. Before leaving the church I noticed a sign in front of it, and felt the words worth recording in my notebook. "The strongest is always the least violent. Henry David Thoreau." A balm for my soul.

Ruby drove me to her house in Bethany. I was so glad I didn't have to walk! It was a lovely retreat in the country surrounded by many trees and much space between houses. Patches of snow still existed in places. The inside of the house was roomy and welcoming. Unfortunately, my efforts to take a shower upon arrival were thwarted by a water pump problem. There was no water. Poor Ruby was trying to cope with a plumber and a family and guest, plus knowing that a group of people from Friends Meeting in New Haven would be in that night for dinner, luckily bringing some of the food with them. We were having a potluck.

The Nolans were Lani's family, the 16-year-old who had stayed at our house when I left on the walk and who walked with Becky and me back in Mendon, about 120 miles ago, when we had looked through the sheaths of shining ice removed from stone walls. Lani, whose straight, light brown hair hung to her waist. Once two years ago when she was camping with our family, our tent pole wouldn't hold. She gave us her chewed bubble gum and we stuck it in the pole and it held. She was a girl with great inner strength and sweetness. She had Ruby's whimsy and sensitivity and compassion.

Julie, her sister, now in sixth grade, was growing tall and graceful. She interviewed me on the sofa for her school newspaper. "What do you hope to accomplish by this walk?" In almost every interview the news reporter had asked me this question. And now even a sixth grader! Why was it so hard to answer?! My walk was more like a witness. How do you ascribe a rational goal to a witness? Yes, I hoped others would find a way *they* could take action in their own way, but it was more than that. I could not answer the question in a rational a way. My walk to me was more like a cry of outrage at the horrors we were committing, it was a prayer that we stop.

In the evening the guests gathered, Friends and friends. It was cozy and informal. We sat in a circle, on the floor, on chairs, eating spaghetti and drinking wine and talking. We all read copies of the People's Peace Treaty, which I had brought with me.

Dr. Marge Nelson, the Quaker doctor who had been captured by the Viet Cong back in 1969, was there. She told of some of her experiences and what she had witnessed, some actions of cruelty, though not to her, some of compassion.

A young man sitting in the circle told a story of his own. He had received in the mail, as a Christmas present from a friend of his (whom he knew to be a fine, young, upstanding Baptist), a Viet Cong ear, with an apology for not having two for him, because the second one got mangled when the fine young man shot the Viet Cong.

The circle of guests felt the impact of these stories.

I made a date to meet with Marge Nelson in the morning. It was one of those golden opportunities to speak with someone whose judgment I trusted implicitly who had actually been over in Vietnam, both South and North.

The guests went home, the Nolans and I visited for a bit and then it was bedtime. What a marvelous feeling to know that I didn't have to get up early the next morning and walk another ten miles. I could just relax, for the first time in two weeks.

Week Three

...South Vietnamese command reported a total of 320 dead, 1000 wounded and 99 missing in action since the operation began on February 8. It is suspected that the numbers are unrealistically small.

— New York Times, Wednesday, March 3, 1971

Day

New Haven, Connecticut – Rest Day   **15**

Wed, Mar 3

It was raining and miserable outside. I was so glad I didn't have to walk. Ruby stayed home for the morning so we could visit and she could drive me into town to talk with Dr. Marge Nelson. We lost our way in the maze of New Haven streets, arrived a half hour late only to find that Marge Nelson had forgotten that she had an 11:00 appointment that morning which she couldn't break. She invited me to go with her. We talked on the way and in the office.

I wanted to know if one of the papers I was using for information was accurate. The article in question was about the Women's Prison at Con Son, Vietnam. The list of atrocities attested to by these women, whose letters had been smuggled out of the prison, were enough to make one weep in just the reading. Were they accurate? Were they exaggerated? She looked at the preface, which was written by Don Luce. Once she saw that name she said she trusted the article. Don Luce knew Vietnam and the Vietnamese language better than any other American, as far as she knew. He had gone over there originally to work for USAID until he could no longer stand the controls put on the populace by the U.S. through AID. He resigned and stayed to work with the people. He had since been asked to leave the country. It was he who arranged in the summer of 1970, for Sen. Anderson and others to visit the Con Son prison, where they discovered the tiger cages.

I asked her whether in her judgment the people of South Vietnam,

107

who were not Communists, wanted us to stay or leave. She said that the people she knew who had originally been for our presence there now felt the price was too great. Even though they feared the Communists, considered them ruthless, they felt the destruction of the people and the land was too extensive and the only alternative was for us to get out. They hoped to be able to work out some kind of a coalition government.

She gave me the articles to read concerning her own capture by the Viet Cong and the respectful treatment she and the others got as prisoners. In her experience at the Da Nang hospital, she had treated prisoners at the prison across from the hospital and often found evidence of torture. She discovered it was being done by South Vietnamese interrogators in the Interrogation Center, built by the U.S. Even though she reported it to the American advisors, they were apparently unable to stop its practice.

The weather became increasingly worse, developing into a wet snow. Ice began to form on the streets. We went home carefully, rested a bit, and then drove into New Haven for a reception at Yale, at Branford College, followed by dinner and a reception at Pierson College. About six young men ate with us and four stayed with us for the evening "talk" which I was scheduled to give. About two more showed up at the meeting. This made a grand total of eight people from all of Yale who gathered to meet me and talk about the war. Clearly, the war and my kind of action was not attracting students.

One of the students at the meeting was Chris Little. He became more interested in the possibilities of the walk especially around the NYC area, and he and Jay decided to work further on it. Chris came to the Nolan's house that night, shaping the possible press releases they could use for New York City. We called home and for a long while had a five-way conversation. Jay had three extensions, and we had two in our Newton house. Jay, Chris and I were on the New Haven end, and Sev and Mary Lou Shields were on our two. After a long discussion, Mary Lou finally said to Sev and me, "We'll leave you two alone," after which she, Chris and Jay hung up. Sev and I were left saying things like, "It's so good to be alone together, darling. This is so *intimate!*"

Lani decided she would walk with me the next day. I was so happy to have her company. It looked like we would be going through some rough weather.

North Vietnamese gunners have fired antiaircraft missiles across the demilitarized zone at American planes flying over South Vietnam, the United States command reported yesterday....the planes did not return the fire.

United States helicopter pilots, who have flown more than 20,000 sorties over Laos in the last three weeks, report that they are encountering the heaviest antiaircraft firing of the war.

—New York Times, Thursday, March 4, 1971

New Haven to Milford, Connecticut

Day

16

Thurs, Mar 4

That day would be a challenge. I could tell. The ground was already covered with some snow and the air was full of it. I decided that I would just keep going as long as I could. "Proceed as way opens," an old Quaker saying, would be my guide. As long as I could make forward progress, I'd keep going. If something stopped me, then I would accept it and wait out the storm.

Before leaving, Jay drove me to see the Rev. Coffin at his home for just a few minutes. I laid before him my quandary, "How can there be two truths colliding with each other?" I told him of the experience I had had at the gas station coming into New Haven.

I wish I could remember verbatim what he said, but in general it was that each of these experiences of Communism was different. The situations were different. One solution could not be applied to both. Whatever his words were, I felt strengthened in my purpose. I felt supported in this witness I had taken on and more grounded in my own beliefs and experience.

And so we drove off to the central church on the Green again. A number of people had come to see us off. A few would walk a few blocks with us, but Lani and I were the only two planning to go on ahead. The wind was now gale force. Some passersby were carrying umbrellas to keep the heavy wet stuff from them, but the umbrellas were blowing inside out. We took turns carrying the pack. At times we leaned on the wind at such an angle that if the wind were to stop too suddenly we would have fallen over. We had to keep looking up so that we wouldn't walk into an oncoming car, but this caused the snow to fly directly into our eyes. It stung. There were times when the gusts were so strong we would have to suddenly turn our backs and wait them out, leaning backward at what seemed a 45 degree angle. I was grateful for the poncho and the balaclava which I could pull down over my face, but worried that Lani was not as warm as she should have been, though she assured me she was "fine." This was one of those days that I wore the boots, and inside the heavy wool socks my feet were well-bandaged with Band-Aids and moleskin. Even so, they soon became very uncomfortable and I had to take them off and put on the sneakers. By noon the wind had abated some, and the clouds turned a lighter gray, almost allowing some sun to shine through. The snow was almost over. We stopped in a diner for lunch.

Initially, entering the diner felt foreboding. The only customers were men. The exceptions were Lani and I and the waitress. The waitress's voice carried to everyone around. She spoke to people in general. She asked what we were doing, and I explained. Once she knew we were against the war, she was right in there pitching. "I'd walk with you, too, if I could. More people ought to do the kind of thing you're doing. This war is awful. We shouldn't be over there." She set the tone. Of all the truck drivers and workers eating there, not one made an adverse comment. There was only politeness. They wouldn't have dared make a comment against us with her there.

As we walked on, a man driving out of a parking lot stopped to ask us where we were going. I said to Washington, D.C. to protest the Vietnam war. He folded his arms. "Have you ever been to Vietnam?"

"No," I said, "but I'll bet you have."

"I fought over there, and I have a 75% disability in my back."

I told him I was so sorry.

He said, "Do you approve of the kind of protest that just took place, bombing the Capitol?"

I said, "No, I don't." I smiled and continued, "I'm certainly not carrying any bombs in my pack," thinking to lighten the encounter.

He said, "How do I know what you have in your pack." He asked me what I thought of the Kent State killings.

I said I thought the National Guard had grossly overreacted.

He said, "Would you like me to spit in your face?"

My recollection is that I stepped far back. "No, and I wouldn't like to spit on you either."

"Well," he said, "that's what the students did to the National Guard!"

Now seeing what he meant, that he wasn't intending to spit on me, I responded, "One doesn't shoot someone in return for spitting."

He went on to tell me how bad things were in the country, how he had lost his job and was trying to win a court case concerning his being fired. More than once he said, "There's nothing you can do. You can't fight City Hall." It seemed to summarize an attitude held by more than one American! "You can't fight City Hall!" That is despair!

After the encounter, Lani and I continued walking. She had felt it deeply. The apparent threat of spitting on me had shocked her and brought tears to her eyes.

One block later another young man stopped his car. "I'm a former graduate of Boston College where your husband teaches, and I just stopped to tell you what a fine thing I think you are doing." We shook hands. It lifted both our spirits, and gave Lani faith again.

We arrived in Milford and stopped in a little coffee shop, ordered some coffee and doughnuts, and I called the Pfaffs to tell them I had arrived. When he arrived we rose to pay our bill. The owner of the store then recognized me and wouldn't take any money. I thanked him heartily and we went out to meet Rev. Pfaff.

The Pfaffs home was fantastic, right on the sea! The great breakers came crashing in against the rocks, whipped up by the gale winds we had had that day. From the inside one could look right out onto the ocean. Their house served as a center for peace and international understanding. Lani stayed for dinner, which we ate by candlelight.

That evening a photographer from a Milford paper came out to the house. Jay came to pick up Lani about 8:00, and our evening came to a peaceful close. We had made it through this day. It was a triumph of sorts.

Punishing winds and driving snow lashed the Northeast yesterday, producing heavy snow accumulations inland and perilous conditions along the coast.

—New York Times, Friday, March 5, 1971

Milford to Fairfield, Connecticut

This morning before I left, Christopher Schmauch came over to the Pfaffs to meet and talk about the Schmauch's World Fellowship Center. Before we finished talking he asked if I could talk to their Fellowship Reunion in Boston on April 21. That seemed such a long way off. I agreed, though at that point I wasn't even sure I would be able to finish the walk. No matter. I would accept, providing I was alive and well.

I was driven to my beginning point, right where I had ended the day before. I hiked off. It was a sunny day, though windy.

I passed a man with a yellow construction hat on that had three American flag decals on it. He seemed the type who would have defended the rightness of the war. He wished me good luck.

Just before crossing the Housatonic River I stopped in a diner for coffee and a doughnut. (One nice thing about all this walking. I could indulge myself in doughnuts and candy bars and not put on weight.) I got into a conversation with the man sitting next to me at the counter. He thought he recognized me from television and then said he had just heard my interview on the radio before coming into the diner. He was amazed at the coincidence. I showed him the Five Theses I was asking people to sign if they wanted to and he said he would be happy to sign. When the owner of the diner found out who I was he wouldn't let me pay. He said it was his way to help.

I crossed the bridge in high spirits.

Walking along a ridge of land, I heard a whistle way in the distance and looked up. On a loading platform that must have been about two blocks away three men were waving. They shouted "Good Luck!" I waved back.

Passing a schoolyard in Stratford, I saw children playing during their lunch hour. A cluster of kids about ten years old noticed me and one said, "You going camping?"

"No, I'm walking to Washington."

"Are you that lady?"

"Yes," I responded.

They followed along inside the fence as I continued on the sidewalk. As we got up to the school itself, they disappeared around the back of it, and as I got to the other end a whole flock of children came running up to me from around the back. They were full of questions. They couldn't believe a person could walk to a point that far away. I took out my map to show them how far I had already come.

We were having a great time out there in front of the school when a man showed up on the stairs. The children said, "That's the principal."

I entered the schoolyard and went up to the stairs to meet him. He was most cordial and invited me in. Since it was still the lunch hour the children waited outside. I went into his office and we had a good talk. I allayed his fears about my political radicalism. I didn't consider myself an extreme radical, just extremely upset by our government's actions in Vietnam. He asked if I wanted to speak to the two sixth grades. That sounded like a fine opportunity. After all, I had once been a teacher of both fourth and fifth grades back in Illinois, and even nursery school. I ate my packed lunch in his office while listening to a news report on his radio.

About 1:00 I went up to the classroom. I told the children how important it was in a democracy for the people to stay informed and learn all they can about what their government was doing. It was especially important for school children to be as well prepared as possible for citizenship for when they grow up. I also talked about the importance of non-violent protest. Both before and after I spoke, the principal underlined that what I was saying was my *opinion* and that I had a right to express my own *opinion* so long as I did it non-violently; there was another side to the problem, he said. And I thought to myself, "Is there another side to murder? Is there another side to rape? Are there two sides to everything? Is everything one says an opinion? At what point does one use judgment and choose a 'side'?" It gave me food for thought for further down the road, but I didn't say anything.

As I continued my journey, walking alone along the highway, I read aloud the beautiful poem Jim Prior had tucked in my pack "for your mind to sing as you walk along." It was from *Gitangali* by Tagore.

On the seashore of endless worlds children meet.
The infinite sky is motionless overhead and the restless water
is boisterous.
On the seashore of endless worlds the children meet with
shouts and dances.

The poem went on for four more stanzas, in that timeless sense, singing of their play with empty shells, floating their boats on the vast deep and not aware of the tempest. The children play on the seashore of endless worlds.

My mind sang and my feet were unaware that they were placing themselves one ahead of the other. My mind sang, and my heart was full. My face and hands were getting quite browned from the sun. That was a fourteen mile day.

That night I was taken to Bridgeport University for an Anti-War Conference. Even there, attendance was slack. There were about 100 people; chairs had been set up for 400. Somehow the war was not getting much attention among the students. I spoke for about 10 minutes on what I was doing and why. Following that, Cynthia Frederick, a member of Concerned Asian Scholars, gave an excellent talk on the political situation in South Vietnam. Such a combination of clarity and passion! Jack Smith spoke for the Vietnam Veterans Against the War. He showed a long series of slides. I braced myself for looking at atrocities, but that wasn't what they were at all. They showed the people in very friendly settings, warmly human; the children were beautiful. Some of the countryside was so delicate. Yes, they also revealed the wastelands that the war had created, and the overpopulated cities with their piles of trash and the army bases. I felt I knew the country just a wee bit better afterwards. After Frank Greer spoke for the People's Peace Treaty, I circulated the Five Theses for people to sign.

Then it was to the home of Dana Jacobson, an old friend. And bed. I got myself well tucked in, when the slats fell out from under the bed. I pulled the mattress onto the floor, climbed back into bed and sank into a deep sleep.

The White House made public today the following recapitulation of American prisoners of war and men missing in action [White House – total 1605; Hanoi's total – 368] since 1964.

—*New York Times, Saturday, March 6, 1971*

Fairfield to Westport, Connecticut

A number of walkers started with me in the morning. As we crossed the line into Westport, about 11:00 a.m., there were twenty people waiting to walk with us. It was beautiful. Before going on we stopped for a drink of water, and a woman, seeing the crowd gathered round at this supermarket parking lot, asked what was going on. When she found out, she said, "What good will walking to Washington do?" She seemed cold and skeptical.

I explained the best I could what had made me walk, and how I felt I had to do it whether it "accomplished" anything or not. When I finished, she clasped my hand in a farewell grip that had great warmth in it, and tears came to her eyes and mine. She then walked on. I had been deeply moved by her response. I felt the Spirit had moved between us.

Yesterday, as we were walking into Fairfield, a man driving alone pulled his car over and asked if I were the woman walking to Washington. He said he was very happy to meet me and thought what I was doing was a fine thing. Today, he came by in his car again, this time with his wife and eight children. He wanted them to meet me. I felt honored.

We reached the vigil in front of Town Hall, which the World Affairs Center has held every Saturday noon since Mothers Day 1967. Usually, they said, there have been four to twelve people present. That day there were about forty. We all made a fine showing for peace. A few people

116

FOR PEACE — Mrs. Louise Bruyn, center, from Newtown Center, Mass., stopped in Westport Saturday during her ten-mile a day peace march to Washington. With her, in front of the World Affairs Center are (l. to r.) Burton Knopp, Mrs. David Newton, director of the World Affairs Center and George Corwin.

The Westport News, March 10

Peace marcher visits center

were handing out cards to be mailed to Sen. Fulbright in support of peace efforts.

Wendy Newton had been the energy behind getting all these people to show up. She had spent about forty-eight hours on the phone. She was the present director of the World Affairs Center, a very active peace group which occupied a storefront in Westport. We stopped in the Center, an esthetically beautiful small place that made peace literature available.

After reaching the A&P in Norwalk, we were driven back to the Center (I hated having to backtrack by car), where I had an interview for the *Norwalk Hour* and *Westport News*, and then was driven to Adelaide Baker's house, where I was to stay that night.

Adelaide's house was part of an estate, with beautiful grounds surrounding it. The interior of the house itself was warm with its dark woodwork; the living room was two stories high with a beamed ceiling. Adelaide was most gracious. She had been a pillar of Women's International League for Peace and Freedom (WILPF) for years.

After a hot bath and a short rest, I made my phone call home and had a radio interview with a Greenwich station, WGCH. We then drove to somewhere, I know not where, because it was dark, and I didn't care. I was too tired and was glad to be riding. But we took a turnpike somewhere to a lovely house where there was a potluck dinner for members of WILPF.

That was Saturday night. Another week had passed and it was time again to talk to Howard Nelson at WEEI. How could a week have gone that fast! With my host's assistance, I shut myself into a room, made the 7:00 call to give him my number, spread out my materials all over the floor, and waited for him to call me at 7:30. It was shakes time again, but not so bad this time.

I was able to pass on information I had gathered during the week. The U.S. bombing in Vietnam had increased, there were 101 more dead U.S. soldiers since last week, and RMK-BMJ, a U.S. corporation that built the "tiger cages," had now contracted to build over 96 more. These were the secret prison cells in which "Viet Cong" and political prisoners were kept, having too low a ceiling so they couldn't ever stand up. (These were the cages discovered at Con Son Prison by Don Luce and Sen. Anderson.) I talked about the corruption of the Saigon regime and how American's fear of Communism allowed them to justify our destruction of a people and their land. And lastly, that I knew that each step I had taken had not yet stopped the suffering.

The call I remember the best was from a man who said in a sneering fashion, "Now, Mrs. Bruyn, why don't you stay home and take care of your husband and children? We all know that all you want is some publicity for your little dancing school."

My incredulity at his statement left me almost speechless. I said, "Sir, I find it hard to believe that you think so little about what is happening in Vietnam that you would attribute such shallow motives to me." The very logic of the situation ought to have informed him that if it were my "dancing school" I was interested in furthering, this would hardly be the way to go about it. If anything, I would *lose* students, besides which I was losing some income, because a substitute was teaching my classes for me. Logic was not his forte.

When the ordeal was over, I again felt depressed. I wasn't shaking, or crying, but just couldn't stand the thought of making "small talk" at the party. I ate my dinner in a corner, feeling very anti-social. I agreed to say a few words before the scheduled talk for the evening. The people there were very receptive to what I had to say, and the following talk by a lawyer on student rights was very enlightening.

Home again to Adelaide Baker's. Another night, another bed, another sleep.

...toll of helicopters taken by North Vietnamese guns. Officially, 38 have been shot down and destroyed in Laos, but the command refuses to disclose how many aircraft have been shot down and later recovered by American rescue teams. An operations officer has disclosed that as of March 1 the number of such planes was 219.
—*New York Times, Sunday, March 7, 1971*

Westport to Darien, Connecticut

Day

19

Sun, Mar 7

That morning was wet and rainy.

When I was thinking about going on this long walk, I thought of all the things that could happen to me. I knew I was a sitting duck for anyone who might want to take out his vengeance on all protesters. I knew, though, that I had to go ahead with the walk; I was ready to face anything. I had had a talk with the girls before I left, to tell them that if anything happened to me on the way, they shouldn't feel bad. I wanted them to know that I felt fulfilled with my family, that they were a joy to me, that so far I had lived fully and would be living in the most alive, human way I could during the walk, and if I were to die or be killed, they must have no regrets, because I didn't.

Every now and then prophetic or foreboding thoughts would brush across my mind. As we left Adelaide Baker's house, from a bell tower I heard a bell tolling. I stopped and looked back. My friend who was to drive me explained, "That must be Adelaide. I've heard she has a bell up in that tower and she does that as a gesture to departing friends." The sound was ominous. All I could think of was "For whom the bell tolls— it tolls for thee." In the gloom of the morning, it didn't exactly cheer me.

We began our walk in Norwalk at the A&P. It was quite a steady rain. Our plan this morning was to walk until about 10:15 when we would be picked up by Wendy Newton and driven to the Wilton Friends Meeting for Worship. The walk itself was uneventful. Just wet. The drive to Wilton took about half an hour and there we hung up our wet clothes over the furnace to dry. Luckily I had a change of clothes.

Someone in Meeting spoke about "Am I my brother's keeper" and "Responsibility." It was a rational discourse. Oh, how I wanted passion! I wanted everyone to jump to their feet and shout "Hallelujah! Amen! Just show us the way, Lord, and we'll follow!" I wanted fervor, enough that would raise us all up to some momentous task together. And instead the Light seemed to come so haltingly, in dribbles, just barely enough to sustain us.

We met my new walking companions back at the gas station where we had stopped for the morning. Some of us had dinner at Old Mac-Donald's Farm, where it was warm and cozy. I did not look forward to starting the walk again, but there it was; we had to go on. The rain had all but disappeared, and by the time we walked all the way to Stamford, past Darien, the sun was shining. I called my next hosts, Sylvia and Robert Reddy, and said goodbye to the wonderful people who had walked all that way with me for almost two days.

Sylvia and Robert were a young couple. Their small but modern apartment contained, besides themselves, two dogs, Happy and Pax, and four cats. They had a system of locking each room as they went in and out to keep the animals where they belonged, either in or out. We were eating dinner and became aware that we couldn't hear the animals. Sylvia suggested that they might be in trouble. Sure enough, when I looked in my designated room, the pups had gotten into my pack. There was lambs wool all over the rug, and sprinkled about were my gloves and Band-Aids and my poncho. Luckily the only thing they had chewed was my Prell Shampoo tube. Small loss. Those scamps! I was careful to lock the door properly after that.

The United States continued widespread bombing raids today, sending more than 1000 planes into action against enemy forces in Laos and Cambodia.

The raids were mounted from at least four bases in Thailand, half a dozen bases in South Vietnam and from carriers of the Seventh Fleet in the Gulf of Tonkin.

—*New York Times, Monday, March 8, 1971*

Darien, Connecticut to Port Chester, NY

Day

20

Mon, Mar 8

I awoke in the morning remembering a beautiful dream. Sev and I were standing in our back yard of our old house in Jacksonville, Illinois, and the grass was growing. We could see it turning Spring right there in front of our eyes. We'd look from section to section of the lawn and see it get greener, growing from seeds in the brown earth. Our garden in the back was thriving. (In real life, it never did.) The tree that had really been an elm was somehow a tree with blossoms beginning to bud, and the back of the house, formerly lacking in paint, was in good repair. It was so beautiful, so hopeful. I awoke right at 8:00 after a wonderful night's sleep

I received a phone call in the morning from Nancy Strong in Newton telling me about the letter written by some women in Norwood, Massachusetts. It was asking the President to stop the war, saying that the mother signing the letter was sending him a picture of her son to let the President know that the price of this war was too high. She was not going to "buy war" any more. Nancy wondered if I would be willing to take these letters and pictures in to the President, if I should get to see him. I said I could. It sounded like a beautiful and meaningful action.

This morning's walk was cold and windy. Going through a run-down section of Stamford, a man said, "You the walkin' lady?"

"Yes," I said.

"You're walkin' to Washington?"

"Yes," I answered.

"And you'll get there 'bout April 2nd?"

"That's right," I said, smiling.

"Yeah, I heard 'bout it on television. Good luck!" he said.

It left me with a warm feeling inside.

One of the women who walked with me that day was a strong women's liberation movement person. She was incensed at the power held by men. She discovered it when she tried to form a women's magazine, own the stock in it and get advertisers who were not exploiting women by their merchandise. It got humorous, because she was mentioning all the things they *couldn't* in good conscience advertise such as bras, cosmetics, nylons—she laughingly decided about the only wholesome thing one could sell was potatoes!

At the Greenwich Library, we met with several women who were part of quite an active peace group in Greenwich. Two women were discussing my hiking garb. One looked at my sneakers and said, "Your shoes stink," and the other said, almost simultaneously, "Yes, they stink" and my mouth dropped open as I looked from one to the other. I thought I had been unaware of how bad my shoes smelled after walking in them for two and a half weeks. But then we all burst out into laughter. They had meant the sneakers were not the best shoes for walking.

We stopped for lunch at a bowling alley and brought our sandwiches in, wanting to order a coffee or soda and eat our sandwiches at the counter. The waitress said, "You can't eat your sandwiches in here." We rewrapped our homemade sandwiches and ordered some of theirs. We had struck up a conversation at the counter with a third woman. When I left the counter to go to the rest room, the third woman picked up my check to pay for my order. I came back in time to hear the cashier say that the sandwich was on the house. She wouldn't accept any money for it, because she learned who I was. She said she was completely in favor of what I was doing and wanted to know if there weren't something else I might want to take with me—a cup of tea? A soda? I didn't need anything more, but thanked her. She was lovely. She wished me good luck on the way.

This time I walked off by myself. The clouds had become extremely dark, and snow was suddenly filling the air. Huge flakes were flying in all directions. My jacket was beginning to get wet. I had walked about a block from the bowling alley where we had eaten, when I heard a man's voice calling, "Louise?" I turned and here was this young man running up to me to say he had been watching for me all day from his store, the Eco-Center, a place for health foods, and he just saw me pass. He just wanted to say hello. It was great meeting him and I decided to walk back the few feet to his store to put on my orange poncho. While I was putting it on, he was choosing some candy bars and packages of organic nuts for me to carry with me. Feeling like a squirrel, my pockets bulging, I thanked him heartily and ballooned out into the wind, the Great Orange Pumpkin.

At Port Chester I crossed the state line into New York. I thought, "My God, Connecticut is big! I've been walking through it since February 22!" I sang a little celebration song in my heart, and passersby might have noticed a smile on my lips. But aside from that, there was no fanfare. I was met at the village Green in Rye by Ruth Bowman, Maida Follini, and a reporter from the *Daily Item*. The reporter did an interview in Maida's VW bus, a warm place away from the chill of the air.

Maida then took me to the Friends Meeting at Stamford, where she had built up a peace center. A poster caught my eye. I wrote down the words in my notebook. "Quakers believe there is something of God in every man. We cannot prove this but we do know that when men act as if it were true their trust is justified."

Later at Maida and Paul's house, friends came over to talk. New York City was coming up soon, where all the networks were.

A lot of planning was already happening over the telephone. Chris Little, who was doing so much work in maximizing the publicity, was trying to get me on the Dick Cavett show. Dick Cavett was the MC whom I really respected. I might be able to speak of my action, my message, to millions of Americans all over the country. The other plans that were taking shape were to have a church service at the St. Clements Episcopal Church. I had no idea how many people would show up to walk with me. There was the possibility that there would be dozens. There was also the possibility that there would only be "us." "Us," hallelujah, would be my family and the Joneses. Becky and Susan and Sev were driving down with Wayne and Jessie Jones to walk with me through Manhattan. That was to be on Thursday. This was Monday. It wouldn't be far off.

Before turning in for the night, Maida shared this poem with me that she had written in January.

AIR SUPPORT
by Maida Follini

I see the bomb as clearly as if it were falling
Through the quiet air
Of the New England countryside,
Although it shafts downwards
In a far place, so far that it is near.
The other side of the earth? Here.
Part of the continent.
The air whistles too brief a warning,
Then the thatched roof, bamboo sides,
Wood rafters, crockery, cotton-clothed
Father, mother, grandmother, burst and shatter,
The mud floor gapes. The splinters, dust and blood
Spray in a widening circle
There/here. Red blotches everywhere;
On my hands, in my eyes, dripping from my arms.
The baby flies, thrown by the shock-wave,
Out of her hanging cradle by the side of the now-demolished hut.
She curves through the air, eyes wide in fear.
Air gives her no support. She cries to be caught.
I cry here, "Catch her! Catch her!"
While as in a dream a thousand uniformed extensions
Of my bloodied arms march past with backs turned,
And with blind eyes pull levers, turn switches,
And there/here
I see the bomb as clearly as if it were falling
Through the quiet air
Of the New England countryside.

The Supreme Court ruled today that young men were not entitled to draft exemptions as conscientious objectors if they objected only to the Vietnam conflict as an "unjust war" and did not oppose all wars.

—*New York Times, Tuesday, March 9, 1971*

Maida put me back on the road at the Rye Green. A group of twenty-eight people had gathered there to walk a ways with me. What a parade we were! Some were high school students who would walk as far as the high school with us. Others were mothers like myself, and there were a few college students.

All of them had dropped off by the time I reached Mamaroneck. I crossed the street to cash a traveler's check at the Mamaroneck bank. I had brought $150 with me in traveler's checks and this was the first one I had to cash.

I decided to stop for a snack at a diner. Upon my entering, a man looked up and said, "When do you think you'll get there?" What a fantastic opener! From there we went on into the details of the trip, how I planned to go from Mamaroneck. He wound up checking the directions on my map for me. The funny thing about this conversation was that neither of us mentioned the war. Both of us knew why I was walking.

Joined again by a companion from yesterday, we walked on toward New Rochelle. A beautiful collection of people met us at the New Rochelle line. We trudged into the city, talking a mile a minute. Others were carrying my pack, so I could really stretch out my legs. At the post office, Rev. J. Ralph Davie presented me with a medallion from the New Rochelle Women for Peace. Written on its face were the words: "War is not healthy for children and other living things." Amen. Now I had a piece of jewelry. Now, when I would attend evening meetings, I could "dress up" just by wearing it. The news media took pictures of the event.

Sister Alice, a teacher at New Rochelle College, picked me up with Ann Schwerner, my hostess for the evening. Sister Alice took me to the house at the College where she lived, we had tea in the kitchen with Sisters Alice and Eugenia, I rested for a few minutes and then caught up on my note taking. On the phone I had a long conversation with Chris Little, who was trying to get Mayor Lindsey to walk with me through New York City. He thought maybe Rev. Coffin could be at the church. An Episcopal minister would perform the simple service.

We went to dinner at the college with Ann and Nathan Schwerner. As an informal announcement to the girls in the college dining hall, I spoke about how we had to keep working for peace. I said that we mustn't give up, because all the time that we were living in our comfort, the Vietnamese were suffering untold agonies, their country was being torn apart, and our young men were laying down their lives. I told them ways I hoped they would keep the protest alive on campus. Sister Alice said it was the first time she had ever heard the girls be quiet for an announcement.

From the college, the Schwerners drove me back to Rye to the Friends Meeting House where a special Tuesday night Meeting had gathered. We settled into a deep silence. After about 10 to 15 minutes, I rose to say the few things that I felt moved to share, and after I sat down, a few more folks spoke their thoughts, including a young boy who shared his feelings of the hypocrisy in the adult world. At the end of the hour, when handshakes all around signified the meeting was over, people decided that Tuesday nights would be a fine time to meet every week to continue thinking about and working to end the war.

Going out to the car, this same young boy who had spoken in Meeting, who was perhaps thirteen years old, walked next to me and said, "I'm jealous of you."

"Why?" I asked.

"Because you can do anything you want to."

"I know what you mean," I said. "You still have your parents responsible for you."

"Yes," he said, "but this summer, I'm going to sit in that tower," pointing to the meeting house tower, "for a whole week and not come down, in order to protest the war."

How our spirit needs expression! It yearns for integrity, dedication, independence. We parted wishing each other good luck.

Yesterday, talking to Chris about the walk through New York City, he mentioned that I should start early enough and plan to walk slowly, "in case they want to shoot you."

I paused. "What?" I said.

"The TV cameras will need extra time," he said.

"Oh, yes, that," I said, relieved.

My thoughts had still not left the idea of an untimely end.

And now I was to stay at the Schwerner's. Their son, Michael was the young man who had been killed in the South working with the Civil Rights Movement. Ann showed me to my room. It was Michael's old room. On the bed was Michael's old blanket, his nametag still on it. I could not help but feel intensely grateful to the family who had given so much, who would share their hospitality with me and allow me to share the intimacy of Michael's blanket keeping me warm.

The Schwerners were beautiful people, full of heart. I ached for their loss, though we never discussed it. Ann noticed my chapped lips and gave me a tube of Nivea ointment. (It stayed with me for the rest of the trip. Whenever I used it, I thought of her.) Wrapped in her housecoat, and surrounded by the feeling of love in that household, I sipped sherry with them in the kitchen until time to turn in.

I rested in the sense of "God's Will be done..."

Quaker takes 450-mile trek to Washington

Hopes her hike will help halt war

By Charles Fager
Special to the National Catholic Reporter

MIDDLETON, Conn. — Louise Bruyn, 40, of Newton, Mass, is going to Washington to speak to America's political leaders about ending the Indochina war.

If her mission is not news, her mode of travel is: She is walking the entire distance of 450 miles from her home near Boston to the nation's Capital.

She began three weeks ago, staying nights in the homes of friends and peace movement contacts along the way. At a rate of 10 miles a day, she expects to arrive in Washington about April 5.

To reassure doubters, Mrs. Bruyn carries with her a letter from the chief of police in her home town. The letter, which she said came unsolicited, introduces her as a woman "of fine moral character, a citizen, wife and mother of our community."

She had not previously been a militant peace activist, and the impulse to walk to Washington was as much a surprise to her as to everyone else. Her normal way of life is not out of the ordinary. Her husband is a sociology professor at Boston College, they have three teenage children, and Mrs. Bruyn teaches dancing part-time to local school children.

She rejects political labels, although she will admit to having worked for Eugene McCarthy and Father Robert Drinan. But she was not prominent in these campaigns and, until she felt the call to her present journey, had not taken any dramatic individual action before.

"The idea came to me on Feb. 6," she explained. "I remember it all very well because I've had to explain it so many times since.

"I was reading an article about the forced resettlement of several million South Vietnamese from their homes in the northern part of their country. And I realized that this, like the Laos invasion, was going almost unnoticed here at home. Americans have become anesthetized about the war, I thought, and myself among them. Then I felt the need to walk."

Atypical as this impulse was for her, it was consistent with Mrs. Bruyn's religious background, which is Quaker. Characteristic of Friends is a style of witness rooted in individual concerns and depending on singu-

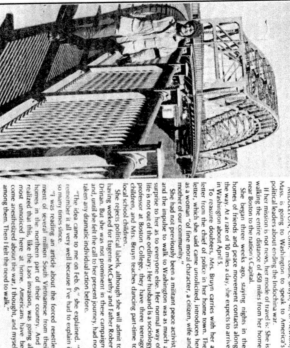

IN GOOD SPIRITS, Louise Bruyn strides across the Connecticut river at Middletown on her 450-mile walk to Washington. (Michael Fager photo)

lar, often seemingly odd personal commitments. In the days following Feb. 6, Mrs. Bruyn followed her tradition and "tested her leading" in long conversations with other Quakers and close friends before finally deciding to act on it.

She said she sought out negative comments especially, and at first she was very worried about the demands such a trip would place on her and her family. But when the day of her departure arrived, she held a quiet meeting for worship at her home with two dozen Friends and supporters. She then felt, she recalled, very calm and ready to go.

After two weeks on the road, winding down through southern Massachusetts into Connecticut below Hartford, Mrs. Bruyn was in high spirits. When she gets to Washington she plans to walk to the Capitol and nail to its doors a list of five theses on foreign policy, which call for an immediate end to the war and a basic redirection of American foreign and military affairs.

Then she plans a walk up Pennsylvania avenue to the White House, to seek an appointment with her president and fellow-Quaker, Richard Nixon. There are already indications that, whether or not she succeeds in seeing the president, she will be greeted on her arrival by Massachusetts Senators Edward Brooke and Ted Kennedy, along with her congressman, Father Drinan.

Much of her message, however, is directed not at Washington but at those she meets along the way, either personally or through the media.

"I'm trying to say to people that if they believe the war is wrong, they have a responsibility to start taking actions to end it," Mrs. Bruyn said. "I don't think anyone ought necessarily to do what I'm doing, but we can't continue to tolerate the war silently. All of us who are against the war have to find our own best ways of witnessing against it and get busy doing it."

The weather has been typically late-wintry along her march, and she has had to slog through wind and freezing rain more than once.

"But the weather doesn't really bother you," she said with a smile, "as long as you're dressed warm. Besides, when it was sleeting, the ice froze on the trees the way it does and the countryside looked so beautiful that way that I forgot about how cold it was."

Week Four

President Nixon, in a rare on-the-record interview, said yesterday that the Vietnam war was ending and added: "In fact, I seriously doubt if we will ever have another war. This is probably the very last one."
—New York Times, Wednesday, March 10, 1971

New Rochelle to Bronx, New York

Ann Schwerner needed to leave early for work. Hannah Ginsburg came over to see that I made connections with my starting point. Hannah had evidently been one of the most active guiding lights of the peace movement in New York. I was honored to have her company and assistance.

She dropped me off in front of the Post Office in New Rochelle at 9:30 and went to park her car. I had been told that some of the other people who had walked yesterday would be there. She walked up about five minutes later, we looked around, saw no one else, and decided we'd start walking. We had gotten only a few blocks when we heard our names called. It was Ted and Mike, both of whom I had met yesterday. In Ted's hands were three flowers. He explained why they were late. He said that after they had arrived at the Post Office, they thought they'd get a rose for me, so they went into a florist shop and explained for whom they wanted the rose, "this lady who is walking to Washington for peace." The florist said "Wait a minute, I know what you want," and gave them three carnations, one red, one white, and one blue. The florist then said "ordinarily that would be $1.50, but for you I'll make it $.50. I'm paying the other dollar myself."

Delighted at the gesture of Ted and Mike and the support from the florist, I had them tuck the carnations into my pack so that they stuck far up into the air, still surrounded at the base by the green florist paper, looking ever so much like a flag. They remained there throughout the entire walk through the Bronx.

Bess Hamers met up with us, and the others needed to go, though Mike made plans to meet me at Howard Johnson's on the other side of the Bronx Park. Bess and I tramped through the prelude to the Big City: still on Highway 1, littered with trash, used car lots coming right up to the edge of the roadway so that our path wound in between the rusty car hulks. Bess and I talked mostly about young people, how many of them have become self-destructive through drugs. She discussed a group she had heard of in which parents of drug-taking young people gathered together to talk about their problems. The families represented every stratum of society, every economic level, every political persuasion. The interesting aspect of the group was the willingness of everyone to listen to one another, because each one knew they themselves had failed in some way. Their own system hadn't worked. The common denominator was the young person. They listened to the kids, and the kids were telling the parents what galled them about their hypocrisy, values, about the war and the draft and the state of the environment. Here was one of those places where creative exchange was going on. Ordinarily we talked to those who agreed with us, or we became arrogant or self-righteous with those who don't, so that in either case no change was possible. This seemed to be a marvelous example of the kind of exchange that we all need that is humbling and yet creative and unifying.

Bess said she could only walk as far as Gun Hill Road with me. Gun Hill Road? There went my imagination again. I laughed this one off, thanked her for her company and good talk, and walked on, knowing it was not more than an hour until I would be meeting with Mike at HoJos.

More and more it became clear to me that it was when I walked alone that people would strike up a conversation with me. If someone were with me, a conversation with strangers would be a rare thing.

I stopped to ask directions at a gas station. A man there recognized me from the news, also from seeing me several miles back. We talked about the importance of every person making his or her feelings known on the war, that it was not enough to just talk about it with friends, that one needed to make a statement to the government or to the public at large and take action that supports that statement such as draft resistance or tax refusal, or at the very least, write a letter to one's congressman or the President. He agreed, yet he said, and I felt he was being very honest, "You know, if you had a letter or a post card already printed up and you handed it to me, I would probably send it. I shouldn't say that, I know, but to be perfectly honest, I probably will not write a letter."

I wondered if the two reasons that follow might be what stop people from writing the government. 1) Perhaps they've been intimidated by those, probably teachers, who have taught the "proper" form, "how you address a Senator," "how you address a President." If people did not have easy access to this form they felt they couldn't properly write the letter that expressed their feelings. They thought they would be labeled "stupid." 2) They might have doubted their ability to "know" as much as the politicians, therefore their opinions were not as valid. They doubted their ability to be convincing, or worried that their arguments were not grounded on as much fact. Therefore they were willing to leave the decision-making completely to the elected officials and then just grumble about those decisions. Yet, our leaders needed to hear from us, in whatever form we knew and with the expression of our feelings.

I had made a decision when I left on the walk that I would not have something in hand to pass out. I still felt that was the right step for me. I was asking people to do what *they* could and perhaps that left them with a greater potential for creativity. Had I had a letter to hand out, the person would be left with the sense that, having signed the letter, that was all that was needed. Of course, everyone I had time to ask I did ask to sign the Five Theses.

I had about reached Fordham Road, and was under the overhead elevated road, when a white haired woman holding a bag of groceries approached me, laughing. She was looking at my pack complete with flowers, looking me up and down and saying, "Well, what have we here? What's this? What's going on?" (I felt like we were on Candid Camera.)

I said, "I'm walking to Washington, D.C. I've already come this far from Newton, Massachusetts, and I'm walking to protest the war."

She became serious and agreed how awful the war was. I told her how the war was draining our resources in many ways. It was costing us billions of dollars that could be used to clean our environment, to solve some of our inner-city housing problems, to eliminate hunger. I said, "When was the last time you wrote your President?"

"Why, I never *have* written the President."

"Perhaps that is something you could do. Write your President or your Congressmen."

This was one of those times I thought about the "Ripple Theory," as a friend of mine back home had so aptly named it. One cannot hope to change the entire world, to eliminate all the problems, but maybe one can set into motion small ripples that will spread out and affect people. Nothing we do is really isolated. It has an effect.

By one o'clock I had reached Howard Johnsons on the other side of the Bronx Park, and there was Mike with Dr. Joseph Gennis. They treated me to lunch and then we all trudged off for the last few miles through the Bronx, down Grand Boulevard and Concourse. I was grateful to have their company, but I also felt there were many possibilities for conversations with passersby that never took place. However, at this point I felt better having the protection of the two men. It was most reassuring. I'm sure people wondered about that pack with the flowers in it.

This was the first time that I felt my feet getting very, very tired. Perhaps it was the city pavement, perhaps the walk was longer than usual. We sat and rested several times, and about 3:30 or 4:00 we arrived near the Third Ave. bridge and I called Jim Niss, my host for the night. After about an hour he and his wife, Martha, arrived, and I parted with my two knights, hoping some day our paths would cross again.

Martha drove us back to their apartment on Riverside Drive, letting Jim off to pick up a ready cooked chicken. Then we drove round and round looking for a parking place. I marveled at how "city folk" could stand life here. She said sometimes she had to drive around for an hour just to find a parking place. She finally found one, only about a block from the apartment and we went in.

It was a spacious apartment, long and thin with six or seven rooms. I felt like a bee in a honeycomb cell. One apartment was stacked on top of and next to another, over and over again, building after building, block after block, square mile after square mile. New York City.

Jim returned with the food and I made the necessary collect phone calls. I called home and was delighted to discover that the family was considering leaving that evening in order to reach the apartment that night. How marvelous! They were going to come down with Wayne and Jessie Jones. It was like looking forward to Christmas. I was so excited! They'd be there that night! It was still a bit up in the air, but I was to call back at 9:00 in the evening. If they had left already, I would know they were on their way because no one would be home. If they were there, but hadn't left yet, I would know they were coming because they wouldn't accept the charges. If they did accept the charges, I would know there was some change in the plan and they would explain it.

The Nisses and I left for New York Monthly Meeting, 15th St. It had been arranged that I present my Minute from the Cambridge Meeting and say a few words. I felt awed by the privilege.

We went back to the apartment in time for me to call the family about 9:00. They accepted the charges on the call, and told me they were just ready to leave; they'd be there about 1:00 in the morning. Fantastic! Now the problem would be to sleep a bit before they came. I prepared for bed, climbed in, but only managed to lie still and *look* asleep for the hours of waiting before they came. Somehow my mind was too awake; I was too excited.

Finally, about 1:15 they arrived. There they all really were! How beautiful to put my arms around my daughters, around my husband. There was so much excitement, so much talk. Wayne and Jessie were there, too, and even though everyone tried to be efficient about going directly to bed, knowing that the next day was one of the "biggest" of the walk, we still didn't get bedded down and quiet until 2:00 A.M. It was the one time I took a sleeping pill. I couldn't trust myself to use the five hours ahead of me for sleeping. I was too anxious. The pill worked. In a matter of minutes I was gone.

A senior official of the Justice Department said today that the department "will vigorously oppose any legislation" that would impair the government's ability to gather information about American citizens.

—New York Times, Thursday, March 11, 1971

New York City to St. George (Staten Island) NY

Day

23

Thur, Mar 11

I was there. I had made it that far and considered New York City the halfway point. It was where access to the news media was greatest, because that was where the news media lived—NBC, ABC, CBS, and the *New York Times*. Reaching deep within me I asked God, my Higher Power, the Universe, to give me strength to speak clearly.

Wayne Jones drove us to where we met up with Jay Nolan and Chris Little. Already some reporters had gathered. They were taking their photographs, asking their questions, and I was feeling my inner tension. How could I speak the most clearly to the issue? Inside myself I was saying, "Don't let the focus stay on me. Let me be a channel for the voice of peace. Let me speak to the problem of ending the war, the insanity of our national policy."

There was joy in our all walking together. Sometimes Susie would carry my pack, sometimes Becky or Sev, but often I had to put it on because the newsmen wanted to see it on me. That was, after all, how I usually traveled, carrying it myself. Over and over again, as we approached a camera, and interviewer, I would need to pull myself together, and say, "Use me, Lord, don't let 'me' get in the way. Keep me a channel," and somehow when the questions came and it was time for answers, the right words came to me.

We walked past Rockefeller Plaza, and Rebecca, seeing the statue of Atlas bearing the weight of the world on his back, said, "Look, Mom, they made a statue of you."

Chris had done so much spadework. I'm sure the presence of all the media was due to his contacting them. My process in the past, when it came to media, was to ask the name of the interviewer and newspaper or radio station he represented. I would write it down in my little red book. It was a way of keeping a record. It also let the reporter know that I was just as interested in the person interviewing me as he or she was in the "walker." I wanted them to know that I was a real person and not an "object of interest." But when it came to New York City, there were so many reporters, I gave up. Chris took care of it all. I just gave up any record keeping or decisions about speed of the walk, or when we had to leave one group to continue on to the next. I rested completely upon his judgment. He was so lovely and gentle about it all. It was reassuring to have him there making decisions.

Somewhere along Fifth Ave. Evelyn Ames, Olivia Hoblitzelle's mother, met us. What a lovely woman! The same light blue eyes of her daughter, the tender, thoughtful mold from which the daughter had sprung. Not far from the Metropolitan Museum of Art I heard that Mrs. Lindsay, the Mayor's wife, had waited to walk for a few minutes with me, but she had other appointments and could not wait. Evidently I was later than expected.

We ate our lunch on the steps of the museum. As we began the walk again, we bought some hot pretzels to share.

I found out later that Mayor Lindsay had sent a telegram to the church which read:

> Welcome to New York City. Your walk for peace is in the great tradition of other walks for justice. As an individual, you are standing up peacefully for what is right. We honor you for your determination, for your cause, and for your faith. We are proud to have you in our city.
>
> John V. Lindsay, Mayor of New York.

Also sent to the church was a telegram from Senator George Mc-
Govern:

> It is encouraging to know of your individual effort to call attention to
> the tragic war in Southeast Asia by your arduous walk from Boston to
> Washington. My best wishes for your continued strength and dedication.
>
> Senator George McGovern

The scene at St. Clements Church, which was on 46th St., was unreal.
I can't remember approaching it. Somehow we were suddenly there.
Had I been talking that much on the way? We walked in and I was
delighted to meet the Vicar, the Reverend Eugene Monick. We spoke
for a few minutes in his study.

He was planning a service there for 2:00 p.m. based on a medieval
service, the Blessing of Pilgrims at a Way Station. I was deeply touched.
He asked me about my faith. I told him I had trouble with the traditional Christian words, the set phrases, so to speak, that seemed to define
the Spirit in such a rigid framework. But I believed in the Holy Spirit,
that power that is more than human, that nourishes us if we will listen
to it. I told him I believed in the love that is divine, the divinity that is
in everyone, that Jesus was the purest example we know of, of a human
filled with the God Spirit, filled with the Power of the Holy Spirit. Yet
I could not say words like "Jesus is my Savior" or "Christ died for our
sins." Gene, as he had us call him, was most understanding and explained his service, which felt beautifully appropriate. I felt that this
man knew where God was, in him, in me, and just wanted to know
what words would best define "Him" for each person. I was reminded
again of the words on the poster in the Peace Center in Stamford, "…
We cannot prove this but we do know that when men act as if it were
true their trust is justified."

I lay down for awhile on the office floor to relax, to think through
what I would say when it was time to speak. I had made very few notes.
I wanted to tell people that everyone had the power to protest our government's policies and I wanted to tell them how they might do it. I
wanted to break through the sense of futility that I felt most of America
had reached. But now I have no memory of what I said.

It was finally time to go into the small chapel, a rather squarish room filled with bleachers on which sat maybe fifty people. There was a little raised platform and a mike and some chairs to the side. We all sat down except the Vicar, who explained what was about to happen. He introduced the young man to my right, who then played an exquisite 16th century Spanish dance on the guitar. The music rolled over us all, delicately, like lace. We were all held in the musical web he was weaving. Tears of joy were in my eyes.

In the past, had I been a witness to a scene like this, I would have broken down into tears. Had I had to speak, I couldn't have. As a child, my brothers called me a "cry baby," which of course would bring on more tears. I was known to have choked up when I gave the valedictory in high school and when I spoke once in church years before becoming a Quaker. When I was moved deeply, tears would come to me, I'd choke up and then I couldn't speak. But this time it was different. As moved as I was by the beauty of the music and the incredible service in which I was a participant, I felt clear and strong. I was coming from a place of power that seemed beyond myself.

Father Gene read from an old prayer book, this ancient service. This was a Way Station and I was a Pilgrim, of sorts. And I felt blessed. I don't remember the words, but I do remember the feeling of his hand as he placed it on my head. And I remember my deep, deep wish to speak with clarity, to keep open to the message.

And then it was time for me to speak. I remember most the inability to see those to whom I was talking. Television cameras were recording the event, and the lights on me were so bright that anything beyond them was black.

Somewhere in the middle of my talking, the bright lights went out. The cameramen were finished, and I was able to see those I loved in the audience and the faces of the strangers, friendly, warm. Finally the ordeal was over, I had spoken from the deepest part of me, and now was a time of meeting the press.

I don't know who this one man was with a mike, asking in a most serious, urgent tone, "Mrs. Bruyn, who do you think will be the next President of the United States?" I couldn't believe his question. I looked at him, laughing inside, smiling on the outside, bewildered. Who cares who I think the next President would be? It was so irrelevant. I said something like, I really didn't know, but that the people who wanted peace in Vietnam would be listening very closely to what the future candidates would be saying and particularly would be watching what they would be *doing* to bring the war to a close.

We eventually all moved out onto the stairs of the church. I had put the pack back on, and there were many more pictures taken and questions asked. It was now around 3:00 and the large contingent (about 20 people, now) walked down to 42nd Street and over to Broadway.

There was one more humorous glimpse of the news process when the newsmen from one of the major networks set up their cameras on a corner and a crowd began to gather. My kids were pushed farther and farther back and they began to hear questions people were asking of each other. "Who is she?" "Did she write a book?" "Is she French?" "She looks French." "Maybe she's a skier."

Not too many people were left to finish the walk down to Battery Park. Jim Bowman, one of the walkers, gave us a running commentary on the details of the architecture of lower Manhattan. Wayne and Jessie Jones and Beck and Sue took the bus down to the Ferry, but Sev and Jim Bowman and I finished the walk. We all met at the Staten Island Ferry, the 5-cent ride that we would take in my forward direction, the only ride I planned. I had never taken it before, and we were all looking forward to the adventure.

The ride on the ferry was fantastic. It was already nightfall, about 7:00 p.m. and lights sparkled throughout the city. They reflected on the water and twinkled off into the distance. The sky overhead was filled with stars. The breeze on the boat was cold, but with our jackets and coats buttoned up and visors pulled down, we were toasty on the inside. Our spirits were expansive. The adventure was so keen, so sharp, so distinct. We couldn't contain ourselves by just standing and talking to each other. We began dancing, swinging around the iron poles on the outside deck, singing, "It's a Grand Night for Singing." Luckily almost all the other passengers were inside the ferry, sitting in the waiting room benches like solid citizens, waiting out the 20-30 minute ride that they probably took every morning and every evening, bored, tired after a hard day's work, thinking thoughts of home and what to cook for supper and what business deal would recoup the day's losses. How could they know our joy, our delight in being together and sharing in this high adventure in faith. I actually swung around a pole, but only once because I could feel that I was tired enough physically that I didn't have the bounce my body would ordinarily have. I decided the swinging was for Sev and the kids. I had a long way to go and didn't need a sprained ankle. But my heart fairly exploded with the pleasure of it all.

The lights of the opposite shore began to be bigger than those of the shore we left. Eventually the boat slid into the docking place, shuddered a bit and the doors opened for the exit. Following the main flow of traffic, we walked off the ferry looking for the Hagenhofers, my hosts for the night. Now my heart was kind of tight in my chest, because I knew I had to leave the family. They had to leave by return ferry. A woman approached, asking if we were the Bruyns, introduced herself as Margo Hagenhofer and warmly greeted us. The time had come. That was it. We all said a quick goodbye, smiling, saying we'd see each other soon again, and we walked our separate directions. Conversation continued with Margo, but my heart was back on the ferry, back with the family, aching for the euphoria we had just known, the togetherness.

Dear Margo sensed all this. She had planned a meeting that evening at her house with her friends, to talk about the war. She kept saying she would be very happy to call it off, that I didn't need to feel I had to go ahead with it. I told her I would probably feel better after a hot bath, and that we should go ahead with the meeting as planned.

I got up to the bathroom, and finally in the privacy of those quarters broke down and sobbed and sobbed. I felt the separation deeply. It hurt so much. I felt so torn. What was I doing?! During the day, my emotions had swung from inexpressible depths to ecstatic heights. I had been under unbelievable tension. I needed to let down, to cry out my pent-up feelings and let the heights and depths flow out to calmer waters.

Afterwards I did feel better. I was still somewhat depressed but I didn't hurt so much inside. The meeting was very worthwhile, lasting from about 8–10:00 and then I went to bed.

Antiwar Woman on Walk to Washington Prays Here

The New York Times/Neal Boenzi

Mrs. Louise Bruyn passing through Manhattan yesterday on her walk to Washington

The Saigon Government's plan to move refugees from the northern part of South Vietnam to the southern part has been quietly set aside in favor of resettling them within their native provinces, American officials said today… "Most significantly," another official said, "finally someone has asked the refugees just what they actually desire."

—*New York Times, Saturday, March 13, 1971*

St. George to Huguenot (Staten Island)

There I was, really on Staten Island. I had never been on the island before. I had been told it was rather rural, but I must confess I had really expected it to look like Manhattan. Instead, it was quaint. The houses on the ridge, the hills, added to this sense. The sea, or the river, whatever it was at the foot of those hills, gave it a special flavor.

Margo and Bob both walked with me, as did one of the young men, David Sahr, who had come to the meeting the night before. It was a lovely sunny day, warm enough for jackets, but with a distinct feeling of spring in the air. I still felt low. I really didn't want to go on walking that morning, but there it was, waiting to be done. Even though I felt refreshed from my night's sleep, I was not as outgoing as usual. Conversation was a little more difficult.

Not long after we left St. George, friends of Olivia's who lived in Manhattan and had wanted to walk with us the day before but couldn't make it, came all the way over to Staten Island this day to walk.

As we were walking along, a man drove up beside us in a car, got out and said, "I was in Detroit, Michigan, this morning and saw you on the 7:00 a.m. Today Show." It was both a statement of fact and one of disbelief. He went on. "I just flew in. I live on Staten Island, and now I see you." We were all amazed at the story, and it was the first time I knew I had been on the Today Show. I had seen none of the coverage of the previous day. He wanted me to know that he approved of my action.

He said that out of 300,000 Staten Island dwellers, 170 had now been killed. He felt this killing had gone on long enough and wanted an end to it. We agreed, and I urged him to do what he could to take action. We parted, all moved by this unusual encounter.

We passed a fire station. A fireman called out from his open, second floor window, "Good luck on your walk."

Farther on, a cluster of construction workers wished me well. One seemed to say, "Praise the Lord!" I waved, smiled and walked on, then stopped and turned to Margo and said, "Did you hear him say what I thought I heard him say?" She said, "Yes, it sounded like he said 'Praise the Lord'." I was perplexed. In the peace movement construction workers were stereotyped as being for the war. If he said it, was it said from his heart or in derision? Would it *be* something one would say sarcastically? I didn't have the courage to go up to the man to ask, nor would it have been appropriate. We just kept going.

We got a lot of advice from a white-haired gent farther down the road. "Vote Republican," he said. "That's the only way we'll get anything done in this country. I'm a retired navy man. I should have been a Presbyterian minister. You get a house and a car. It might not be the best, but what do you want, a Cadillac?" His advice continued at some length. He didn't think my solution made much sense, but he thought I was "courageous." We parted with his calling after us, "Remember, vote Republican."

A woman stopped in a car to wish me well. She knew the island was conservative and wanted me to know that she agreed with what I was doing. Margo and Bob said that the fascinating thing was that there was no negative response at all to my walk, to my presence on the island. Both seemed surprised because they lived on the island and knew, or thought they knew, the feelings of the people.

By the end of the day, I felt I knew Margo and Bob like old friends. Margo had to go back a bit earlier because she was concerned about her teen-age daughter's health, but David and Bob finished with me, all the way up to the Maliks' house on Sequine Ave. We were mighty glad to be through walking.

I couldn't help but bemoan the condition of the island. Underfoot there was *so* much broken glass, beer cans, paper. Somehow the glass was the most obvious. What would happen to it all? It couldn't dissolve. Supposing *all* the jars we used were returnable, pickle jars, tomato juice bottles, jelly glasses, soft drink and whiskey bottles—just think of the remarkable savings. They could be used over. All we needed was a system for returning these to their manufacturers.

Edith Malik was there to welcome us and offer us a delicious piece of pie. The ride came soon to pick up Bob and David. Edith showed me to my room and the tub, and soon I was clean and relaxed again. I called home, and the family was safe again in Newton. I called Chris Little and he had watched the news shows, all three of them, the day before and said they were all pretty good, that the message I was bearing had gotten through. He was happy. I was happy.

According to a previous agreement, I called Cathy Perkus to see about returning to New York City for a Steering Committee meeting of the National Peace Action Coalition, the one working on the April 24 March on Washington. She thought there might be some benefit to the both of us if we met together, but hard as we tried, there was no way we could figure how I could get to that meeting. A car was just not available in that short a time. Then, Lisa Hammel of the *New York Times* phoned to find a time when she could do an interview for the Women's Page. We planned to meet on Monday night in Princeton at the Quays'. I had one more phone interview with someone from the Staten Island newspaper, and then it was dinnertime and I could really relax.

In the Malik's kitchen was a plaque made of wood with a painted inscription, "A wishbone ain't as likely to git ye sumplace as a backbone—." I liked it. I copied it into my notebook.

That night I didn't do much. There was no meeting planned. I was grateful for that. I spent some time on the telephone and reading the news, trying to catch up on the happenings of the day. I watched some television.

I was enormously pleased to see Joan Baez on the David Frost show. What a beautiful woman. They were speaking of anarchy. David Frost said, "But if you had anarchy, wouldn't you have chaos?" She answered (in my rough paraphrase), "There already *is* chaos, but you and I don't feel it. We travel from New York to San Francisco to Los Angeles and we eat. There are those who don't eat. The criminals are the ones in command. You have defined the hardened criminal as the one who doesn't feel his crime. That sounds to me like the man flying the airplane and dropping a bomb by pushing a button. He does not witness nor feel the death he has caused." She kept trying to pull people back to the realities of life. The hostility she aroused in the faces and voices of the audience was palpable. And yet, when she sang, her music reached the people. They were softened by it and thanked her each time with strong applause. What a dilemma. What do you do with a person who speaks of love and sings with such beauty and strength and delicacy and yet challenges all the basic assumptions of one's life?

I began to worry that I would need a rest day later in the walk. I knew my second rest day was coming up on Tuesday of the following week. I wondered if there were a way that I could proceed as long as my well-being allowed me, which meant pushing the entire schedule ahead by one day from Princeton on. That was what some of the phoning was about at the Malik's. It seemed possible to shift those days in the following week. I called Jessie Jones and talked with her. She was perfectly willing to go ahead with this providing I felt I really needed the extra day.

The number of war refugees in South Vietnam has risen dramatically—perhaps by as many as 150,000—since new allied operations in Indochina were begun late last year... The cumulative totals since 1965 are about 5 million refugees.

—*New York Times, Saturday, March 13, 1971*

Day

Huguenot, New York to Nixon, New Jersey 25

Sat, Mar 13

The morning looked a bit rainy and foggy. But as I began to walk the haze lifted and I was just left with the gray sky and the mud. It was pretty open country there. It looked like there might be a lot of new building coming in soon.

About an hour later I reached the bridge at Outerbridge Crossing, across which I had to leave the island. I would have to find a way to cross because it was restricted. No pedestrians were allowed. I went into the toll booth and explained that I would like to get across and wondered how I could do it. The policeman who was in there was very friendly and said that he would be very glad to take me across.

I decided to rest there for a few minutes since I had been walking for about an hour. I had worn my boots that day because of the mud, but already they had given me blisters!! That was the last day I wore them. So I took them off, put on my sneakers, and took a drink of water. The police woman at the desk offered me some Life Savers and I took them with me. I explained what I was doing and they recognized me from the news. The policewoman agreed that something needed to be done. She knew she wasn't doing anything but she wished she knew what she *could* do. And I said again what all the things were that I knew there were to do. After about a ten minute rest the policeman showed me the way to the car and drove me across. He said one of the reasons why they had to close this to walkers was that kids had walked across the bridge and when they got to the top of it they threw things down on the boats below.

The ride was almost two miles long. The bridge itself from the beginning to the end was about a mile and a half. Since I had gotten the ride in my forward direction I was able to walk further that day than I had originally thought, past Nixon, New Jersey.

I was walking through Fords, a small town, when a gray-haired couple, the Russens, stopped their car and got out. They came up to me to ask if I were the woman walking to Washington. They were so sweet. They were in tune with what I was trying to do. They asked if I'd like to stop at their place for a cup of coffee, and I looked at my watch and saw that it was a good time for a rest, and was happy to stop in with them. It was about 11:00 by then. They drove me to their house, which wasn't too far away.

We had coffee and cookies. I was telling them what I had heard from Cynthia Frederick at the Bridgeport University teach-in the previous week about a company called RMK-BMJ, an American contracting firm, which had contracted to build 90 more tiger cages in Vietnam. This man knew a lot about contracting firms. He recognized the initials and tried to fit the names to them, a fact I didn't have. This remained one of the things I tried to pass along in my walk.

The Russens wanted to know what they could do to help on the walk. They wondered if I needed any financial help. I told them the walk itself wasn't costing us anything. I wasn't paying anything for transportation and very little for food, but the one expense we were incurring was the big telephone bill at home. They said they couldn't do much but they'd like me to take a $10 bill. I accepted it. It made me feel strange, accepting money, but I knew they wanted to help and it was a *real* help. Mrs. Russen spent a good deal of time on the telephone trying to contact the New Brunswick newspaper to no avail. They then took me back to where they had picked me up, and I walked on from there.

That area of New Jersey seemed very desolate. There were long stretches of road in open country interspersed with factories surrounded by lots of land. At one point a car came up and pulled over to the side and a man asked if I wanted a ride. I said no, I was walking.

"Are you that woman that's going down to Washington?"

I said, "Yes."

He shook his head and he smiled and said, "And you're not afraid to walk on these roads?"

I said, "No, I haven't had any trouble so far."

He took out a card. The card introduced him as being a leader of the young political party in that area, and he said, "I just wanted you to see this so you'd know who I was."

I thanked him for it. He kept shaking his head and laughing at this preposterous thing of my walking down the road and not being worried about people coming up and molesting me. We exchanged a few words about what I was doing. He said something about my "twinkly blue eyes" and still seemed to be responding to the idea that I would "risk" myself in this way by being alone on the highway. I finally said goodbye to him. As I walked off I was chuckling to myself and thinking, "Brother, if there's anyone I have to worry about, it's people like you."

I got as far that day as New Brunswick. When I got to the Great Eastern Discount Center, I called the Kleinmans who were my hosts for that evening. Pretty soon Toby, the Kleinman's daughter, came by in her car, and she took me to the Kleinman's house.

Gertrude and Milton Kleinman were most gracious. I was shown to my room, where I was able to relax and take a hot shower. That evening there was a party at their house and some Vietnam Veterans came with their wives. It was a fine gathering of friends who had been active in the peace movement and even those who had not.

This was Saturday night again, and that meant I had a date with Howard Nelson of WEEI. I went into Dr. Kleinman's office, closed the doors and laid out all my papers on the desk. I made the 7:00 phone call and then waited on tenterhooks until I was called back at 7:30. I can't seem to remember anything that was said during that interview. I just remember sitting there with all the papers spread out all over the desk and some on the floor. I was not as shaken as I had been in previous times. I hadn't been able to eat before this interview, but with the ordeal over by 8:00 I was able to go in and enjoy the party.

About 10:00 I was beginning to droop and knew I had to walk the next day, so I went on upstairs. It seems most of the guests left by 10:00 anyway. They had been told, as I recall, that 10:00 was the end of my ability to respond to other people. That's when I rolled in my antennae, and just had to go to bed.

An Army judge, one of seven black officers and enlisted men who have asked that an Army court of inquiry investigate housing discrimination against black American troops in West Germany, has been returned to the United States and has been talking with Pentagon officials for a week...sources have indicated that the Government would like to convince the officer to have the application for a court of inquiry withdrawn...During a recent interview in Germany, Captain Smothers said: "The fact that housing discrimination continues against black soldiers shows that the military does not consider this a high priority matter."

—New York Times, Sunday, March 14, 1971

Franklin Park below New Brunswick, New Jersey

Day

26

Sun, Mar 14

This was one of those mornings that I felt downhearted. For one thing, I was walking along a divided highway and it just seemed to go on and on in a very uninteresting way. There was nothing beautiful around to look at. It seemed like an endless task. I was frankly bored with it.

I had been walking for about an hour and was approaching a turn-off where cars could come up off the highway. A car stopped on that turn-off ramp and the driver hailed me. I walked up to him. He said, "Here's something for your walk."

Since he looked sort of familiar, I said, "Did I meet you at the party last night?"

"No, we've just known about your walk. We know what you're doing and my boys would like you to have this." He had two young boys in his car, perhaps ages 8 and 10, and he handed me a paper bag. I opened the bag and inside were four sweet rolls and two cartons of cold milk. He was so dear to have passed that nourishment along to me, though I wondered if "the boys" really approved of dad giving away their breakfast. It wasn't only nourishment for my body but it really picked up my spirits at that point, because I felt that if somebody was still aware that I was plodding along the highway, it wasn't such a futile task ahead of me. He drove off. I walked on until I found an industrial yard with an old pipe on which I could sit. I removed my pack and ate some of the sweet rolls and drank the milk.

As I was sitting there, another car drove through this parking-lot-type of yard and a woman spoke to me from the driver's window asking if there were anything she could do. She, too, knew who I was and what I was doing. I said, "No thanks, I'm really well taken care of here."

She said, "I own the Carriage House down the road and I'd love to have you stop by there for coffee if you like."

I said, "Well, do you know where Cozzins Lane is? That's where I have to turn off. I'm following this route exactly because someone is meeting me today on the route."

She said, "Yes, that's just beyond the Carriage House. If you stop in there I can show you where it is." So I thanked her and she drove on. When I finished my sweet rolls and milk, I walked on again.

I kept walking and walking, still looking for the Carriage House. By now it was about 11:30. Pretty soon the same car approached me as before, from which the woman spoke to me. She pulled over and she said, "I'm *so* sorry; I gave you the wrong instructions. Cozzins Lane is *before* the Carriage House. I just realized it and I came back out to tell you." She had found me perhaps three blocks past Cozzins Lane, and drove me back to that point. As we parted, she said, "Is there anything that I can do? Do you need any financial help?" Again I said that the only thing that would be a big expense to us as a family would be the telephone bill. She reached in her purse and pulled out a twenty dollar bill. She said she had hoped that I would stop in the Carriage House and have lunch with them, but realized that it was out of my direction and it was too early for me to eat lunch. It was a beautiful gesture on her part. She had done such a caring thing to see that I hadn't gone too far out of my way and to take me back onto my route. I thanked her, got out of the car, and went on my way, this time on Cozzins Lane.

This road was much prettier to walk on than Highway 1. It was a residential area, but also had open country, with farmland visible in the distance. That little jog over to the other highway was a pleasant walk. When I reached the intersection with the next highway, I sat on the grassy corner, on my poncho, to eat lunch and rest. It was about noon.

Several cars stopped to see if they could help. They seemed to know who I was and wanted to know if I needed coffee or anything. I said I was well-stocked and felt that I had to stay there. It was the day that

Chris Little would be meeting up with me. He wanted to take some pictures. Besides his efforts to alert the media for our trek through New York City, Chris was a freelance reporter for *Time Magazine*.

After about a twenty-minute rest eating my lunch, I walked on as far as the next gas station. I needed a rest stop. It was a small place, quite run down. I asked the old man running it if he had a rest room. He did, and handed me the key. I noticed the building next to him. Several Blacks of differing ages were sweeping the porch of an empty store and fixing up the grounds. The old man explained that they were going to make the storefront into a church. I went in to use his dark, somewhat unkempt restroom, and when I came out, the man began talking to me about what the "Spooks" had done in New Brunswick last week. An awful murder. I said, "Who? Spooks? Who are they?"

He leaned in a little closer, and he said, "You know, Niggers."

"Oh, you mean Blacks," I offered.

"Yes," he chuckled, just like it was all the same. And here, next door to him, these people were trying to start a church. I could just see the tensions that would be coming up. On my way back to the road, I went up to a few of the workers and told them how great I thought it was that they were building a church out of the old store. It was all I felt able to do.

While I was standing out there, two cars drove up, bringing me three new walking companions, Sarah Boyd, Rev. James Robinson, who was a minister from New Brunswick, and Chris Little. One of the drivers would meet Sarah later to pick her up.

So now there were four of us walking. It was a great pleasure to be tromping down the road with these friends. My spirits were greatly lifted.

We came to a small town. A young boy, perhaps eleven years old, asked, "Where are you going?"

I said, "I'm going to Washington, D.C."

He said, "You're going to Washington? And you're walking?"

"Yes," I said, "I'm going down to tell my senator and representatives and the President that I don't like what we are doing in Vietnam." We filled him in on the fact that I had already walked this far from Boston. We said goodbye and went on, but James Robinson, the minister, went back to the boy and talked with him further. When he was through he came up and told us the conversation he had had. He had said to the boy, "Do you know why she's doing this?"

And the boy said, "No."

And he said, "She's doing this for you."

And the little boy said, "For me?"

And he said, "Yes. Because she doesn't want boys like you to have to grow up and go to war anymore."

And the boy said, "Gee, thank you."

James Robinson's son had been killed in Vietnam.

We got to our destination of Franklin Park about 2:00. This seemed too early to leave Sarah and Jim and Chris, so we decided we'd find a cup of coffee somewhere. Jim's car had been parked in Franklin Park so we all got in and drove back to Chris's car, which had been left in front of the church-store, and then we continued to drive to Howard Johnson's on Route 1. The way back to Howard Johnson's was by the same route I had walked. It really made me crumble inside to see all of the effort that I had expended that one day collapsed into a ten minute drive.

About 3:00 Chris drove me back to the place where we had ended the walk, and I called Alice and Gene Glazer.

When Alice and Gene came to pick me up, it was like I had always known her. Alice's way with strangers was so immediate, direct, welcoming. The banter and small talk she was able to create made me feel completely at home within a matter of minutes. The Glazers had an open house that afternoon and evening. People kept dropping in. There was a total of perhaps ten to twelve people with whom I had some conversation.

A photographer arrived from the *Home News*. He was sort of a short stocky man. He came in rubbing his hands together and saying, "Now, I want to set up a little gag shot here. I want you to put your feet in a bucket of water. We're going to pretend that its hot water and that you're soaking your feet."

I said, "I don't want to."

He said, "You don't want to? Why not?"

I said, "Because it wouldn't be honest. My feet don't hurt."

He looked at me with some astonishment and some hurt. "We've got to have a picture that tells a *story*. You know, you have to have a *story*."

I said, "Well, I understand that you have a problem, that you need that kind of a picture. Would you like to use my pack? Or perhaps I could be looking at a map?" He had me bring the pack down from upstairs. Before we had completely set up the picture, I said, "You know, I know what I *really* should have that tells a *story*. I have some pictures in my pack of napalm-burned children. That's what the story is. It's not my feet." So I took out those pictures from the Committee of Responsibility, which I had carried in my pack, and showed them to him. The look on his face told me the horror of their plight had gotten through to him. He didn't say anything about that, though, just that the pictures were too small. "They would never show."

I then got out copies of the People's Peace Treaty from my pack. On the back of each there was printed in large letters WE WILL MAKE THE PEACE. He saw that and said, "Let's use that. You can stick that in your pack."

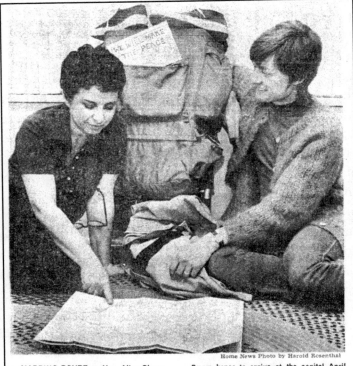

Home News Photo by Harold Rosenthal

MAPPING ROUTE — Mrs. Alice Glazer, 8 Dundee Road, South Brunswick, helps Mrs. Louise Bruyn, right, of Newton Center, Mass., map route to Washington, D.C. Mrs. Bruyn hopes to arrive at the capitol April 2 to post her theses on the door of Congress. Her orange jacket and black armband have become a familiar sight along the road.

So we set up the picture so that Alice and I were sitting on the floor looking at a map with the pack behind us. Tucked in the pack was the piece of paper that said "We will make the peace."

Alice continued to work on the photographer to get him to see what the real issues were. He was one of those who couldn't believe that he should do anything different than what his government had arranged for him to do. If there were a war he would have to fight it. He had been in World War II. He supposed his sons would have to fight in this one, though he didn't want them to. He noticed a quote that was up on Alice's bulletin board. It was a quote from Martin Niemoller, a German pastor who initially supported Hitler but in 1937 was arrested by the Gestapo and sent to Sachsenhausen and Dachau concentration camps.

"In Germany they first came for the Communists and I didn't speak up because I wasn't a Communist. Then they came for the Jews, and I didn't speak up because I wasn't a Jew. Then they came for the trade unionists, and I didn't speak up because I wasn't a trade unionist. Then they came for the Catholics, and I didn't speak up because I was a Protestant. Then they came for me—and by that time no one was left to speak up."

After reading it, he asked if he could take it with him. Alice gave it to him.

I was still concerned about the problem of saving my rest day until I needed it, but it became apparent from Jessie, who had talked to many others along the line that it would be a large planning problem. All that day, I had been feeling the soreness in my eye of a beginning sty.

The one thing that became difficult was the fact that my host did have an open house for the rest of the afternoon and evening. This became somewhat tiring, trying to relate to the people and still trying to adjust the schedule ahead in order to save the rest day until later, and being interviewed by two newspapers.

One of the people who was there was a man probably in his 80s, who felt that he and I had much in common and he wished we could speak more about it. I believe he had been a Quaker at one time.

I got to bed about 11:00 that night. I was very, very tired. Drained. And to think that I began that day by being bored.

Senator Edward M. Kennedy has estimated that at least 25,000 civilians were killed in the war in South Vietnam last year and that 100,000 were wounded...based on official figures [this estimate is not disputed by Government officials.] "By this yardstick alone we can see that the war in Indochina is not winding down for the peoples of the area," Senator Kennedy said.

—*New York Times, Monday, March 15, 1971*

Day

New Brunswick to Princeton, New Jersey 27

Mon, Mar 15

The man from last night who felt we had much in common called in the morning to ask if I couldn't please come over and talk for a few minutes before I started the walk. I felt rushed for time, but did want to talk more with him. Alice drove me over there, a few blocks away and we had an interesting conversation. (All the time I was soaking my sty with hot water.)

I had a basic disagreement with this man. He was deeply into the Communist ideology. He said that in order for us to change the world or the inequities or injustices of the world, we must inflict pain on those who held the power, on the "superrich." (There was that word again.) I did not agree with him. At what level did one inflict pain? Did this mean hurting their status through embarrassment? Did it mean hurting them financially? Torturing them? Killing them? Whatever the pain, it was "eye for an eye" revenge. Gandhi said, "an eye for an eye' only ends up making the whole world blind."

Yet one was faced with the fact that through the actions of some people and institutions a terrific amount of violence had been done to others. How to make the changes? Through law? A law itself might be unjust, as it was during the time of slavery in this country. How then? Many non-violent tools were available. Through such actions as personal confrontation, demonstrations, strikes, boycotts, and other techniques documented by other writers, immense changes had come about.

It is desperation and fear that have led people to inflict pain on those they identify as the "oppressor." If there were no larger community to support those being hurt by individuals, corporations, government, whatever entity, then a struggle was more likely to turn violent in return. That was why we needed to organize. It was a question we needed to keep in mind in terms of the methods we chose to make change. Though Communism seemed to hold out to many a solution to injustice, it itself became unjust. This man and I may have shared our concern for injustice but we did not share the ideology.

Back on the road, Alice Glazer walked with me for a ways. It was a beautiful day, warm, sunny and windy. It was the first time I walked without my jacket. Spring was really in the air.

Sarah and Dick Boyd met me again along the way. We discussed the possibilities of adopting Vietnamese children or racially mixed children—what the value was to the child or potential damage, what it meant to the family, etc. We discussed the need that we felt existed to try to right the wrongs that we were creating as a people—righting them on a very personal basis. She told me that only 12 Vietnamese children had been allowed out of Vietnam for the purpose of adoption. [This became a very complex issue in the years to come.]

Finally I made the decision to send my boots back. I had carried them (or wore them, with regrets) through the last half of February and the first half of March, and would celebrate the Ides of March by getting rid of this three-and-a-half pound weight which no longer served a purpose. Sarah kindly took them in their car. With a much lightened pack I said goodbye, and went on my way.

It was windy, *very* windy. Though it was a beautiful day, it was extra hard walking. Heavy gray clouds began to fill the sky as I got into Princeton.

Coming into the main road, I removed my pack and sat on a bench to rest my weary bones for a few minutes—a bench placed there for people waiting for a bus. A young man came up to me, introduced himself as the reporter from the *Trenton Times*, said he had been looking for me and wondered if we could talk. On the bench we had a fine conversation. I told him all I could about the whys and hows of my walk. At the end of the interview, he asked if he could sign the five theses. I was more than happy to get them out of the pack. It was the first time a news person had asked, in his private capacity, to sign the theses.

The rest of the walk was not too difficult. Several people stopped to say a few words. One college girl walked two blocks with me, a woman offered overnight hospitality, a professor from the art department of Princeton University stopped to talk a few minutes and finally a reporter from the *Princetonian* accompanied me to the end of my walk for that day. My destination was the Fund for Peace Education, a second floor art/crafts/gallery/store and office, which was a center for peace action in the area.

I was *so* tired and thirsty. Someone brought me a large iced soda which was very refreshing, but I even lay down for awhile on the floor because my body was so tired and my feet ached. I'm sure I was unpleasant to talk with at this point. It was hard to relate well to people.

About four o'clock I walked over to Palmer Square, a block or two further down the street, where a group of women sold peace literature from an outdoor table, which they did regularly. It was just at this point that the rain, which had been threatening earlier, now began to fall, and we all helped to move the card table and literature into a dry area.

Mrs. Quay drove up to our appointed meeting place. She and Rev. Quay, a retired minister and fundraiser for the Princeton Seminary, were the parents of Ginny Hutchison, from Friends Meeting at Cambridge, who had driven out to meet me in Storrs, Connecticut. I was to stay with them tonight. The drive itself was about 10 minutes to their modern, neat apartment. When we got there, about 4:45, there was Lisa Hammel waiting for me, the writer for the *New York Times*. I begged leave to retire for about an hour with a hot shower and rest and by 5:30 or 6:00 I was fresh enough to begin.

There were frequent interruptions for telephone calls, but aside from that the time was intensely hers. Never before have I been so closely questioned about what I thought and felt. She was very keenly tuned in, very sensitive, listening with her inner ear. She delved into my brain in a way no one else ever had, trying to get to my reasons, my rationale for doing what I was doing. The interview lasted through dinner and up until we drove her to her bus stop at about 10:30.

One of the calls was a decisive one in which I talked to Jessie Jones in Newton. I decided that I would take my rest day as planned and therefore not throw off the schedules of all the people who had planned ahead to have me be at their place on a certain day. The strange thing was that by this time I knew I really needed that rest day. My sty had become more fierce, and my whole self, feet and all, just didn't feel like going ahead.

When I talked to Susan that day during one of my regular phone calls home I felt she was very depressed. She said that a teacher had said to her that when I returned I would be embarrassed about what I did. I know Susan's faith was shaken by that comment. I assured her that I would not be embarrassed. What I was doing was at too deep a level to have anything to do with embarrassment! I felt strongly about the walk and would continue to feel that I had to take the action that I did.

South Vietnamese troops abandoned a fire base in Laos under heavy enemy pressure overnight, leaving behind their artillery pieces, military sources said today. Abandonment…was ordered because United States helicopters could no longer supply the base…. The outpost was the second South Vietnamese fire base abandoned in recent days under renewed North Vietnamese pressure.

The Secretary of Health, Education & Welfare, Elliot L. Richardson, said today that the nation "must develop the means of controlling the potential for harm inherent" in the Government's computerized data banks of information on citizens.

—New York Times, Tuesday, March 16, 1971

Princeton, New Jersey—Rest Day

Day

28

Tues, Mar 16

It was my rest day. I didn't have to get up until I felt like it. The long, luxurious sleep really made me feel good. Rev. Quay played the harmonica, an old skill that one doesn't hear very often, which gave the morning a jaunty air. Mrs. Quay fixed a lovely breakfast. How nice to linger over it.

Since I didn't have to walk on that day, it was a day I could shop for another pair of jeans. The ones I had been wearing since Feb. 17th were beginning to fray on the bottoms and wear out on the seat. It was the first time in my life that I had ever worn out a pair of jeans on the bottom edge before getting a hole in the seat or the knees. However, there was the possibility that at some point the seat would wear through, and there I'd be…. The other item I needed was sneakers, since I had sent the boots back home. I needed a second pair in case the first got wet. It was also time for me to get a haircut.

Much to my surprise and delight I got a phone-call about 11:00 that morning from a friend I hadn't seen in years, Carolyn Hill. She said, "Louise, this is a former neighbor of yours…" I recognized the voice immediately. Our families had lived in opposite ends of a veterans housing unit at the University of Illinois during the 1957–58 year. That was the year my husband went back to school to finish his work toward a doctorate in sociology. Bill Hill was getting his in chemistry. Our preschool children played with each other during that year. Carolyn had heard of my walk and had found the right number to call somehow.

Here she was on the phone saying it was possible for us to get together and she would be glad to pick me up. We could go shopping together.

I had made a 1:00 appointment at a beauty shop to get a haircut. Carolyn took me there. All over the shop I noticed a number of pieces of beautiful sculpture. When the man began to cut my hair, I asked him whether he enjoyed cutting hair. He said he really preferred to sculpt. That's when I found out that the pieces were done by him. (After looking at my finished haircut, I thought it was a shame he couldn't sculpt full-time!)

How strange it was to be in a store again, shopping for sneakers and jeans. It felt so ordinary, yet so unreal. It was such a different orbit. I got what I needed as quickly as I could. I found a pair of boys' white sneakers. Before I could do anything about it, Carolyn was putting the sneakers on her charge card. I tried to stop her, but she said she wanted to help in some way. It was a very real help. Then she took me to her house where I met Bill, whom I hadn't seen in years and two of their three children, Kenny and Cheryl. Freddy was at a play rehearsal. After some reminiscences and fast synopses of our lives up to the present day, Carolyn took me back to Palmer Square, where I was to be picked up at 5:30 by Grete Otis who had invited me for dinner that night. Somehow being with Carolyn that day re-humanized me. I felt more like myself again. We parted with the promise that we would see each other soon again, and then off I went with Grete.

This was a grand opportunity to see a little more of the countryside of New Jersey. Grete and Sandy Otis, two very warm and welcoming people, were friends of Chris Little's mother. They lived about 40 minutes out in Belle-Mead. I found this part of New Jersey absolutely beautiful. At one point driving along the darkening road, we saw three wild deer poised in silhouette against the pale sky. Suddenly they bounded off. As we pulled into the driveway at the Otises a rabbit dashed into the bushes. In the distance there was the lovely pulsing sound of crickets—or birds—or frogs.

We sipped sherry in front of the burning logs in the fireplace, which took the chill off the mid-March air. What a shame it was to have to rush dinner with the Otises. It was one of those places and evenings that would have been ideal to continue on into time. After what seemed less than an hour we had to dash back to Princeton University where I was scheduled to talk at 8:00.

The group I met with informally consisted of about twelve townspeople and eight students from Trenton University. There wasn't one student there from Princeton itself.

Marjory Pratt, one of the coordinators of this part of my journey, an energetic, strong, and lovely woman in her seventies, was there. In my talk, I tried to give out all the facts I knew about the war and all the possibilities for action that I was aware of. The students from Trenton University wanted me to come to see them the following nights. We made arrangements for that. Though this meeting was small, I could only measure it against the no-meeting had I not come at all. Had I stayed at home and only thought about walking I would have talked with no one about the bombings, the atrocities, the defoliation, the population relocation, the utter inhumanity resulting from our misguided Indo-China policy. I had three theories about why the Princeton students didn't show up. One was that they were already in tune with resistance to the war, had many speakers every week, and were therefore too busy to come to this meeting. Another was that they were suffering from the same deadly apathy that existed on so many campuses. A third was: Who would want to go listen to a "housewife"? That didn't explain the Trenton University students being there. But I think they came because they knew Marjory Pratt.

Some time during that day, I had spoken to George Hardin of the Peace Education Office of Philadelphia Yearly Meeting in Philadelphia. I discovered for the first time that there were grand plans for my arrival at the City of Brotherly Love. The Peace Education Office had gotten together with The Action Line of the *Philadelphia Enquirer* in order to publicize my walk as much as possible. They were already making leaflets headed "What Can One Person Do?" I found the idea very exciting, that I should be speaking at a rally with the former Sen. Joseph Clark. It was to be at Independence Mall.

At the end of the Trenton meeting I was taken home to the Quays' and dropped gratefully into bed.

Week Five

Vietnam Veterans Against the War announced today that the organization, which claims to have 8000 members and chapters in every state, would hold a five day encampment here next month "to protest the war and the lack of adequate services for returned veterans....It plans to hold teach-ins to send delegations to lobby in Congress, to put on displays portraying alleged war crimes in Vietnam, and to try to call on President Nixon.

—*New York Times, Wednesday, March 17, 1971*

Princeton to Trenton, New Jersey

Day

29

Wed, Mar 17

Mrs. Quay drove me to the beginning point of my walk, Palmer Square. The weather was beautiful again. My feet felt ever so much better. It was amazing what one day of rest could do.

A photographer met me within a few blocks to take pictures for the *Trentonian.*

A young man wearing a broad-brimmed felt hat ran over to me from his car and said, "Do you have anything green to wear today?" It wasn't until then that I realized it was St. Patrick's Day. I was wearing a heck of a lot of orange, but no green. So he handed me a green ribbon and I wore it for the rest of the day, looped through the belt of my pack.

On this day Mrs. Heymann walked with me for part of the morning. She had been at the meeting the night before. She was of Dutch Jewish parentage and had lived through the Nazi occupation of Holland. She felt keenly aware of our policy in Vietnam. She not only brought with her a box of imported Dutch cookies but handed me an envelope with a $10 bill.

Marjory Pratt met up with us about 10:00. Marjory brought with her a letter, which had been forwarded from home.

March 13, 1971

Dear Louise,

At monthly Meeting night before last we followed your route in our mind's eye and blessed you in our hearts. The Meeting asked about the stages of your journey and asked me to tell you that we think of you in love and friendship day by day.

You have read Svetlana Alliluyeva's book? An extraordinary hymn to freedom and humanity. I was struck by the sentence from Gandhi which Svetlana found in Chester Bowles' *Ambassador's Report*. "It is possible for a single individual to defy the whole might of an unjust empire to save his honor, his religion, his soul, and lay the foundation for that empire's fall or its regeneration."

Gandhi acted on this principle. Svetlana acted on it. You are acting on it in a special way, and you are setting in motion waves that can bring regeneration.

You must think of fifty signatures along with mine –

> Our love to you,
> Jim St. John
> Clerk

When Marjory and I were alone I was struck by the beauty of a large gray tree, perhaps a sycamore, symmetrical, full branches, bare. It was reaching up, the grayness of the large, heavy trunk extending up through the branches and out further to the gray twigs, all of this against a steel gray sky. We had to stop and just look at that for a minute. It was intensely beautiful.

As we walked on, Marjory began quoting poetry to me. She said, "This is Shropshire Lad country." I admitted my ignorance and she mentioned the name of A.E. Housman. Then she began:

> Loveliest of trees, the cherry now
> Is hung with bloom along the bough,
> And stands about the woodland ride
> Wearing white for Eastertide.
>
> Now, of my three score years and ten,
> Twenty will not come again,
> And take from seventy springs a score,
> It only leaves me fifty more.
>
> And since to look at things in bloom
> Fifty springs are little room,
> About the woodlands I will go
> To see the cherry hung with snow.

There was something very special about this poem today. Marjory Pratt was in her "three score and ten" and quoting a poem she had learned in her youth. The sense of blossoming was there, of promise coming to fulfillment, the gray tree against a gray sky, the blossoms coming soon. Awareness was there. Awareness of awareness.

And then she went on to quote another poem:

> What shall I think when I am called to die?
> Shall I not find too soon my life has ended?
> The years, too quickly, have hastened by
> With so little done of all that I'd intended.
>
> There were so many things I'd meant to try.
> So many contests I had hoped to win
> And lo, the end approaches
> Just as I was thinking of preparing to begin.
>
> Anonymous

Marjory left me with one other quote, this one from Gandhi. It was so pithy. I asked her to write it in my notebook, which she did:

> nonviolence does not seize power;
> it does not even seek power;
> power accrues to it.

Marjory and I parted company near Rider College at which point she took the bus back to Princeton.

I hadn't passed the college by too far when Debbie Opdycke caught up with me. She was a student reporter for the college newspaper. We had lunch together during the interview. One of the most interesting things she mentioned was the fact that someone's class at the college had invited a Ku Klux Klan member to talk to them. I hadn't realized I was in Klan territory. How fascinating it would be to talk to a Klansman and try to follow his thought processes.

About 2:00 I arrived in Trenton. At one intersection a man stopped his car and we carried on a conversation for quite a few minutes. He was someone who obviously came from what one would call the "working class"; his car was an old one filled with work tools of some sort. He wanted me to know that he approved of what I was doing. He didn't believe in Communism but he thought the war should end. He said a most interesting thing. We were parting and he said, "You and I might disagree about a lot of things, but I think you're right." I hadn't gone but four more blocks when this same man drove by again. This time he handed me a $10 bill and said he wanted me to be careful of the neighborhood I was about to go through. I thanked him for his caring and his financial help.

I walked past a housing project. Several blocks further down a woman drove up from that direction. She had seen me walk past the project where she lived and just wanted to come meet me and shake my hand.

I walked past some liquor stores. An old man staggered out of one and wove his way over to my side of the street asking me what I had behind my ears. I didn't know what he was talking about. He explained. He meant the pack. I laughed with him and told him what I was doing. He took my right hand in his two and said, "Don't walk at night. You don't walk at night, do you?"

I said, "No, I don't ever walk at night."

He went on, "Promise me, you won't walk at night, will you? Don't walk at night. Don't ever walk at night."

I promised, and assured, and restated that I would never walk at night.

He went on and on until he had said the same thing about twenty times.

Finally I said, "Look, I promise you I'll never walk at night if you promise me you will write President Nixon and ask him to see me."

This pact appealed to him. He assured me he would write the President and I began to step away from him, gently letting my hand slip out from between his two, his arms extended, and as I turned my back and then glanced back, I saw that his eyes were glued to the seat of my pants. In my heart, though I felt tenderly toward this old man, I felt glad I was not walking at night.

A few blocks further on, about 2:30, I passed a car sales lot. Some men standing outside waved as I went by and asked if they could do anything. I called back and said, "Have you got a drink of water?" They said, "Yes, come on in." I was very thirsty. They handed me a soda, just what I needed. I sat and rested just a couple of minutes thinking I would go on. After a few minutes I decided that I might as well stop my walk at this point and call Lisa Brengle who was my hostess for that night in Trenton.

Lisa came by and picked me up. From there we went to the railroad station to pick up Jane Slaughter who had traveled up to Trenton from Washington, D.C. especially to talk with me. She was a worker for the People's Coalition for Peace and Justice. They wanted to know in what way they could coordinate activities in order to make the most of my walk as I came into Washington.

We went directly to Lisa's apartment and there Jane and I talked for about two hours. I tried to clarify the way I saw my walk, the kind of witness that it was, that I didn't want to be identified with any specific group, though I welcomed anybody who wanted to join, either walking with me or trying to extend the effects of the walk. I wanted no placards or banner waving. When I got to Washington, D.C. I wanted to enter in silence with the greatest degree of intensity rather than counting on crowds for quantity.

We talked about the fact that April 2 was a time being planned to commemorate the assassination of Rev. Martin Luther King, Jr. Activities were being planned in capitals throughout the country on that day, and I told Jane that a number of people were planning to take the Five Theses to their state capitals at the same time that I was arriving. We cleared up the fact that there was no planned activity for Washington, D.C. on April 2. I agreed to write a letter to Hosea Williams of the Southern Christian Leadership Council to suggest that groups cooperate if they could.

At about 5:45 the students from Trenton University came to pick me up. These students ran the campus radio station and they had time from 6:30–7:30 to broadcast. We went into a large lobby where they had set up their microphones. There were only about six people present in the room at the time. The way they planned to proceed was for the announcer to introduce me, to ask a few questions, and then I would take it from there. I would talk about my reasons for taking this walk and what the situation was in Vietnam as I understood it, and what I thought people could do about it.

The way these young people used the facilities they had was the most creative of any place I had been. The number of people in that room was very small, but the broadcast was beamed into the recreation areas, poolroom, etc. of the University. The directors of that program had gone to those areas to ask people to please leave their station on, so the effect was that we were reaching a much larger audience than just those in the room in face-to-face contact. I noticed that after I began talking people began filtering into this room.

We got back to the Brengle's apartment about 7:40. After dinner I called home.

At the beginning of my trip, when I first started calling home, the operator would say, "I have a collect call for anyone from Louise Bruyn. Will you accept the charges?" And generally the response was, "Delighted!" "Marvelous!" "Most certainly!" "With pleasure!" Every night it was different, but always it was reassuring. Then about three weeks later, for fun Sev said, "I don't know if I'll accept the charges or not." I burst into laughter, called him a few names, and then he said, "Okay," and we went on talking. Tonight, when the operator asked her usual question, "Will you accept the charges?" he said in a pseudo-hostile voice, "Well, it's mighty late to be calling! It's eight o'clock! I don't know if I should accept the charges!" I mock pleaded with him, "Please dear, I'm sorry I'm late. I couldn't help it." After begging a little and his holding back a little, and the operator being thoroughly confused, he finally said, "Okay."

At about 8:30 visitors were expected to arrive. People from the peace groups came over for coffee and cookies. Some of these people had been doing an awful lot to work toward draft resistance and other war protests. The evening ended about 10 or 10:30. Again I was extremely exhausted because of the continual demand on my brain to attend to matters at hand, and the demand on my body to make it another ten miles each day.

I had received a piece of mail from Cathy Perkus of National Peace Action Coalition. In it she enclosed all the literature about the April 24th March on Washington and a button advertising the date. In a note she said, "Here is a button for the 24th. Wear it." And she went on with other statements about the March. I wasn't about to wear something just because I was told to. Not only that, part of my intention was to go without buttons or slogans or signs. This was part of what I thought had been cleared up when I was talking with Jane. Also, I wanted Gill

Anderson to be the coordinator of the activities when I got into Washington.

Lisa pulled out the hide-a-bed in the living room. This was one night when I didn't sleep well. Light came in through the windows from the street, I didn't have enough covers, even though I wore my hat and sweater to bed, and in general I was a bundle of nerves. I know Lisa and her husband didn't sleep well either because they had kept their kitty in their room so it wouldn't be bounding all over me. Instead it was all over them. Altogether it wasn't a very pleasant night, but we managed to get through it.

South Vietnamese troops evacuated another base in Laos today. ...the base has to fall, one pilot said, because the North Vietnamese are "hitting it around the clock."

The United States command in Saigon has told Washington that a lack of money for the Vietnam war has been more crucial in determining the rate of troop withdrawals than has the progress of Vietnamization or what the enemy does on the battlefield [sic].

—*New York Times, Thursday, March 18, 1971*

Trenton, New Jersey to Penndel, Pennsylvania

Day

30

Thur, Mar 18

The Brengles drove me to the bridge, which was a few blocks past the point where I had stopped the night before, and I crossed the Delaware River into Morrisville, Pennsylvania. It was a beautiful morning. The birds were singing. The air was clear and cold, the sun was shining strongly on the houses and yards. I had the sense that Spring was really on its way. But in my heart I felt very alone and sad. Part of it was not having had a good night's sleep the night before. Part of it was because the walk seemed so endless. I was feeling sort of crumpled inside.

A taxi stopped by me in the road. The driver said, "Are you the lady walking to Washington?"

I said, "Yes."

He said, "I drove by you once, and then turned to drive by the other way, and decided I had to come back to tell you what a wonderful thing it is you are doing."

I thanked him and tears welled up in my eyes. "I needed that," I said. A few more words and he was gone. I waved goodbye with tears openly running down my cheeks. They felt good.

I called Cathy Perkus from a phone booth and told her my intention for Gill to be the coordinator in D.C. I also said that I would not be wearing any buttons, but would be talking about the April 24th demonstration as being important for people to go to in Washington. She seemed to understand very well.

As I was walking along I remembered how Sev had said when I left Newton that I shouldn't feel that I had to continue. He said that whenever I felt I had come to the end of my energy I should feel free to turn around and come home. I was suddenly aware of what I was going to do. I laughed out loud. And smiled for at least the next mile.

Along the way, I met a young man who was hitchhiking. He was going in my direction so I asked him if he'd like to walk along with me. He said he'd be happy to. He was a Quaker who was doing his best to resist the war. One way for him was to do draft counseling. It was good to fall into step with somebody of like mind.

From a gas station I made the phone call to my hostess, who came to pick me up. While I waited for her to come, I spoke with the gas station owner. He reflected the weariness of the people with the war. His grounds for being against it were that it was already so long. "Eleven years we've been fighting," he said. "We've never fought a war that long before."

"Have you ever protested against the war?" I asked.

"No, I never had," he responded.

I said, "The young people need gray heads like yours and mine to be in those marches. Our government has to hear from us, that we are against their policy."

He agreed in principle, but I don't know that he was ready yet to go out and march.

During this part of the walk I'd been envisioning a way of getting more people to visibly protest. I felt that people would respond if others came and took them by the hand and said, "Come with me." I pictured whole cities dividing up into circular areas, perhaps related to high school districts. The students, because they could be organized and there would be enough of them, could fan out to the outer edges of the district and go door to door, knocking on the doors. They would say, "We're going to the center of this district and we're going with our neighbors, because we are opposed to the war. We want to register our protest." And because one person would see that his neighbor was going, he would know that it was all right, that it was "safe" to protest. The idea of safety I couldn't handle yet because I knew that protesting a policy of this sort shouldn't involve a concern for "safeness." Yet I felt so many people felt threatened by the very idea of speaking out against their government that they would do it more readily if they saw co-operation from other people in their own neighborhood. I envisioned great crowds of people gathering in a friendly manner talking with their neighbors, maybe for the first time. They would be agreeing that, "yes, we have to register our protest and we have to do it together." And then, when all these people would gather in the center of their district, wherever it would be, there would be some event there when someone would speak for them. What could make this any stronger than a regular march? I didn't know. Would the culmination be picture-taking at the end to show how many had shown up? Would it be signing a petition? Would a few do civil disobedience and risk arrest?

Rene Hepburn picked me up and drove me to her house, where shortly after, a lady from the *Bucks County Courier Times* came to do an interview.

That evening the Hepburns had company. Some people were active in the peace movement and others were neighbors who were just interested in coming over. It was most interesting to see the beginning of awareness in some of these people who had previously not thought about the war and what it meant. They seemed to need to have personal contact with someone who had strong feelings about it.

Later someone at WCAU interviewed me at the radio station. It would be broadcast live from about 11:00 to 11:30 p.m. I felt the hostility of the interviewer, perhaps because he kept pursuing the question, "What would you do if China attacked the United States?" If I didn't believe in war, he wondered what I would do if a war happened. I kept holding to the point that we've got to seek justice. We had to find out what the *reasons* were for wars to begin and treat them *before* hostilities broke out. He wanted to make an assumption that the Chinese would drop nuclear bombs. What would we do then? I could only say that if they dropped nuclear bombs, I felt it was over for all of us. Then he said, "Supposing they dropped bombs that were not nuclear, then what would you do?" At that point I said that this was a hypothetical situation and I was more interested in speaking about the real situation that existed right now. I couldn't be trapped into that kind of thinking. During the whole interview I was very nervous, to the point that my knees were shaking so much that the table rattled. Those of us who were in the kitchen could hear the table rattling and found it a humorous sidelight. I don't think the shaking showed up in my voice. I tried to keep my mind as clear as possible for speaking to his questions and to what I felt the issues were.

Before the broadcast took place, which I knew would be live, I decided to call Sev so that he could listen to it. The program was to reach 35 states, I was told. This was also my chance now to get back at him for the two times he had told me that I was late in calling back or that he wasn't sure he'd accept the charges. I called and after he had accepted the charges I said, "Dear, I've just decided that I'm not going to go any further. I'm coming home." There was this long pause. He must have heard my suppressed giggle. He started calling me names. By that time I was laughing and he was laughing. I had really gotten to him, because he realized how much *he* had become invested in this walk of "mine." Even though he had said when I left the house that I should feel free to come back and not feel I had failed if I couldn't finish it, and I felt he meant it sincerely, he realized the deep disappointment he would have felt had I not finished the walk. The knowledge that I could shake him up like that delighted me. I told him how I had laughed for a long while that day just thinking about that prospect.

In the midst of my serious commitment to this journey, it was still possible to find humor.

The United States command said today that 45 Americans were killed in combat in Indochina last week, an increase of one over the previous week. It listed 156 Americans wounded, compared with 434 the week before. South Vietnamese head-quarters reported 773 Government soldiers killed, compared with 650 the previous week. The United States command listed a total of 44676 Americans killed in action since January 1, 1961, and 296,034 wounded.

—New York Times, Friday, March 19, 1971

Day

Penndel to Pennypack Park, Pennsylvania   31

Fri, Mar 19

That was the day I would be walking into Philadelphia. Rain was com-ing down so steadily that I kept up a fast pace and arrived at my des-tination of Pennypack Circle at 1:44. I stopped in a cafeteria to have lunch before I called my host and hostess. A group had been ready to meet me at 2:30 with signs, but I got picked up around 1:45 and went di-rectly to the Cohens' house—soaked through. The first thing I did was take a hot bath and warm up, then put on dry clothes. Rae and Charles Cohen came over with the signs from the demonstrations that never happened, and we all had a cup of tea together. Donna and Dawn, their daughters, came in after school, also drenched to the skin.

That Friday the article, written by Lisa Hammel, came out in *The New York Times*, so we bought a number of copies at the drug store before going home to the Cohens.

About five o'clock when I called home I found that Susie was going to come walk with me in Philadelphia. She had tried to come by way of a car ride with some friends she thought would be making the trip. The ride fell through, but Susan wanted to come so badly, that our friend Valerie paid for her air fare to fly there. She had wanted to surprise me, but because of a misunderstanding with the Cohens' daughter, I had been called to the phone.

That night the Cohens had a large gathering at their house. There were people in the peace movement, young and old. I met George

Hardin, Exec. Secretary of the Friends Peace Committee. He looked like a modern-day Ben Franklin with a lovely sense of humor. I talked with Stewart Meacham on the telephone. He was going to try to come over but he was unable to. Chris Little was in Philadelphia that weekend, and he came over to the house with his friend, Nelly. Nelly was a young beautiful woman who had been in an automobile accident a month or so previous and was in the process of recovering. Here was this beautiful, glowing young woman, almost blind, walking hesitantly, terribly tense because of her motor nerve problems from brain damage, but still radiant. How much more radiant she must have been before the accident!

When I had last talked to Susan we had made the arrangement that she would call me when she got to the Philadelphia airport. We also agreed that it would be easier for her to take a cab from the airport to the Cohens' house because the drive itself was about an hour long. It would mean two hours of someone's time, which didn't seem necessary.

It was getting on to be about 11:00 p.m. and her plane was to have arrived around 10:00. We received no phone call. By 11:15 I was so worried—my fifteen-year-old daughter was alone in an airport and I hadn't asked for somebody to personally pick her up. I had been asked very thoughtfully if I felt comfortable with the arrangement, and I had said yes. How would she manage with the taxi driver? I envisioned all sorts of problems. I could feel the tension mounting in me, the worry. Finally about 11:30 a car pulled up outside. A number of the people who had stayed to meet Susan called out, "She's here!" I was *so* relieved! I ran out to greet her as she came up to the house.

Apparently she had forgotten to call, and it had taken her awhile to get a taxi. It was wonderful to see my Susie again and to know she was safe and would be there the evening with us. We talked furiously for about an hour. She had brought a lot of mail with her, which had come to the house. It was astounding support for the walk. She also brought a special card signed by some of our friends with meaningful comments on it.

Louise: I did *my* thing, organized Houghton Mifflin around your resistance, a core group has connected themselves, more are joining every day—it's so exciting. Thanks for inspiring this activity and commitment! Valerie

You shall see storms arise,
> And, drenched and deafened, shall exult in them.
You shall top a rise and behold creation
> And you shall need the tongues of angels
> To tell you what you have seen.

> —Nancy Newhall from
> *This is the American Earth*

We are *very* busy getting others very *very* busy!
> Olivia Hoblitzelle, Sharon Satterthwaite,
> Phil Snodgrass, Marjorie Snodgrass

A Gaelic Prayer:-

> I am going out on thy path
> God be behind me
> God be before,
> God be in my footsteps.

> Betty—with much love to you.

And all this signed by Chuck and Peter Woodbury, Char and Bob Seeley, Jerilyn and Jim Prior, Carolyn Henderson, Jessie Jones, Valerie Kreutzer, and my beloved Sev.

I knew that the next day was the supposed "big day" with my walking into Philadelphia. I was to deliver a speech at Independence Mall. By 12:30 a.m. I still had not organized what I was going to say. Even when I had gone to bed, sharing the double bed with Sue, I felt very restless and unsure. I got back up, went into the living room, looked over notes, scraps of ideas that I had, wanting to put down into the best form what I felt was important to say. About 1:00 a.m. I finished. Even though it was late, I knew that I would speak better for having stayed up. When I did at last go to bed I wasn't at all tense because there was Susan in bed next to me. It was very reassuring, very comforting.

...the House Armed Services Committee voted today to eliminate draft defer-ments for divinity students and to extend the required civilian service for conscien-tious objectors to three years from two. The committee votes...are subject to final committee approval next week.

The South Vietnamese command announced yesterday that it had withdrawn 2000 to 3000 of its troops from action in Laos in 48 hours.

—*New York Times, Saturday, March 20, 1971*

Day

32

Sat, Mar 20

Pennypack Park to Philadelphia, Pennsylvania

We left from Pantry Pride, a grocery store in Philadelphia, at Penny-pack Circle. A number of people had gathered to walk with me. Ben and Elaine Cohen, their two daughters, my Susie, about six other young people, and some others who weren't so young. This was the first time that there was leafleting along my walk. The leaflet explained that there would be a rally at Independence Mall at 2:30 p.m. and urged people to come, saying who the speakers would be. Two of the young people were from United Farm Workers. They were very buoyant leafleteers, running up to cars at intersections, politely, happily, handing out the leaflets to waiting drivers, giving them to everyone along the way who would accept them. We were a happy band.

The length of the walk was somewhat more than what I would be doing normally. It was farther to walk into Independence Mall than had I gone directly on my way to the Schuylkill River, continuing in a straight line. So we took a car ride for a mile or two from the turning point of my forward direction in toward town. We got out again where we were to meet some Veterans for Peace. The veterans turned out to be one man, a veteran of World War II, with a hat on that said "Veterans for Peace."

We proceeded on our walk down into the center of town, walking un-der the tall building with William Penn atop it. From where we stood, he looked so small up there. (Yet, I was told, the brim of his hat was wide enough to hold an automobile.) Going through the city some people spoke to us who were from Boston. They had been following my trip and were very surprised to see me there. They said they would continue to follow it and wished me well.

By the time we got to Independence Mall, the light and sparse snowflakes were beginning to fall. It was very cold and windy. There didn't seem to be a crowd anywhere. Hardly anyone had gathered for this so-called "rally." Some people said it was because there was a very important basketball or football game, and everyone was home watching their television. They were being kind.

Three people spoke. There were about 30 to 60 people gathered around a stone bench in the outdoor cold. We each took turns standing on it to address the "crowd." I've always worried that people didn't really want to hear what I had to say, so I didn't say an awful lot. I didn't say nearly what I had written down the night before, because I felt people were cold and wanted to get on with other things. When I thought I was through, U.S. Senator Joseph Clark (President of World Federalists USA) called out, "Tell us about the Five Theses, Louise." So that's when I read the Five Theses aloud and explained how I felt about having a stronger world government so that we wouldn't get into these Vietnam-type problems. I was shaking like a leaf, partly due to the cold, partly to nervousness.

There wasn't a TV camera in sight until we began walking away from the mall, where a TV crew had been assigned to take pictures of some other event. That event, for some reason, hadn't happened. They mentioned that it had something to do with Angela Davis, a radical African-American educator. Here they were without a story. So we told them what *we* were all about and the man started taking pictures. They finished filming the interview outside of the restaurant, after which we all stopped for some coffee to warm up and relax.

I found out one of the things that had gone wrong, in terms of what George Hardin thought was going to happen and what actually happened. It was that the *Philadelphia Inquirer* disowned the backing of my walk which had been written about in their column called *The Action Line*. That column was supposed to tell what was going on in Philadelphia for the day or week. The editor of that column was severely reprimanded for having taken an active stand in backing the rally. He was almost fired from his job. Whatever else went wrong, I didn't know. Somehow the word did not get out, or else it just didn't get the people out.

Susie and I turned into our respective beds about 10:00 p.m., tired from this day, but looking forward to the next.

Staff Photo by Pat Crowe
Mrs. Louise Bruyn on Philadelphia Pike yesterday

The Evening Journal.
March 23

Day

Philadelphia to Swarthmore, Pennsylvania 33

Sun, Mar 21

Some good soul drove Sue and me to the Schuylkill River where we were met by the Sibbets, John Logue, Paul Mangelsdorf and two others. We walked across the bridge together. Our route carried us past the television station WCAU, channel 10. I almost walked past it and then I stopped and thought to myself, "Why not try." So we went around to the back, even though it was Sunday, and announced the fact that we were passing through. Would they like to give us any coverage? John Logue talked to Jay Silber who was their news producer. John used to have a program at that station on current issues. They agreed to send a crew out about 2:00 p.m. We set a general meeting point where we thought we would be at that time.

We finally did meet them along the road. Again I tried to center down to the best of my ability, to use those moments to the best advantage. A good bit of footage was taken. When we saw it later on the 6:00 news they had cropped a lot of it out, of course. The interview was nerve-wracking, as usual, just to try to control the information that got out, to keep the focus on the war and the issues and not be led into focusing on my feet or my pack.

We evidently passed within a block or two of a local congressman's house. John Logue had talked me into stopping by there to ask him to take stronger peace actions. I hadn't made an appointment ahead of time. Paul said to me privately, "Are you sure you *want* to do this?"

Stopping by a Congressman's house unannounced was different to me than stopping by a TV station. That was one of those moments when I felt that I had been pressured in a very subtle way, and given Paul's gentle question, I thought better of it and didn't stop there. I was glad that I didn't, partly because of the time problem, and partly because it was just too casual..."I just happened to be walking by your house and I wondered if..."

Susie walked almost the whole day with me, but she had to make her airplane ride back. About 4:00 she hopped into a waiting car and zoomed off to pick up her things at the Mangelsdorfs' and then to go to the airport. It was so delicious to have had her with me. I now had about two more weeks left and then I would be home with my family.

Walking through the Swarthmore College campus was such a beautiful experience. I wish she had been able to be with me during that, because the trees, the buildings and the shrubbery reminded me so much of the Illinois College campus where Sev had taught, one block from our old house.

When I did call home that evening, about 9:00, I was very glad to hear her voice and know that she had arrived safely.

That evening there was a potluck supper at the Swarthmore Friends Meeting. Barbara Reynolds was there. She had been working with a group whose main aim had been to educate people to the fact that nuclear war was unthinkable, that war today could not work, that we had come into the nuclear age and we had to think differently now to solve our problems. The group's approach was to show the film that they had made about the nuclear age to a group of teachers within a school system. After seeing the film, if any of these teachers would like to show it to their classes they did so. (I did not remember the age level of the students.) They then would try to get the superintendent to back the showing of the film to the entire school. By this time enough parents had heard about it through the children who had seen it; they knew the value of the film and were not frightened off by it.

There were about 40 people at the supper. I asked if they would all introduce themselves and tell how they learned about the meeting. I always found it fascinating the ways in which people found out about something and how they decided to get involved in an activity. Was it by word of mouth, the newspaper, the radio, did they accidentally pass a place and walk in? We found there were many people at that meeting who would not have been at a Quaker Meeting ordinarily. There were new faces. Many of them had seen the article in the newspaper the week before. Some were responding because of friends. I then spoke for about 20 minutes and following that we had a brief period of silence, which was a partial substitute for the Meeting for Worship that I had missed that morning. After all the talking and listening, and being present to so many others, the silence brought back serenity to my inner being.

I also was talking to a young man who was in the Reserves. He told me about the way different groups in the Reserves study the problems of how to reconstruct the government and economy of a country after it has been hit by an atomic bomb. His project was Czechoslovakia. The concept behind this project was that if any of these places had been hit by a bomb, a person would just reach up on a shelf some-where and find a masterplan of how to reconstruct that society along democratic, capitalist lines.

The frightening thing about this system was the kind of thinking that was involved. It encouraged becoming accustomed to the idea that there is a ready-made solution to a society after an atomic explosion. One just picks up the pieces and goes on. These studies were done as "exercises." Apparently they were being done for every country that ex-ists. The government tried to keep these plans secret, but this young man would not cooperate and as a result, he had been given a number of different assignments in the Reserves, so that he would not be al-lowed into planning sessions. He had openly told them that he didn't intend to keep silent about it.

We went back to the Mangelsdorfs' where I would be staying for the night. I was reading the news-clipping about my walk through Philadelphia which was juxtaposed with a story about a rally held in Washington by a pro-war fundamentalist radio preacher from New Jersey, Rev. Carl McIntyre. The pictures were even similar as far as expressions went, a small two-inch photo of each of us, separated by two columns of words. I was looking down to the right, he was looking down to the left, both looking away from each other. In a sense, it was really a humorous article, that pitted our two styles against each other. But this is what caught my eye:

> "When the President said on March 8 that he was a dedicated pacifist, that turned me off," said the Presbyterian minister. "We don't want a dedicated pacifist leading our boys into battle. The time has come for the President to step down and let Agnew run this government. Let's have a President who will bring our boys home in victory."
>
> *The Philadelphia Enquirer, Sunday morning, March 21, 1971*

When I finished reading that, the telephone rang and it was Gill Anderson in Washington, D.C. She wanted to know why I thought I should see the President. It was as though I had read the reason the second before. She was now calling for that reason. President Nixon apparently had said he was a pacifist. I felt that I could speak to that part of his humanity, his identification with his Quaker beliefs. In his role as President he had tremendous power over the fate of other humans. I hoped I could give him a greater sense of what the people of the country wanted, and of faith that if he were to take the road of peace that the people would follow him.

How often I had thought, over and over in my mind as I walked, what I would say to the President if he would see me. I had even considered only meeting in silence with him, letting that which was holy between us speak to both of us. I had thought of speaking to him from everyone who had spoken to me as I walked, letting him know their interests. Yet how could I say that I was moved by the Holy Spirit, that I had a "message from God." I could hardly even think that. I only knew that I was moved to speak with him, and somehow, if he would hear me, I could reach him.

The other person that I tried to contact was Brian McDonnell, the man who had fasted for forty days outside the White House and was instrumental in getting a small group of people in to see Kissinger. I made arrangements to call him the next day in order to meet together.

One of the things that Gill had said was that Senator Kennedy wanted us to have lunch with him. I had been so moved by his leadership and that of his brother, President John F. Kennedy. I felt truly privileged at the prospect of spending time with him at lunch.

I called ahead to my next host and hostess, thinking it would be Dolores and Alden Josey, friends of ours from Urbana, Illinois. I had a great conversation with Dolores, also a dancer whom I knew back at the University of Illinois, and a Friend. As it turned out, she was to be the hostess for Tuesday night instead of Monday, so I called Elizabeth Pattison in Wilmington, Delaware. Elizabeth told me of their vigil, which they would be holding in front of Naaman's Teahouse at 2:30. I couldn't be sure of the time I would be arriving. Alden Josey would be participating. If I were to arrive in the middle of the vigil I would want to greet Alden, a very dear friend of Sev's and mine, and not hold to the silence, since I hadn't seen him for such a long time. We agreed then, that I would promise not to arrive before 3:00, so that the silent vigil could continue for at least half an hour, but if I were later than that, it would be okay. I really looked forward to the next day's walk.

More than 2000 South Vietnamese troops retreated hastily from Laos yesterday and today while North Vietnamese forces pursued them, posing a possible threat to American installations supporting the six-week-old campaign. Virtually every American helicopter here was thrown into the effort to bring back the South Vietnamese. The helicopters again ran into heavy anti-aircraft fire...

Two platoons of American armored cavalrymen refused orders yesterday to advance along embattled Route 9 near the Laotian border, and their commanding officer was relieved of duty, United States military spokesmen reported.

—*New York Times, Monday, March 22, 1971*

Swarthmore, Pennsylvania to Claymont, Delaware

Day

34

Mon, Mar 22

I began the walk right from the front door of the Mangelsdorfs'. Two young men and a young woman whom I had met at the meeting the night before walked with me. One of the young men, Bill Stanton III, quoted all 59 lines of the poem "The Box," by Kendrew Lascelles, as we walked. It was the story of war, told in fairy-tale-like language, both gently humorous and powerfully serious. We walked to the sound of Bill's voice, our minds and hearts in tune with the words.

It was a sunny day and the air was bracing. We made good time. Such good time, that we were going to be early. We stopped in a Gino's hamburger place for about an hour to use up some time. It still appeared that we would arrive at Naaman's Teahouse by 2:00 unless we did something drastic. Rather than get to the vigil before the appointed time, I stepped off the road into a patch of woods, spread out my poncho and used the time to write in my notebook, to catch up on the events that had already happened. The three young people went on ahead. The meeting place was only about two blocks away, one block forward and one to the left. My walking companions sort of peeked around the corner at the vigil. It seems someone saw them and began to speak to them. The walkers, through gestures and signing suggested that I was down the road apiece and would be along at 3:00. The walkers returned to where I was and reported that a television truck had been driving around looking for me. I felt very awkward, like I was playing hide and seek. At that point it seemed hilarious.

Finally at 3:00 I emerged. As I walked toward the vigil I passed the Channel 12 TV truck. The crew said they were glad to have found me and said they were in a hurry. I told them that I needed to arrive at the vigil about 3:00 and would come back to talk with them. They were very kind and allowed me to go on, whereupon I walked the last two blocks to the place where about 15–20 people had gathered. And there was Alden. It was delightful to again see this very dear friend of ours. When we came up to the vigil there were reporters there taking pictures. Alden read a minute from the Wilmington Meeting and I was introduced around. The Minute read:

> TO WHOM IT MAY CONCERN:
> At the Monthly Meeting of the Society of Friends held on March 14, 1971 at Fourth and West Streets in Wilmington, our attention was drawn to a walk by Louise Bruyn from Newton, Massachusetts to Washington. The Meeting expressed a deep appreciation for her concern to draw attention to the tragedy of the Vietnam War. We join with her in spirit and are looking forward to meeting her on March 22 as she passes through Wilmington.
> Sincerely, Richard H. Rhoads

They were a warm welcoming group. Somebody there said the State Police were there with their television, and I thought they were joking. I didn't think the men in the TV truck were State Police, but clearly the vigil people were aware that this was the kind of surveillance that was happening. Then a man from a radio station began interviewing me at length, asking me questions about my stand against the war, sounding both superior and hostile to my action. At one point he said, "Mrs. Bruyn, I see your lips are chapped. What has been the hardest thing about your trip?"

I looked at him in silence for a minute and said, "Talking to newsmen."

He laughed in an embarrassed sort of way. I went on to explain that I had a letter from my police department in Newton. He was quite interested in that. He wanted to see the letter, so I took it out of my pack. He read it into the mike, including it in the taped interview.

By this time the TV crew wanted to get on with their business so they could get back to the station. So they asked if they could do some footage of me walking. The interviewer, Charles Tornell asked me questions as the crew took pictures. I tried so hard to make the seconds count. And then he asked me that question. "What do you hope to accomplish by this walk?" And I could feel my voice becoming more and more strident, trying to say that sometimes people do things without the hope of an "accomplishment," but just because they feel it's right to do. They have to express the depths of their feelings. At the same time I was feeling, "I'm wasting my time—my news time—trying to explain this point. I'm not saying enough about the war itself." In a few seconds the interview was over and the cameras were turned off and I broke down in tears. The men said, "Is anything the matter? Is there anything I can do?" Charles Tornell said, "Can I get you a cup of coffee? Would you like to sit down?" I pulled myself together again and apologized for having cried. It was just that I felt that I had wasted an opportunity again having been caught in that question. Then I said, "Please don't report in the news that I cried," and Charles Tornell was very considerate and said that he wouldn't. I felt it was so important to not be "weepy" even though at times I felt so distressed. I did not want tears to be part of my mission.

I remember the day before I left Newton, when I was being interviewed by the *Boston Globe*. I had gone through about fifteen interviews previously that day, speaking on the phone to every radio station Jim Prior had contacted, giving my reasons for doing what I was doing. On that final interview with the *Globe*, Cindy Smith had asked me, "Who are you doing this for?" It hit me. I had said, "I'm doing it for us. I'm doing it for all of us," and I broke down and cried then. I felt so bad that I had cried. It turned out that she used that as the very opening of the article the next day, that I had broken down into tears. Somehow it seemed weepy and weak and I didn't want that.

How we all do try to hold back the tears, I thought. Somehow they were the badge of weakness, of futility, of powerlessness. Yet how deeply we felt the tears of another, the anguish. Would that we could feel the tears of those whose homes we were bombing, whose rice paddies we were destroying, whose children and mothers and brothers and fathers we were killing, maiming, burning. Yet there, the anguish goes too deep even for tears. My thoughts swirled, then cleared for the ongoing task.

We got into the television truck and the men drove me back the few blocks to the vigil. In the truck everybody was very relaxed. The driver said, "You're a Quaker, aren't you?"

I said, "Yes."

He said, "Well, how do the Quakers feel about Nixon? He's a Quaker, isn't he?"

I said, "He pains them very much."

When we returned to the group and began walking the rest of the way, I began thinking about what I had said and what the interview was like. It hit me that I had made a statement about the president which I felt would not be helpful at this time. First, I was only speaking for the Quakers whom I knew. I could not know that he distressed all Quakers. And second, I did so want to get in to see him, to bring him my witness. I didn't want to say anything hurtful to that mission. So when I got to the house where I was to stay that night, with Elizabeth Pattison, I called the television station and once more talked to Charles Tornell. I said I had made an off-the-cuff comment in the truck and wondered if he would please not use it. Again he was very kind and said he had thought about using that but he himself had felt it would not be a good thing to put in his report. So he agreed with me that he would not use it and could see why. Then he said, "Is there anything that you feel that you weren't able to say, that you would like to say now?"

I said, "Yes, one of the things that I have wanted to say is that Nixon has labeled those who want to stop the war as neo-isolationists. To me this was not isolationism, to want to stop the war. We would want to continue working in peaceful ways with countries, but he was unfairly equating the concept of stopping the war with not wanting to be concerned about other countries." He took down the ideas, the words that I felt had such import at that moment, and later I watched the six o'clock news.

The report of my walk was at the very end of the news hour. There was a lot of photographic coverage that even extended into the credits at the end. I heard myself repeat the reasons for my doing what I was doing, "what I hoped to accomplish" and my voice getting more and more strident, getting a higher and higher pitch, and I cringed inside. But the tag that they put at the end of the interview while the walking footage was still going on, was not about Nixon's "neo-isolationism," but rather that the state police had been at the vigil and were taking pictures of all of us there. This was the news. Delaware had been going through experiences with the state police, enough that some residents were likening Delaware to a police state. I thought this was the reason also that the interviewer from the radio station had shown such an interest in my letter from the Newton police department. It was certainly unusual for a "protest" to be backed in any way by the police.

Most of the people who had been at Naaman's Teahouse for the vigil were connected in some way with the organization "Another Mother for Peace." One of the women told me as we finished the walk that day that the police had asked for a list of all the members of their organization. This woman said to the policeman in tones of disbelief, "You don't want *mothers* in your files?!"

At the Pattisons' I was interviewed by Cathy Wolff of *Wilmington Morning News* for about an hour before and during dinner for a news article. After dinner, Elizabeth drove me to the Wilmington Friends Meeting where a special meeting had been called for me to talk about ways of resisting the war. It was there that I saw Dolores, my dear friend, lovely as ever, wife to Alden. It was a good meeting. There were a variety of people there, perhaps thirty altogether. Some of them had excellent questions about whether the war was right or not. One such question I remember in particular, in which a woman asked, "Well, if we're supposed to be defending democracy over there, how come our friends (other countries) aren't helping us?"

Alden Josey's answer was classic. "That should give you a clue."

A man was there who had come to defend the administration's position. He was an older man, perhaps retired, definitely against Communism. Though he seemed armed with literature, ready to tear me down on any of the positions I might take, he wound up being very mild. For some reason, he was not as vehement as others had expected him to be.

About 10:00 I began to fold, as usual, and Elizabeth took me to her home, where I got to bed as quickly as I could.

Elizabeth was fearless in her handling of the State Police. Her view was that this was an opportunity to educate them about the peace movement, so she was very cooperative with the police. She showed her views clearly at the vigil at Naaman's Teahouse. She didn't give them the names of the individuals who were with the organizations, but gave the names of any organizations that were backing it, trying to explain what Friends were and Another Mother for Peace.

A "national week of concern" for the American prisoners of war and servicemen missing in action in Indochina opened here today amid growing Congressional feeling that an alternative to President Nixon's policy on the prisoners must be found. The Defense Department said that 462 men were believed to be held captive as of mid-March...

The Defense Department argued today that tear gases and plant killers were legitimate, humane weapons of war that should not be abandoned by the United States.

—*New York Times, Tuesday, March 23, 1971*

Day

Claymont to Hares Corner, Delaware 35

Tues, Mar 23

The next morning I was driven back to Claymont to where I had been picked up. Alden was there as well as about eight other people. It was a beautiful morning, sunny, exhilarating. Alden stayed with me for the entire day and carried my pack. That day I didn't have to carry the pack at all.

One of the women who walked with us was exquisitely beautiful. A young mother, she could have been a cover girl for any beauty magazine. She felt so bad, so guilty, that she had seen the light about the war only recently, that she had formerly accepted the war as being the right thing, almost on the basis that because our country was doing it, it therefore must be all right. But when she began to see the series of wrong moral choices and immoral actions, she became suddenly aware of the need to take action to stop the war. She was now in the process of converting her parents. (This was the woman who had said, "You don't want *mothers* in your files?!") She walked as far as she could with us that morning and then left. Most of the walkers dropped off before we got to Wilmington Square.

When we got to Wilmington Square Alden told me about how the State Police had put microphones in the trees to bug the demonstration that had happened there several days before. The microphones were discovered by a janitor who was cleaning in the government office building. In one of the rooms he kept hearing birds singing. He

195

looked around for the birds. In the process he found the speaker that was broadcasting the sound of the birds from the trees outside in the square. In the paper the next day there was a marvelous cartoon. Two birds were in a tree. One was twanging a worm-like guitar, and another was playing a corrugated worm-like accordian, both birds singing. The caption read, "Auditions for Battaglia." Battaglia was the head of the State Police Intelligence.

Alden and I talked about many things for the rest of the walk. He was interested in what I had been thinking about during the five weeks that I had been walking. I was able to talk with someone for the first time about how my whole sense of time and space had changed. At the very beginning, planning out three days walk from Newton meant three ten mile segments. I had looked at it and suddenly realized that that point thirty miles away was a place I would think nothing of driving to in thirty minutes, but if I were walking it would take me three days. I thought about how people at this time were talking about the super-sonic jets which would get people to Europe three hours faster and for that they were willing to jeopardize our environment with large sonic booms. It seemed such a misuse of public money. The values were so strange. Walking every day, covering inch by inch of the ground was somehow so much more human than anything I had ever done. Every tree, every rock had meaning to me. There was time to appreciate the wildflower or the branch.

We talked, too, about communal families. How separated we were from one another the way our families were organized. Mothers went through the same routines over and over again, cleaning and cooking, and fathers worked to support a single family dwelling. Better use of time and effort could be made if work were shared. Living could be made richer.

We talked about the quality of life, how we wanted to make our lives have greater value. How much of our lives today was taken in by the "Big Sell." We were confronted on all sides by the urge to buy this image, that product, a certain way of life. We had been sold on the idea that bigger and faster means progress, that technology was the answer to any problem. To have taken an action myself that was slower and smaller, the pace of a snail, a unit of one, somehow flew in the face of that belief. I found the power of the spirit in me was unleashed in the process. The action for me was humanizing. The response from others had led me to believe it was also humanizing for them.

Yes, on that day especially, I felt the luxury of five weeks of walking. It was filled with new experiences, with meeting old friends, with the excitement of the unknown, with the unifying of my innermost longing with outward action. I felt so enriched. I could imagine people saying, "Yes, she could afford to take time out from her regular life." Yet what I felt was that I was taking time to step *into* life.

We walked on further on the right side of the highway. A car pulled up and stopped by us. A young man got out and asked if I were that lady walking to Washington. I said Yes. He said he was so glad to meet me. He knew I was coming and had driven along the road looking for me. He just wanted to tell me that if I got in to see Richard Nixon, I should tell him that he should do something about jobs. He was having trouble finding one. I assured him that I would pass on the message, and after shaking hands and bidding him farewell, he got back in the car, and with a fast U-turn, zoomed back in the other direction.

We reached Hare's Corner and sat in the median strip awaiting Dolores, whom Alden had called when we passed a phone booth, at about 3:00. After about 45 minutes she arrived in her little VW and we piled in, tired and cold, but satisfied at having done what we had done. During the afternoon, the clouds had become heavier and gray, and the sun had disappeared. The temperature dropped. As we pulled up to the house it began to snow.

A hot bath and a short nap later, I felt revived. After my bath and nap I looked out the window and all over was a blanket of white. How kind of the weather to wait until we were inside before loosing the frosty white stuff.

We had a quiet evening of conversation. Dolores and Alden had invited in a few friends. Later that night we watched the replay of the "Selling of the Pentagon." We need so much more illumination by the news media of what was happening in government.

Week Six

Day

Hares Corner, Delaware to Elkton, Maryland

36

Wed, Mar 24

That day I walked all alone. The snow had melted, but the day was extremely chilly. It wasn't that the sun wasn't shining. It was just that the wind was so raw. It seemed to go right through me. My path ahead was a short-cut. I got away from the four-lane highway and my route took me through Cooches Bridge. The road was black top, two-lane. A car seldom passed. Early in the morning a pick-up truck stopped and the driver asked me for my autograph. It was one of those sweet ego-boosters. I obliged. How difficult it was to not get affected by the "fame" syndrome. I didn't even remember if I told him that I felt there was something that everyone could do to stop the war, and hoped he'd find his thing. I had tried to do that in every contact, yet I knew there were times when I didn't, or couldn't.

It was lucky that I had in my jacket pockets the chocolate, nut, and raisin mixture, which had been given to me by a Quaker doctor at the meeting the night before. It was so thoughtful of her. She had prepared two bags, one with raisins, chocolate bits, and peanuts and the other of sugared orange rind. There were no coffee shops, no roadside stands, no grocery stores, no restaurants—no place where I could buy any refreshment. Certainly there was plenty of nourishment in my pocket, including an apple, but how I longed for a cup of hot coffee to get shelter from the cold and to warm my innards.

My feet hurt a lot that day. I rested often. At one point a young man passing in a car asked, "Would you like a ride?

I said, "No, thank you."

Pretty soon he came back and asked, "Would you like to rest?"

I said, "Yes, it's a good time for that."

"My place is just down the road a few miles," he stated.

"Oh, no thanks. I don't leave the road," I said. "I'll sit by the road and rest if you want to visit here with me." He made me very uneasy. It was a desolate road.

He talked a bit about having been to Washington with his motorcycle group. He told about how some of them had been arrested. I'm afraid I wasn't very outgoing with him. I talked about the war, but gave him no friendly encouragement. Soon he'd had enough and left. Maybe he got cold.

I discovered a good way to warm my fingers, which were almost numb from the wind. I balled my hands into a fist, removing my fingers from the finger parts of the glove and let the sun shine on the palms of the glove. I could feel the warmth radiating into my fingers. But it sure looked silly. Limp empty glove fingers bounding up and down with each step.

Around noon I changed sneakers, hoping that would relieve some of the aching. I put on two pair of the heavy wool socks so that I could tie the laces tighter. That would give me more support for my foot. It was an improvement.

I finally walked into Elkton. I got my first thumbs down sign from a truck driver. I also saw a bumper sticker on another car that said "God Bless Spiro Agnew."

I had arrived about 2:30, had my lunch in a little restaurant in town, and called Gertrude Malz, my hostess for the evening. She arrived in about half an hour and drove me to her apartment in Newark, Delaware.

After the supper, at which there were a number of students from the nearby university, we had a discussion. We talked about the kinds of avenues open to people to take action against the war. Two people remained very silent until the group broke up, ready to leave. That's when one of the girls who had not spoken came up to me and said she was part hawk. She said she knew the hawk's position and the dove's position and felt the answer might be somewhere in the middle. I said I was afraid one had to make a choice.

If one were for armed intervention in the affairs of another country and another were against armed intervention in that same country, where was the middle ground? A little armed intervention? Just kill a few people? Was it handing the rifle to the other guy and saying, "You shoot your enemy. I'll stand here and show you where to point the gun, and how to pull the trigger, and give you more ammunition when you've used up what you have, and I'll cheer you on." Supposedly that was "Vietnamization." Or might the middle ground be diplomacy? Or the multitude of non-violent ways of dealing with problems.

The girls may have been afraid to voice their opinions in the larger group. However, if they had spoken, it might have given everyone the opportunity to face the challenge of an opposing idea.

After the dinner and discussion, several of us went to the Episcopal Student House. We were seventeen altogether. There we talked about world law and our war in relation to it. Afterwards I asked any who wanted to sign the Five Theses. When I looked at the names later I saw that one of the girls had written her name, followed by "in Jesus' name."

Rev. Hummel, at that center, passed this prayer on to me:

PEACE ON EARTH

"Oh Lord in Thy mercy and wisdom
hear the prayers of Thy people
who are beset with war.
In this season of Thy birth,
grant us peace.
Thy people cry out,
and are not heeded.
Our sons go out from among us,
to a war without victories
and return not.
The people turn one against another,
and are divided.
Oh Lord, give wisdom into the hearts of the mighty;
give understanding to Thy people,
and grant us peace."

"A Service of Lessons and Carols for Christmas,"
Willimus Byrd, Durham Cathedral, 1643

Copies of Federal Bureau of Investigation documents that have been mailed anonymously to several newspapers and individuals indicate that the agency is engaged in active surveillance of student, Negro and peace groups.

—*New York Times, Thursday, March 25, 1971*

Elkton to Weigh Station on Rt. 40, Maryland

Day

37

Thurs, Mar 25

Gertrude dropped me off in Elkton at the restaurant, where I met Sharon Dickman of the *Baltimore Sun* who wanted to walk with me for a way while interviewing. It was a pleasure to have company. My country path had ended at Elkton. We got onto the main highway, four lanes with median strip, and together battled the backwash of trucks roaring by. It was an effort to speak, to hear, to write, but we were both in good spirits so it all worked. About 11:00 we had arrived at the YMCA. We both thought it would be nice to stop for a cup of coffee, if they had one, but were I to leave the road I would miss meeting the two women from *Good Housekeeping* who would be looking for me about this time. So we decided that I would wait by the roadside while she went in. I took off my pack, leaned it against a post and lay down on the curb for a few moments to rest my back and feet. Wouldn't you know it, that's when Alice Lake and Kathryn Abbe arrived, finding me stretched out, looking as if all the world were my couch.

After a short cup of coffee for all of us, we started on our way again. Sharon Dickman left and I continued on with Alice Lake. Kathryn would drive on, and as we approached, she would take pictures.

Alice had many thought-provoking questions. She tried to get as clear a picture of me, and what I was trying to do, as she could. Her questions were sensitive. She listened carefully. I could feel that she was listening to the deeper level of this experience, as well as picking up surface details. After lunch we walked on and Kathryn Abbe spoke of her wish that I could be photographed talking to someone, but we were walking along a four-lane highway. Small chance of finding people to talk to.

Just a few minutes later a car pulled over. The driver asked if he could take us anywhere. I laughed and said no, we were walking, but "You don't know what you just walked into." I told him what I was doing and who the other two women were and asked him if he would mind getting out of his car to talk for a few minutes about the war, because Kathryn wanted to take some pictures. He laughed and said that would be fine and then he told us that he was a returned vet from Vietnam. When I asked him what his experience had been there, he said, "Vietnam is rotten!!" He went on to explain how if any Vietnamese wrecked an army truck nothing would happen, but if an American did the same thing, he'd receive Holy Hell. The words may not be exact, but that was the general idea. And he talked of the corruption of the government in Saigon and how he was trying to get himself "back in shape as a civilian." Kathryn took the pictures she wanted and he drove on.

Later down the road a minister stopped in his car to tell me that I couldn't cross the Susquehanna River by foot. I hadn't known that it was a toll bridge, not for pedestrians. He said if I had trouble I should stop at the school and someone could drive me. I didn't know what school he meant, though he explained that it was near the bridge. I tucked the note in my brain for the next day. I asked him how he knew who I was. He said he knew I was coming.

When we got to the weigh station on route 40, Kathryn and Alice drove us all back to Gertrude Malz's apartment. That was the one time when I stayed two nights with the same person because Jessie could not find another home for that second night. It was also one of those times that I felt the incongruousness of my action with reality. Here I was walking to a point 450 miles from the starting point, but being picked up at the end of each segment to be whisked to some other place for an overnight stay. To have to backtrack over my trail left me with that peculiar feeling of purposelessness. How much better I felt when I actually walked up to the house where I was to stay and left from that door by foot to continue through the next day.

Alice stayed for a bit more to finish asking me questions, and then left. Gertrude and I had a delicious dinner which she had prepared. I spent that evening quietly, reading some of the materials I had in my pack, writing notes, making phone calls, and doing laundry. I was very, very tired. It felt so good to finally turn in.

United States bombing raids over the southern provinces of North Vietnam have caused some 100 casualties since the beginning of the month, according to a communiqué published here today. During the same time period, United States aircraft have carried out "daily reconnaissance flights over nearly all of the provinces and cities of North Vietnam, including Haiphong and Hanoi," the statement by the "Commission of Investigation into American War Crimes," said. It said that from March 1 to 22, American planes made 1440 reconnaissance sorties and 220 tactical sorties, bombing several populated regions of the provinces north of the 17th Parallel. Over this area, it said the United States planes dropped 2,220 demolition bombs and 120,000 small demolition bombs. B52 strategic bombers dropped an additional 2,600 tons of bombs, the communiqué said.

—New York Times, Friday, March 26, 1971

Weigh Station to Stepney, Maryland

Day

38

Fri, Mar 26

One day blended into another. Gertrude drove me to the Weigh Station on Route 40 where I started again, another farewell, another trek. This day was marked by the fantastic excitement of a hamburger at Gino's, doughnuts, coffee and peanuts at a diner. I reached the Susquehanna River about 11:00, looked at what was maybe the school where the minister, whom I had met the day before, had taught, looked at the police office on the bridge, and thought I'd try first to get a ride across from the police. They seemed very happy to oblige, so there was no problem. There was a weather warning of snow. I wondered when it would fall. It never did.

When I reached Stepney I called Margaret Hopkins. I waited for her in the VW auto sales building. She came to get me in about twenty minutes, a woman in her 60s. She drove me to her farm in Darlington, much farther away than I had thought. Her farm was lovely—secluded, clean and simple and pure, away from the pollution of truck and auto exhaust, away from the pollution of noise. It was peaceful. It was like going back in time, rediscovering the connection between human and the earth, so easily forgotten in this day of instant frozen TV dinners, canned entertainment, plastic trash. I longed to be a part of that life. I think I was born 100 years too late.

That evening we went to dinner at the home of the four Allen sisters. Though only one still retained the name Allen, the four sisters again lived together, now in their seventies and eighties, forming a primary community, living in harmony with one another. What a beautiful evening that was. Their house was new, modern, sturdy. We took time to appreciate the beautiful sunset outside their window. They said it was beautiful every night, but always different. (Will even beautiful sunsets be gone someday?)

The dinner itself was served with elegance—shining silver, sparkling crystal and warm linen. The offerings included creamed chicken and peas and biscuits and jam and butter and Jello salad and ice cream and cake and coffee... The meal seemed so special. It wasn't just the food that was served. It was the presence of life and light at that table. I was awed by the age of the women at this table, by their sensitivity to life and the world around them, by their care of one another. And not just of each other. They were concerned about the Young Friends Meeting at the Meeting House, whether to bring enough food for thirty people or for sixty.

Later, two of the sisters, Margaret Hopkins and I went to the Meeting. The young Friends had gathered for a weekend there. They were just like our kids. I spoke to them for a few minutes about what I was doing and why there was a need. I told them I would tell my children and their friends that there were young people in Maryland they would enjoy knowing.

"The papers and the radio in Saigon kept on saying there was a Laos victory, I have learned now, but what a joke," Corporal Ti said. "We ran out like wounded dogs.".... "The most heartbreaking thing," he continued, "was that we left behind our wounded friends. They lay there, crying, knowing the B52 bombs would fall on them. They asked buddies to shoot them but none of us could bring himself to do that. So the wounded cried out for grenades, first one man, then another, then more....We ran out at 8 PM and about midnight we heard the bombs explode behind us. No more bodies! They all became dust."

—New York Times, Saturday, March 27, 1971

Day

Stepney to Joppatowne, Maryland

39

Sat, Mar 27

Margaret Hopkins told me at breakfast, as I was admiring again the expanse of farmland, the cleanliness, the wholesomeness of the scene, that soon this whole area would be under water. Somewhere they were building a dam that would make a reservoir that would inundate the entire farm, house and all, and all the neighboring area. People were fighting the project, giving arguments that it wasn't needed, that it could be built somewhere else. But arguments notwithstanding, she felt that in a few years all that she knew there would be gone. I did not absorb all the details of who was building the dam, who needed the water, what the alternatives were. I could only ache for the people who would have to leave their homesteads and watch them fill up with water.

Margaret took me back to the VW car sales place. The weather was beautiful. It was sunny and cool-warm. We parted with a bond of affection and I walked on.

About 11:15 a car pulled over. It was two workers with the AFSC, Jane and Chris Motz. We spoke briefly and they wished me well. Just before they left a man pulled up to see if I were "that woman." He was a chemist for the army. He wondered if he could take me to lunch, since he wanted to talk further. It was about 11:40, so it seemed a good time to break for lunch, and though he thought it was silly, I made him promise to bring me back to the same spot after lunch.

At lunch we had a long talk about the army and the kind of research they were doing. Some of it he found abhorrent. He told of the cold way scientific reports could be given which were dealing with the chemical means of destruction. Yet he felt that his own research was more basic. It was like working for a university, he said. I suggested that all chemists for the army go on strike until the war was ended. (Sometimes I took delight in coming up with a naïve suggestion.) Perhaps the army could change its image. Instead of working on ways to kill people, it could use its scientific power to solve the car problem, such as how to get rid of exhaust fumes (something I had felt keenly in the last month!). He drove me back to the place on the road. It had been good to talk with him. He seemed to be a very concerned individual. He was against the war, yet he could not see the connection between his work and the continuation of the system that waged the war. In the name of science, horrors had been perpetrated. Technology had shown us a cleaner way to kill people. We didn't have to get our hands dirty.

I walked on until about 3:00 when again I saw the chemist's car. This time he had with him his wife and three daughters. They were lovely. He had wanted me to meet them. They even brought with them some food and drink for me for later in the day. It was so thoughtful. How I wished that he didn't have to be a chemist for the army. Yet being a chemist for a corporation might not necessarily leave one free of involvement in the war. Many a private company was doing research for the Defense Department, such as Dow Chemical, which produced napalm.

I finally got to the Joppatowne shopping center. From there I called Adelaide Noyes, who picked me up about an hour later. Not only did she live a long way off, but we were waiting for each other in two different places at the shopping center. What a shame!

Adelaide Noyes was one of those people who had been working for peace for years and years. Everybody in the area knew who she was. She lived all the way in Bel Air. Her house was a beautiful, one-story mansion. The ceilings were 15 feet high. The appointments were elegant, yet it was still cozy.

I was about to get into the shower, when I was called out by none other than Gillian and Woody Anderson, our friends from Washington. It was Gill who was doing so much to prepare for my arrival in Washington.

They had much to tell me about who was doing what and when and how. Adelaide Noyes invited them to dinner and to stay all night. They had looked for me all along the road, because they had wanted to walk with me. But they were looking in the wrong place. The itinerary was not accurate at that point. But at least now we could visit.

Adelaide Noyes had invited a number of people to the house for the evening. There were 20–25 people there. Unfortunately, I was not as open to all of them "timewise" as I would like to have been. Saturday night was my "date" with Howard Nelson on WEEI. I needed to call him at 7:00 and then wait for his call back to me at 7:30. I spread out my papers in readiness for the onslaught of callers. Howard called me back and we were on the air. And who were the first callers? My own daughters! It was such fun to speak to them in this way. They had called in early to be sure there was a line for them.

Another caller said, "Mrs. Bruyn, just what roads have you been taking?"

I told the man that I had started out on route 16 from Newton and then said I didn't remember which ones came next but that if he really wanted to know we'd be glad to send him an itinerary.

He said, "Well, you know, a couple of years ago a man went up into the north woods and said he was going to live off the woods itself, by eating berries and trapping his own game, and a couple of months later he returned and the people gave him a big parade. You know, they found out later that all that time he had stayed in a motel."

I said, "You don't believe that I'm really walking!!"

He said, "Well, how do I know you're really doing it."

I couldn't believe *him!*

Howard Nelson jumped to my rescue to say there were ways of telling, such as the fact that reporters had met me along the way...

It still was a marvelous example of disbelief. In the face of huge amounts of evidence, we still refused to believe something if we didn't want to. It is no wonder that some people have refused to believe the My Lais. They don't want to. I read a marvelous capsule statement describing the way some people think in terms of the reported atrocities: "Our boys wouldn't do such things, and besides they deserved it."

I had the chance also to speak to Fred King and Peg Michaud. Peg told me of the plans for women in Boston to walk "with me" on April 2. So many people were doing so much to expand the action. God bless them all for catching the spark and carrying it further.

Aware again of the guests at Adelaide's, I met Cathy Mink. She was busy organizing my walk through Baltimore. We checked a map together to agree on what the best route would be to take.

Gill and I talked more about the arrangements in D.C. and then it was time for people to go. Ten o'clock seemed to roll around very early. But I had another ten miles to go the next day. We retired about 11:00.

ALONG THE WAY—Mrs. Louise Bruyn pauses in Baltimore during walk from Newton to Washington, D.C., to protest war in Indochina. (AP)

Boston Globe, Mar 30

The United States command in Saigon…raised its estimates of the damage caused by American airpower during the operation in Laos. It said airstrikes killed an estimated 4,100 enemy troops and destroyed 69 tanks and 14,000 tons of ammunition….

The South Vietnamese say that nearly 14,000 enemy troops were killed and that 176,246 tons of munitions were destroyed. [figures include results of ground action]

—*New York Times, Sunday, March 28, 1971*

Joppatowne to Overlea, Maryland

Day

40

Sun, Mar 28

Since Gill and Woody had to return to Washington anyway, they drove me to Joppatowne. We said goodbye to Adelaide Noyes. It was a beautiful morning. Outside of her house we heard the birds singing with fervor. The sun was bright and clear. For the first time I felt that Spring was a reality, the warm Spring that brings with it flowers and leaves and birds. Easter was now only two weeks away.

Gill and Woody left me at Joppatowne and I continued walking. After about an hour's walk, I saw the familiar car, the familiar face and smile. It was the chemist again. He was on his way to get the Sunday paper and just happened to be going by. I really felt part of the "neighborhood." We exchanged a few friendly words and he drove on.

My path now left the main highway and I cut through a section of small homes in a country setting. The area was so beautiful. Everything was coming up green. Yards were large enough to pasture horses, but small enough to make neighbors feel close to each other. The air had a soft, sweet smell. I walked for another hour and felt ready for a rest. I found a telephone pole against which to lean, took off my pack, sat down and stretched out my legs. I began to peel an orange.

A car pulled into a small road leading up to a house. The driver waved in a friendly manner, went on, then stopped and backed up. She asked me, "You wouldn't be that lady who is walking to Washington, would you?"

I said, "Yes, I am."

She said she was very happy to meet me, and would I like to come to her house for a cup of coffee. "It's instant," she warned.

"That would be just fine," I said, "most welcome." I put the pack into her car and she drove me up to their door.

I met the rest of their family; they were all dressed up, ready to go out somewhere special. One of the children wanted my autograph. One of the parents said, "Too bad there's no film in the camera." They were awfully sweet, but I couldn't help but feel like a bear who had lumbered past their house, whose presence had to be recorded or no one would believe them. But wasn't that the American way! I've done it myself. The autograph, the picture, the souvenir. Proof of the experience. Maybe it wasn't just American. Maybe it was the human way. They drove me back out to that telephone pole, though it was so close I wouldn't have minded walking. It had been a refreshing rest stop.

In the next hour or so I learned to read the modern road signs. The Native Americans were able to tell what animals were ahead by their footprints or by fur caught on branches or by broken twigs. I learned that if there were sandwich wrappers and milkshake cups marked "Gino's" on the left side of the road, a hamburger stand would be coming up in a mile or two. It would take about that long for someone to finish their lunch before throwing the remains out the car window on their way away from the place. Sure enough, I was soon at a Gino's.

A number of people spoke to me that day, some stopping their cars, some speaking from their front yards. They knew who I was.

The day's walk seemed very long. My feet were tired. It seemed ages before I got to Overlea. I called Peggy Neustadt, my hostess, and within minutes she was there with the rescue car to whisk me to her house, a hot shower, and a rest.

All along, every night I called home. Many plans were made, ideas exchanged. The calls were very important to us all. I was about to make the usual collect call home, when Peg said that she really wanted to pay for it. She wanted to help in some way. This, then, was my chance. For a long time I had thought of the fun I'd have if I could do this. I asked her daughter, Kathy, if she would play telephone operator. With a bit of practice beforehand, and much clearing of the throat in preparation, she dialed the number and then said, in her best Southern drawl, "This is Houston, Texas. I have a collect call for anyone from Louise Bruyn." (My mother lived in Houston.)

My husband responded, "Where?"

Kathy said, "Houston, Texas."

"From whom?"

"From Louise Bruyn." We were all quiet for a second, then we broke into laughter. The rest of the conversation was more sane.

In the evening Peg had invited over some guests for conversation and about 10:00 I retired.

Thirty-three American soldiers were killed and 76 wounded early yesterday when enemy forces attacked and partly overran a United States Army artillery base in northern South Vietnam....The toll of American dead and wounded was the highest in more than eight months...

—*New York Times, Monday, March 29, 1971*

Overlea to Baltimore, Maryland

Peggy and her daughter Kathy took me to the beginning point in Overlea. A number of other walkers met us there, some with children.

Somewhere along the way that morning, a reporter from the Washington Star met us. He asked many questions. At one point he said, "Many people have said, 'I'd be glad to push if you'd just show me the wheel I could put my shoulder to.' You seem to have found that wheel. How does it feel to be putting your shoulder to it?" What a marvelous image. It put together the experience of physical exertion with the concept of goal to be attained. Would that our goal could be achieved that easily, that simply. We would be more in keeping with the times if we said we yearned to push a button that would stop the war. But we knew that neither a button nor a wheel was going to do it.

Somehow, knowing that this reporter was from Washington did strange things to me. I had a belief that I wasn't aware of at the time, that if someone were from Washington, they must really be smart, they must really know everything. Knowing he was from Washington I felt he would of course understand why I was walking, what my whole mission was about. I held Washington on a pedestal, and therefore he was on a pedestal. The upshot of this was that I failed to inform him clearly, as I had done so many times before, what I felt the role of the news media should be, how important it was that a reporter not focus on my blisters or my pack or my person, but to use the opportunity to write about

217

the incomprehensible brutality we were wreaking upon Indo-China in the form of bombs, napalm, and herbicides. I failed to tell him about the birth deformities, the five million people who were refugees in South Vietnam, which was almost one third of the population. So, not bolstered by my information, he wrote the article stressing the "heroic" aspects of my walk, the kind of personality oriented, human interest article that said very little about what the war was doing to the people of Indo-China. It was only in reading the article and thinking about it later that I realized where my failing was.

Another person who walked with me that day greatly challenged my thinking. He had worked closely with the Berrigan brothers, two Catholic priests who were very active in their protests against the war. He felt that my action was weak because I was doing it alone. He saw no Christian community involved. He said to me, "Where two or three are gathered together, in my name, there am I also."

I considered this deeply. I decided that to accept that exclusively would be to deny the existence of God in each individual. As single individuals we can walk in the presence of God and communicate with that loving spirit, and when we come in contact with another human we can share that love. At that point the Christ within us can reach out. This person wanted me to know that he wasn't against what I was doing. He was there, walking with me, in support of the action. It is true that in taking individual actions there is the awful pitfall of the ego. And I realized when deciding on this witness that I would be in for that accusation and that real temptation. But to me, to take action was more important than the fear of how it might be perceived or that I might fall into that ego trap. And even though it began as an individual act, it was supported enormously by the deeply spiritual community of the Quakers.

On that day my feet hurt a great deal. But I wasn't far now. Two more days of walking and then a rest day, and then I would be there. Actually, I was walking farther each day, twelve to fourteen miles in each of the next three days in order to allow for the rest day on Thursday. That meant condensing four days of walking into three.

Those who walked with me handed out leaflets as we went. They were lovely people. This was the day for which Cathy Mink had organized.

We walked right through the center of Baltimore. There, at a department store was the vigil, waiting for my arrival. Once there, I helped pass out leaflets. The leaflets called for an end to the war, for people to take action to stop it. An old man walked up to us, in an old frayed dark coat, stocking cap on his head, thick glasses, and said, "Is this about God?"

And I said, "Yes, it is about God."

He took one and held it close to his face, scanning each line. He said, "I don't see the word God in here."

I explained as best I could that this was part of God's message to us. The word God wasn't in it, but the spirit of God was, that the war went against all that we have been taught through Jesus.

He slowly folded the paper and put it in his pocket and said, "We have to listen to God's Word. If we don't listen to God, we're lost." And he walked away.

That evening Matt Storin of the *Boston Globe*, Washington Bureau, took me to and from WMAR TV, all the while asking me searching questions.

At the TV station, where I had been told I would be on for two minutes, I had thought two minutes would be long. I was used to interviewers asking lots of questions, and photographers taking lots of footage, and I had forgotten that out of all that, they only clipped a minute or so to show on the program. This was live. It was so difficult to think fast enough and speak fast enough to get in what I wanted to say. Before I knew it she was thanking me for coming, and that was it. I was really frustrated at myself.

The rest of the evening I spent reading the paper and making a phone call to my brother Edgar in Chicago. It was great to talk to him and his wife Nancy. Ed used to live in Washington when he was a violinist in the Air Force Orchestra. (He was now in the Chicago Symphony Orchestra.) I couldn't believe how close I was getting to the city. Ed knew the area well. We reminisced briefly about the first time I had gone to Washington in 1947 to visit him. I was 17 and he was 19. I remember how he took me on a tour of all the monuments, and how he built up into high drama our approach to the Capitol. Climbing the steps he told me how this was the symbol of the United States of America, the seat of government of our great nation, atop which flew the flag—the red, white and blue... Both of us were moved. He was enjoying his role as guide, educator, revealer of great wonders, and I was thoroughly soaking up the majesty of that symbol, the great power it expressed. I was awed.

Now again I was going to the Capitol. But in such a different time and for such a different purpose.

First Lieutenant William L. Calley Jr., was found guilty today of the premeditated murder of at least 22 South Vietnamese civilians at Mylai three years ago....He faces a mandatory sentence of death or life imprisonment...

...An appeal is automatic within the military court system...

—*New York Times, Tuesday, March 30, 1971*

Baltimore to Laurel, Maryland

Day

42

Tues, Mar 30

I was driven to my beginning point, the intersection of 695 and Alt. 1, ready for another long walk. As usual, my hands were slightly sweaty and my pace initially sluggish until my legs and feet again got used to the steady pull of one foot in front of the other. After the first few "blocks" the circulation improved and the pace became freer, more elastic.

I was walking past an apartment complex and asked a woman how far ahead the next restaurant was. It was about 11:30 in the morning and it looked like there might be long expanses of road ahead without a place to get a meal. Remembering the time I went through Cooches Bridge, I didn't want to be caught without a lunch place. The woman recognized me and warmly suggested a place not too far down the road, the Log Cabin. She said, "Hop in, I'll drive you there."

I said I couldn't accept her ride; I'd have to walk. It was early enough; I still wasn't that hungry and it would be about the right timing for me to walk there.

She insisted. She said it was really no trouble at all to take me there. Why didn't I just hop in and she'd whisk me down.

I said, "But if you did that, then you'd have to drive me back to this point so I could walk from here."

That baffled her. "No, you wouldn't have to come back here. Just go on from there."

"But that would break my discipline," I said.

221

Pres. Nixon has begun to review the post mortem studies of the South Vietnamese invasion of Laos, which cover some serious military misjudgments as well as claims of strategic benefit....Mr. Nixon is being told that no one expected the North Vietnamese to be able to reinforce their units in Laos as quickly as they did or to supply them with 150 tanks and other heavy equipment in time to stage a massive counter-attack....Flights by [U.S. air cover] helicopters and tactical support aircraft were hampered not only by poor weather but also by poor coordination with South Vietnamese guides and controllers on the ground.

—*New York Times, Tuesday, March 30, 1971*

It was with great effort that I finally convinced her that I could not, would not, accept a ride, and so, humoring me, she drove ahead to the place, waiting for me along the road, so that I would finally find it. She then went in with me and bought my lunch. She was lovely. It turned out that she even knew the people I was staying with that night. Since I was planning to speak at a meeting in Columbia that evening, she thought she might be there.

While sitting in the Log Cabin, we struck up a conversation with a man sitting on my left. He said there would never be peace, that the Bible told us so. He told about his experiences in Vietnam, about what he knew the Viet Cong had done to innocent villagers. His thinking was based more on the "eye for an eye and tooth for a tooth" principle. My own position was that I could not condone atrocities on either side, but that our daily bombing amounted to technological atrocities. I said I felt we had to grow beyond this point of retaliation and dependence on violence to solve our problems. And certainly to wreak the havoc we have on Vietnam has been no solution to *their* problems. I didn't reach him. I felt that his mind, and the minds of many, many Americans were still operating under very primitive principles. All of us, being human, needed to look closely at our responses to difficult situations, and our reliance on violence as an accepted solution to them. Being human, we had the capacity for hate and revenge and destruction. But also, being human, we each contained a segment of the divine, of potential for change and growth. If we spoke to this divine center, we would call it forth, develop its power. If we spoke to it in others, it would have more chance of being called forth.

A young man in an army jacket came in for lunch. Somehow he found out who I was. He wound up saying if he didn't have to go to work, he'd love to walk with me. He left to go to work. Just before we left, he was back. He said, "I got off work. I'll walk with you." He stayed with me the rest of the day. He was in the Reserves, and somewhat uncomfortable about being identified because of his Reserve status, yet he wanted to go along with me. He felt he might get into trouble, yet he was willing to take the risk. For the rest of that day's walk he carried my pack.

Further down the road, a man who looked down and out, walking in the opposite direction, wished me good luck. We stopped to talk for a few minutes. He said his son was just reported wounded in action. He and his wife had just gotten the message two days before. He talked about all they had done to keep the young man out of the army, how awful the waiting was to know he was wounded but to not know where, how bad it was... He was truly anguished. He said, "Someone ought to tell Nixon about that. Someone ought to go in and *shoot* Nixon!" He went on, "You know who they should send over to Vietnam. They should send those men in the penitentiary," and he waved in the direction of one that was close by. "*They* ought to go fight." He continued, "I'm on welfare, but I don't want to be. They're forcing me to be on welfare. I'm not like those niggers who get welfare on one hand and drive around in Cadillacs on the other."

At this point I broke in. I said, "I have to take issue with your calling anyone a 'nigger'. Anytime you call anyone a name like that it diminishes their humanity and yours. This was the same technique that was used in Germany before World War II. The Jews were referred to as vermin, lice, and it became much easier to exterminate them. I can't approve of using the term 'nigger' for Black nor 'pig' for policeman nor any other term that dehumanizes a person."

"Yes," he said, shaking his head thoughtfully, "I suppose you are right there."

How much I left *un*said: shooting Nixon? Convicts fighting instead? Blacks not needing welfare as much as whites? Where could I have grabbed hold? All I could reach for at that time was 'nigger.' He was filled with *so* much hostility, *so* much anguish. I told him I'd pass on to the President his message, and I meant it. I would pass on to the President his despair, his desperation. The young man walking with me and I turned and walked on.

At the end of our walk, I contacted Virginia Bates, my hostess for the evening. My walking friend got a ride back from another friend. Virginia had been very active in the peace movement in Maryland. Such a sensitive soul. She lived about 40 minutes by car from my pick-up place, way out in the country. Virginia was a poet.

That night she drove me to Columbia, Maryland, that new city, built between Baltimore and Washington, D.C. I spoke for a few minutes at a planning meeting for a peace group and then we went back to her house.

Virginia gave me a poem she had written.

PIETA FOR TODAY

Eat your Wheaties, eat the seventy-cent spread and don't forget your vitamins;
I will wash and iron your clothes for almost two decades
And my eyes will shine when you are properly attired, all spic and span;
I will do for you whatever I can
To nurture your mind and spirit—teach you Love and Brotherhood
And Thou Shalt Love the Lord Thy God and Thy Neighbor as Thyself.
I will do what I will
          To teach you not to kill—to Love Thine Enemies
I will unceasingly, tenderly, do what I can
          To make you a Man;
For I love, you, you are my son.

And when they find you a perfect specimen of manly manhood,
Because I saw that you had rest, and food for body and for soul,
They will strip away your lovely individualized colors,
The blues and whites that bring out all the golden in your hair,
And give you the muddy, murky mantles of murder
And leave you with a number, and me with despair.

And when the letter comes, and the trumpet blows
And they hand me a neatly folded flag from off the coffin
With a precise salute and chin up and all that bloody rot,
When they exchange a rag, or flag, for my boy-child, my wonderful son,
          my life,
I shall spit in their eye, and die.

          V. Bates

Gasping for breath, First Lieut. William L Calley made a final plea for understanding today as he faced the military jury that convicted him yesterday... The 5-foot 3-inch platoon leader...said he never "wantonly" killed anyone. Shaken with sobs, he said the Army never told him that his enemies were human....The enemy was never described to him as anything but "Communism," he said.

—*New York Times, Wednesday, March 31, 1971*

Day

Laurel to College Park, Maryland

43

Wed, Mar 31

I had arranged to meet a very close friend of mine, Marge King, at the beginning of that day's walk. We had danced together in the same group at the University of Illinois and one time we had all been together with the Joseys, our friends in Wilmington. I had not seen Marge in several years. I was so happy when she arrived,

It was wonderful having Marge's company during this last day of my walk. We talked about old times, about family relationships, about matters of deep import to us both. The time flew. In a way, I even forgot I was walking. We could have been any two friends out on a hike in beautiful weather. Her presence gave me a chance to share feelings on a very deep level.

We arrived at College Park about 3:00. I called the Conways, and Jean picked me up within about 20 minutes. I left Marge to be picked up by John, her husband, a few minutes later. I would see Marge again on Friday. She was planning to walk the final distance with me.

Jean Conway drove me to her home. She and her husband Bill were instantly knowable. They made me feel at home, offering all kinds of assistance. "Our house is your house."

I couldn't believe that I had arrived. I was actually ready to walk into Washington! I was there! I had been walking for 43 days and I was ready to go into Washington! Nothing had happened to stop me—I had neither been sick, nor had I suffered a sprained ankle nor had I given

The Senate Foreign Relations Committee decided today to push ahead with public hearing on "how to end the war.",...Senator J.W. Fulbright, its chairman, charged that the Nixon Administration was guilty of either "massive deception" or "massive misjudgment" – and perhaps both – in the American-supported South Vietnamese invasion of Laos.

—*New York Times, Wednesday, March 31, 1971*

up. I was amazed. And I even had a rest day ahead of me before finishing. The realization of these things left me in a peculiar state...one of detachment, wonder, unreality. And how sensitive my hosts were to my inner condition. I was grateful for their tender caring.

That evening Gill came to the house. In her hands was the fate of Friday. That is to say, she had planned the speed of the walk, the route, had contacted the congressional offices and the press. She had done a fantastic job of organizing. I asked her if she had checked on the permit I would need to post the theses on the Capitol doors. She said she would check into that the next morning.

Only one more day until Sev would arrive. Tomorrow I was to go to a radio talk show and then Jean would drive me to the Snyders.

How nice to sleep and not worry about getting up in the morning.

House Democrats called today for an end to United States involvement in Indo-china by the start of 1973....The action was almost identical to that taken by Senate Democrats a month ago.

First Lieut. William L. Calley Jr. was sentenced to life imprisonment today for slaying at least 22 South Vietnamese civilians three years ago at the hamlet of Mylai 4....His sentence could be overturned during the automatic appeal process, and the term could be shortened at any time by the exercise of clemency by the President or the Secretary of the Army.

—New York Times, Thursday, April 1, 1971

Day

College Park, Maryland — Rest Day

44

Thurs, Apr 1

In the morning I stayed in bed. But I was busy. I was writing down what I felt I should say on the Capitol steps. What *was* the distillation of my trip? What was uppermost in my brain, my heart, if I were to say something to the country, to the government? I recorded in little tiny writing in my little red notebook what seemed important. Yet in looking at it when I was through, it sounded too emotional, too pretentious. These then were only to be guides for what I wanted to say. I would leave myself open to the Spirit to speak through me and help to form my words.

Gillian called to say that it was not possible to get a permit to put anything on the Capitol door. I couldn't believe it. I wound up calling the Chief of the Capitol police myself and was told by him that under no conditions could I affix anything to the building, whatsoever. I asked what the penalty was for doing it anyway. It was either arrest, or a fine. I don't remember.

There was my dilemma. I had said I would attach the Five Theses to the doors of Congress. I had also said I was not interested in committing civil disobedience at this time, so I would not nail it, I would only scotch tape it. And now even holding it against the door was civil disobedience. Incredible. I knew the Capitol police would not be in a gentle humor. Should I risk their arresting me? What would that do to my chances of seeing the President? Was I being cowed by unjust authority? Would my action have more weight by actually affixing the

227

The campaign against Communist supply lines is over, but statistical warfare continues to rage, reminiscent of the days when American commanders put the stress on "the body count" to demonstrate success in the Vietnam war....The figures at issue these days are those provided by the South Vietnamese Government on the invasion of Laos...It is an old controversy, now attracting new interest because the Saigon Government and, to a lesser degree, the American command are still providing a heavy dose of numbers to try to cure the public discomfort over the Laos campaign in Laos. The list is long, from enemy killed and munitions destroyed to field radios, trucks, anti-malaria pills and chickens and ducks captured.

—*New York Times, Thursday, April 1, 1971*

papers to the doors or would it have less weight because of a skirmish.

My final decision was to consider Senator Edward Kennedy and Representative Robert Drinan the symbolic doors of Congress. (Representative Drinan was a Catholic priest who had been Dean of the Boston College Law School before being elected. He was affectionately addressed as "Our Father Who Art in Congress.") After all, it was Congress's attention I was trying to gain. Had they not been there, my problem would have been a different one. With them present, the important thing was to put the Five Theses and the People's Peace Treaty into their hands. It took me all day to make the decision. Part of me still wished I had attached them to the doors, but another part of me realized that I probably did the saner of the two possible actions.

Jean drove me to the radio station for an interview that lasted about half an hour, and I felt great support from the staff at the station. I had had the opportunity to go to a TV station that day and other interviews could have been set up, but I had wanted to keep that day clear because of the import of the next day. In doing so, I was more concerned for my person than for my purpose, and to that extent, weakened whatever public message could have been built during that time. When did one say "Enough"? Could one? Could one spend more than one is able to give? I was afraid of that possibility and therefore held back. In retrospect, I wished I had not.

Jean took me to the home of Ed and Bonnie Snyder, where I stayed for that night. Ed Snyder was the Executive Secretary of the Friends Committee on National Legislation (FCNL). Their family was open and lovely and in the evening I studied my materials a bit and then finally

Sev arrived. My dear beautiful husband. Tomorrow was the big day. Gill came over that night to make some last minute plans and both agreed that I was probably doing the right thing to give the documents to the Congressmen rather than try to post them.

How fine to nestle down into bed beside my husband. I felt reasonably secure, enough that I was able to fall right to sleep, knowing he was beside me.

The House voted overwhelmingly tonight to continue the military draft until the middle of 1973 and sharply increase pay and allowances for servicemen.

President Nixon yesterday ordered First Lieut. William L. Calley Jr. released from the stockade at Ft. Benning, Ga., and returned to his quarters on the base while his murder conviction is being reviewed.

—New York Times, Friday, April 2, 1971

Day

College Park, Maryland to the Capitol

45

Fri, Apr 2

I awoke after a good night's sleep refreshed and somewhat calm. But there was still confusion over what would be the order of events. I was to arrive at the steps at 12:10, climb to the top, have a silent witness of 10-15 minutes, then say a few words and hand the Five Theses to Senator Kennedy and the People's Peace Treaty to Congressman Drinan, and then I would be finished. But Gill and Sev and I were still trying to figure out if the silence should come before or after the "few words." How long should the silence be? Should we break it by shaking hands?

The Snyder children ate breakfast first. It was a school morning. Sev and I sat down at the table with Ed and Bonnie when the children were through. I tried to eat the scrambled eggs that Bonnie had fixed, but my stomach tightened up on me. I had the feeling of jumping off a high dive. I said, holding my stomach, "I have butterflies." Ed responded immediately. He said, "Gather round kids, and hold hands. Let's have our silent time." They immediately jumped up from what they were doing in their preparations for school and held hands around the table. The supportive calm I received was so beautiful, so deep. It brought me back to the essence of what I was doing; there was no need for nervousness. If I kept faith, kept close to the source of life, kept the core of my mission uppermost in my heart, I could walk on in calm and assurance.

About 8 a.m. Bonnie drove Sev and me to the corner where we would begin. Out front Marge King was waiting. Beautiful Marge! What a

230

shame that on that last day I had no record of those who walked with me. I knew many of them but not all. Whoever we were, there were about eight of us starting out together. Some news people arrived early. I was without my pack; I just had my poncho handy. It was threatening rain. All these people to walk with me and it had to rain!

Before we started I asked Marge to be the pace watcher. Gill had planned when we would be at each major intersection, based on 2 miles per hour, and had put it on a mimeographed sheet. But I didn't want to have to think about it. So I put it in Marge's hands, who accepted it kindly. We joined hands in a circle, had a minute or two of silence and then we began to walk, keeping silence.

People joined up with us, one or two here, another few there, waiting along the route, recognizable by their black armbands and welcoming faces. Then, about 9:00, figures began appearing in clusters—It was Susan, and Becky and Pat and Valerie and all their friends and all my friends. Unbeknownst to me, they had chartered a special bus down from Newton, had driven all night long and here they were now, tired, but with happy faces! I threw my arms around them all. Yet, I had pledged myself to silence and did not want to break that.

I fought with that pledge of silence. I kept trying to figure whether it was better to keep the discipline or to let the Spirit flow freely. At one point I wanted to gather everybody into a circle and thank them for coming and to tell them how I loved them all for making the trip with me and what the timing of the walk was. I wished I had had courage to break my own discipline at that time. Instead, I made a feeble attempt to hold hands in a long thin "circle" along the sidewalk, but nobody knew what I was doing and it didn't work. How could they read my mind!

We were by now some 40–50 people. Several police had been put on our "march." They rode up to intersections on their little motor scooters and waited for us to pass, then buzzed on to the next intersection. One policeman began to harass us. His final salvo was, "Is this all you could muster? You're not doing too good." He buzzed past. I had decided if he would make one more comment I would break silence, because it seemed to me that he didn't know how to take our silence. He was threatened by it. He needed to know that we were not against him, that our silence was for a deeper reason. This was another time when I felt the rigidity in what I had asked of people. Words were needed to communicate ideas. Silence might bring each of us closer to our commitment, to our cause, closer to our center of being, for me, closer to that source of strength I needed to keep me an open channel when I arrived at my destination. Yet, in ways the silence closed off that channel in terms of each other.

Within the external quiet I was aware of the beautiful people who had come with me, of my husband at my side, my lovely daughters, their faithful friends, of Pat and Valerie and Marge. I was aware of the weather—moist-humid, warm-cool, gray sky, the switching between light showers to brave sun cutting through the clouds. Washington was in bloom.

We rested often, as Marge would stop us because we were ahead of schedule. Never had I walked so slowly in all the 44 previous days. It was much more tiring than a faster pace.

There was a beautiful moment when we rounded a bend and there, shining in all its alabaster splendor was the Capitol. This was what I had been walking toward for a month and a half, and now it was almost within reach. I felt sure and exultant within. Yes, Washington was within walking distance of Boston! Yes, I had done what I had set out to do! Almost.

We arrived about 15 minutes early at the little park below the steps of the Capitol. We were ahead of schedule. We sat on the stairs near the empty pool, waiting, silent, praying, loving one another with our eyes, and our arms. We were one band—asking our government to stop the brutality, the bombing, the inhumanity—my

Photo by Valerie Kreutzer

God how we yearned for it. And then, a bit ahead of schedule we stood to travel the final block or two. Sev put in my hands the stacks of signed Five Theses, signatures that I had collected on the walk and that had been mailed to us from across the country, and the People's Peace Treaty, and clutching them tightly I turned and we all walked the last few hundred yards.

The scene that opened up before us was becoming more and more unreal. I saw a crowd of people up on the top landing of one set of stairs of the Capitol. They stopped to look in our direction and then they hurried on. I wondered if they were there for us or the Cherry Blossom Festival. It became clear; they were not there for us. Band music became audible and grew louder. A high school band was playing on the far steps of the Capitol.

A man sauntered up to me, waiting for us to approach and said, "Mrs. Bruyn, I'm from *Time Magazine.*"

I don't remember if he asked me a question. I just remember saying, "I'm not speaking yet" and feeling stupid.

And the closer we got the more newsmen became evident, TV cameras, reporters with mikes, and photographers with still cameras. They were all around and in front of me. I stood at the foot of the steps looking up to the top of the stairs. It looked so far up. I turned, and looked at Becky and Susan. Becky was crying. I threw my arms around her and hugged her. Half way up the stairs coming down toward

Photo by Rich Sobol

me was Congressman Drinan. I started up the stairs and the amoebic presence of the newsmen kept in front of me. I heard them say things like, "Back up now, give her room, let her go." It all felt so eerie. It was reminiscent of being rolled down a corridor in a hospital and hearing the doctors speaking about the patient but not to her. It was being a "third person." All this time the band music in the background and the Cherry Blossom tourists swirled about.

Then on my right up strode Senator Kennedy, supportive, quiet, gentle, compassionate. By this time, I had arrived beside Congressman Drinan. Flanked by both and surrounded by the press and cut off from my friends, I walked up to the top of the stairs where we turned to face the others. Try as I could, I couldn't see the people I wanted to talk to, my husband, my girls. All I could see was the technological presence before me of the press. Somehow their color was black; it must have

Concludes 450-mile peace march *Schenectady Gazette*, April 2, 1971

Mrs. Louise Bruyn, a dance teacher and housewife from Newton, Mass., concluded her 450-mile peace march from Boston to Washington, April 2. She was greeted on the Capitol steps by Rep. Father Robert F. Drinan, D-Mass. (left) and Sen. Edward M. Kennedy, D-Mass. Mrs. Bruyn is in Washington to protest the war in Indochina. (NC PHOTO by Michael Fager)

been the cameras, the cords, the mikes held up before me.

Gillian was there, and I said something about having a period of quiet and many of those who heard my request, gathered into silence. My God, how I asked for strength to speak at that moment what my 45 days had given me—to be a channel for the culmination of my "leading." To speak honestly and simply of what I felt and knew others felt about the war and our country and our being humans together. The silence was all too short, all too incomplete—not the 10–15 minutes we had originally envisioned—partly due to the gay marching military music, partly due to tourists suddenly recognizing Kennedy and shouting "There's Teddy Kennedy." (I don't actually remember that, but others later told me that was so; I was involved in my inner call for strength.)

Meanwhile, other Senators and Representatives had gathered on that top landing, including Sen. Jacob Javits, Rep. Margaret Heckler, and Rep. Jonathan Bingham.

After the silence I tried to speak to those who wanted to hear. I first asked where the public address system was, that Gillian had told me would be there. It turned out to be a small battery operated megaphone, clumsy to hold. But with the help of Sen. Kennedy, I caught on to how to use it and began.

I spoke of the response of so many people I had met who wanted the war to end. I spoke of the great number who had said "You are walking for me," that I hadn't walked alone. I spoke of people's despair and of my hope for the future if people would recognize the power they have. They just needed to use it. And I read the Five Theses aloud.

All the time I spoke my legs shook. Dear Gill was kneeling, holding on to my right leg trying to keep it from shaking. I handed the Five Theses to Kennedy and the People's Peace Treaty to Drinan.

I do not remember the following remarks, but Sen. Kennedy reportedly said, "No statement by any member of Congress can carry the sense of commitment that Mrs. Bruyn has conveyed."

The press reported that Fr. Drinan urged others to follow my example and said, "Evil grows because good men are silent."

Rep. Robert F Drinan, and Senator Edward Kennedy speaking to Louise Bruyn

And then it was over. I had done what I had set out to do. Sen. Kennedy asked, "Shall we go back now?"

And I responded, "I need somebody to tell me now what I should do."

And he said, "You come with us," and took me by the arm, followed by Rep. Drinan, my husband and two daughters, into the Capitol for lunch.

The walk wasn't completely over. At lunch with Rep. Drinan and Sen. Kennedy, our daughters asked searching questions of them both. Sen.

Kennedy then introduced our family to a number of other senators in the lunchroom and later we met with other legislators in their offices. Finally the girls had to return with our friends to the bus which traveled back to Newton that day.

Sev and I walked on from the Capitol building to the White House. President Nixon was out of town, but we were invited in to meet with Clark MacGregor, Nixon's Counsel for Congressional Relations, who listened thoughtfully to our concerns about Vietnam and International Law.

Sev needed to leave on Sunday to teach his Monday classes, but I stayed on, hoping to speak to Nixon when he returned from San Clementi, California. On Monday I went again to the White House, this time to be met by Robert Finch, another aide of Nixon's.

Since Nixon was expected to give a major speech on Wednesday, I decided that, rather than spend the day in meditation at William Penn House, I would meditate outside of the White House. By this time I figured I'd done so many crazy things, I might as well do this, too. When I arrived at the guardhouse where twice before we had been ushered in to the White House, I said, "I would just like you to know that I'm standing out here, in case the President wants to see me."

"And who are you?"

"I'm Louise Bruyn. Some Congresswomen have sent in a telegram saying the President really should see me. So if he wants to do that, would you please tell him that I'm out here?" At that, followed by their quizzical looks, I walked over to a fence and stood there for the rest of the afternoon.

Gill picked me up at 6:00 and took me to the airport to make an 8:00 plane. That evening I was back home.

———————

The end of an adventure in faith. A fantastic, beautiful, shaking, deepening experience—a merging with humanity, a bearing of a message for millions, a drop in the bucket. It was all these things. It was big and it was small. It was a public outcry against the inhumanity of war, it was my prayer.

Looking Back

I am writing this now from the third floor of the same house from which I began my walk 42 years ago. In rereading the journal that I wrote the summer after I had returned, I am left with a feeling of deep gratitude to so many, many people. Over and over people said I was walking for them. My hosts extended such tender support, physically, emotionally and spiritually. I had the sense I was being passed from hand to loving hand. The efforts of my husband and Jessie Jones made the transitions from one day to the next seamless. I was always uplifted after calling home. Even our daughters took on responsibilities, such as answering phones, speaking to the media, answering letters. It was truly Our walk.

I had said in the beginning of this memoir, that the words "dramatic action," which I had read in the Ben Avram book, were italicized. Several years later, I looked for those words again in that book. They were not italicized. My inner state had made them so.

After the walk, I thought about my action a lot. A recurring question was—Why did I do this? What motivated me beyond my awareness of my own sense of being anesthetized? I remembered my childhood. My family had strong German roots, since my father had emigrated from Germany in 1921. Even my stepfather, present in my teen years, was German. I was 11 when Pearl Harbor happened, in World War II. We lived in Chicago and at about age 15, around the dinner table my family was discussing what we had been hearing about the systematic rounding up and killing of Jews in death camps in Germany. My stepfather, Dr. Max, said that was propaganda. He recounted his mother seeing an American poster of a German soldier in World War I, hoisting a child on a bayonet, with some language about the "Huns." He recounted that his mother had said, *"Ein Deutscher tut das nicht!"* (A German doesn't do that!) I was much relieved.

Later that year I was in a dime store and found a paperback book with photographs of the Nazi ovens and the skeletons piled high.

During World War II, I was caught up in the patriotism of the times and the belief that our country was on the side of right and good. We all sacrificed so that democracy would win. "Use it up, wear it out, make it do or do without" was our patriotic duty. I believed as a child in the glory of our flag, in our heroic history. And in my later years I wondered how the Germans could have allowed the Nazi government to take over their country and allow the extermination of the Jews, the gays, the gypsies, and others. How could they have allowed it? Many Germans said they "didn't know." Or they did know and believed they couldn't have done anything about it. In our country, these were called the "Good Germans."

On learning of our atrocities in Vietnam, which went far beyond cutting off the ears of dead Viet Cong, I was stunned. I thought, "Our American soldiers wouldn't do such things." And then I came to realize that any country could have soldiers who abrogate human rights, could torture, could act out the brutality that is war. Soldiers "follow orders." War itself creates these conditions. To allow that to happen without protesting or trying to stop the government from continuing the war, we were the "Good Germans." And I didn't want to be a "Good German."

Following the loyal coverage of the walk by the *Boston Globe* and the *Herald*, plus TV coverage, I became a well-known personage when I returned. I was amazed by the number of people who knew about the walk and recognized me. That familiarity followed an arc that I was initially honored by and later found increasingly humorous. It began with "You must be Louise Bruyn, the woman who walked to Washington for peace in Vietnam." Later, it became "You look familiar. Didn't you walk somewhere once for something?" and years later to "You look familiar. Didn't you work at the drug store?"

Upon my return I was asked to be present at a meeting of the Cambridge City Council as they debated passing a resolution deploring the continuation of the war. I was sitting in the audience with hundreds of others, when someone from the podium introduced me, and there was a standing ovation from everyone in the auditorium. I was amazed. Then a woman just behind me who was furiously clapping, shouted, "How much weight did you lose?"

Upon returning from the walk, I realized how much I had experienced of the highway in a physical way. Riding again in our car, and seeing the metal guardrails along the road, I didn't just see metal guardrails. I felt the cold of sitting on them, the slanted edge of their support against my seat. Looking at the road, I felt the tilt of the slight embankments on the left side of the road as the angle that made my left leg ache. Lamp posts and highway directional posts were things I had leaned against. The swirl of dust and exhaust from trucks, which we feel from inside our cars, often with closed windows, now had a visceral effect on me as I remembered trying to make headway through it, leaning into its backwash. And then there were the moments of exquisite beauty, like the squeaking of the ice-clad branches, the sparkle of the snow, the songs of birds along country roads in the Spring.

As I reflect back on this imprint of my experience, I think that so much of our living these days is virtual. We are protected from contact with the elements; we experience the world from pictures, radio, television, computers, through windows in a car or plane. The thought leaves me cherishing our natural environment even more.

It is strange to think back over those times. The intensity was palpable. It permeated everything in the country. Just last week, in looking through an old 1971 knitting magazine for a pattern, I saw an ad for a crewel stitch embroidery pattern containing the serenity prayer, with the words "Amazing Embroidery Offer—Beautiful 'Silent Majority' Serenity Prayer Now Yours in Fabulous Crewel Stitchery." Those who didn't speak up during the Vietnam War were considered the "Silent Majority." They were the enigma. Which side were they on?

The demonstration called for April 24th, 1971 was a great success. The Vietnam Veterans Against the War camped on the Washington Mall in a campaign called Operation Dewey Canyon 3, and many of the decorated veterans threw their medals over a fence on the Mall in their show of rage at the continuing war. Susan and I attended. I took the opportunity again while I was in D.C. to ask to see President Nixon. A response from Clark MacGregor, one of his aides, told me he was out of town during that weekend.

During that Spring and Summer, I, who had never spoken in public before, was asked to speak to various groups in the area. For the first time I participated in civil disobedience and paid my due to society by spending six days in jail for refusing to pay a $20 fine. In 1972, Margery Swann and I helped raise money for children in Buddhist orphanages in South Vietnam. Later, I lobbied and leafleted and fasted, and sat in some "tiger cages" on the steps of Congress with others. My last major attempt to stop the war was in January 1975. Ten of us from regions across the country demonstrated in Saigon in front of the American Embassy to call for stopping the funding of the Thieu government. Each of these actions had interesting details that are too numerous to include here.

My friend, Pat Simon, had reached out to other Gold Star Mothers in Massachusetts. Later, on a church grant, she, with other parents, organized Gold Star Parents in many states; they worked for amnesty for draft resistors, deserters, and vets with less-than-honorable discharges as a living memorial to all the young dead soldiers. In 1980 she was nominated as a Vice Presidential candidate on the floor of the National Democratic Convention in order for her to make a statement to the assembled body against the reinstatement of the draft.

People worked night and day to stop the war. People demonstrated, stood in vigils, resisted paying taxes, resisted the draft by burning their draft cards or escaping to Canada, committed civil disobedience, poured blood on draft files, sat in mock "tiger cages" on the steps of the Capitol, lobbied Congress.

From 1971, it took four years more of protest before it ended, with an overall total of more than 58,000 U.S. soldiers killed and 75,000 severely disabled (total of 303,616 U.S. wounded), either in combat or non-hostile action.[1] The numbers of Vietnamese dead between 1961

1 Shannon, Paul, *The ABC's of the Vietnam War*, Indochina Newsletter, copyright 2000, Special Teacher's Issue, c/o 2161 Massachusetts Ave., Cambridge, MA 02140, p. 21.

and 1975 soared to more than 3,000,000, which included all factions in the struggle. Civilians accounted for two-thirds of the above figure.[2]

In his book, *Kill Anything That Moves: The Real American War in Vietnam*, Nick Turse writes of his findings that explain the incredible proportion of civilian over military deaths. Using our own government's records and interviews with the soldiers, he found the slaughter of unarmed civilians in Vietnam was actually not the result of rogue soldiers or "bad apples," but was the result of our government policies.

The deaths of Cambodians and Laotians raised the figure by 300,000 to a total of about 3,300,000 deaths suffered by the Indochinese.[3] Guenter Lewy, author of *America in Vietnam*, calculated Vietnamese civilian wounded to be 5.3 million.[4]

Finally, on April 30, 1975, the war ended. Though my walk clearly did not end the war, it was part of the movement across the U.S. and the world that strongly impacted both Nixon and Congress. U.S. combat troops were withdrawn once and for all in 1973. In the Summer of 1974, President Nixon resigned, passing the presidency to Vice-President Gerald Ford. In the Spring of 1975, when it became clear that only the reintroduction of massive U.S. bombing might possibly save the Saigon government, President Ford requested a big jump in military aid to the Saigon regime. But Congress felt the pressure and voted it down. The Saigon government totally collapsed.

When one takes a step, it often leads to many more. By answering the call that I felt deep within me to refuse to stay anesthetized, I grew in my understanding of the causes of war and of many of our other problems; I grew in my confidence to speak out and in my faith that change can happen. I became much more open to possibilities for action. Trying to change things educates one. One becomes aware of the obstacles to change, both in the system in which we live and in our mindset. Some of that I met on that journey, some I grappled with later.

---

2 Turse, Nick, *Kill Anything That Moves, The Real American War in Vietnam*, New York, New York; Metropolitan Books, Henry Holt and Company, 2013, p. 13.

3 Shannon, Paul, *The ABC's of the Vietnam War*, Indochina Newsletter, copyright 2000, Special Teacher's Issue, c/o 2161 Massachusetts Ave., Cambridge, MA 02140, p. 21

4 Turse, Nick, *Kill Anything That Moves, The Real American War in Vietnam*, New York, New York; Metropolitan Books, Henry Holt and Company, 2013, p. 13.

The need to change our way of thinking today is great. Our reliance on oil, so responsible for our comfort, has been largely responsible for war after war, as well as for global warming. Both have resulted in a plethora of devastating conditions, human and environmental....And hanging above it all, the threat of nuclear weapons, the use of which, war or no war, intentional or accidental, can bring an end to most life on this planet.

We need to learn what these dangers to people and planet are and join together with others to change our direction. There are so many ways people can become involved to bring this about. Paul Hawken, in his book *Blessed Unrest*, tells us that globally there are at least one million non-profit organizations working on our local to global problems; he fills 200 pages with types of groups and their interests and says their number is growing.[5] There is hope.

Inaction, I believe, comes from denial, from not wanting to feel the depths of despair that can arise when faced with the realities of life today. I have experienced that despair. But the words of people working over the last century in the peace and labor and justice and environmental movements speak to my condition. They have said, "Don't mourn! Organize!"

People have more power than they think. It is through working with others, merging their energy, that hope is generated. Some feel that all is in God's hands, that all will work for good. Some feel that the End of the World is coming anyway, so just have enough faith that one's self can be saved in the Afterlife, but no need to do anything now except pray. My belief is that the divine spark that is in each of us is the way God, the Universal Love, the Divine Creator, works in this world. If people don't do the work, how will it come about? It is with faith in this power to bring about a just and peaceful and sustainable world that I urge us all to take heart, pick up the task with affirming, loving energy, and move forward.

---

5 Hawken, Paul, *Blessed Unrest; How the Largest Movement in the World Came into Being and Why No One Saw It Coming*, New York, New York, Penguin Group, 2007, p. 191.

She Walked for All of Us
Olivia Ames Hoblitzelle

It all started over the morning paper. That morning, in the winter of 1971, several of us read the same article in the *Boston Globe* about a woman named Louise Bruyn, a housewife, mother, and dance teacher who had made the astonishing decision to walk from her house in Newton, MA to Washington D.C. as a peace witness against the endless horrors of the war in Indo-China. The article quoted her as saying,

> I can no longer sit in the comfort of our beautiful home, knowing the death and destruction we are causing in another land.... By taking an INDIVIDUAL action, by walking—so that you're available to people who want to talk to you—I am trying to make my deep feeling visible. You just have to act on that little bit of light.

In her departing press conference, Louise said,

> If what I'm doing could move a few other people to take a strong action, in their own ways, to protest the war, then I would consider the walk a successful demonstration.

Louise's decision to walk ignited the hearts of countless people across the country to initiate actions of their own. Her words as quoted in that *Boston Globe* article propelled a small group of us into action in ways none of us could ever have imagined.

We were an unlikely group to launch what subsequently unfolded. We were eight young mothers who gathered at the Friends Meeting House every Wednesday morning. We would pool our children with a babysitter so we could discuss books and parenting. Louise's action abruptly changed all that.

Our first meeting after the article was memorable. Suddenly we were on fire, inspired by her action. We had to do something, but what? How could we support Louise? How could we spread the word about her courageous action?

First we decided we would walk with Louise for the first few days until she was too far out to reach easily by car. We agreed that if she didn't have someone walking with her at least part of every day, she would never make it, as though she were heading off into the vast reaches of the Arctic tundra instead of into the most populous urban areas of the country!

For three days, we drove out to rendezvous with Louise—our strollers, toddlers and babies in tow—to walk quietly with her through the gently falling snow. It was immensely moving and dignified to walk along beside her. No placards, no leaflets, only black armbands to indicate our grief over the death and destruction of the Vietnam war.

Like others, we were struck by the dramatic power of Louise's decision to make the walk alone. It symbolized the impact that an individual's action could make a difference. All those photographs of Louise walking along with only her backpack and black armband invited people to identify with her very personally. "If she can do something like that because she feels that strongly, then I must do something!"

And so we did. Our second plan took off in unimaginable ways. It was extraordinarily ambitious: we would contact people across the country, reach into every state of the union, tell the story of her courageous walk, and encourage them to initiate peace actions in their own states. In particular, we encouraged them to organize an event for April 2nd to coincide with Louise's proposed date of arrival on the steps of the Capitol.

Could we pull this off? Her walk was to take forty-five days and she'd already been gone a week. We flew into action. We called everyone in our circles of friends and family. In turn, we asked them to reach out to their friends. Here we were, suddenly galvanized into action. Infants sat in Easy Babies, toddlers wandered among papers strewn across the floor, determined mothers bent over lists and telephones. We were now meeting daily. We had dropped everything to support this ambitious campaign on Louise's behalf.

As of March 20th, our small group of friends and supporters had sent Louise's *Five Theses, the People's Peace Treaty,* and form letters to hundreds of individuals and groups across the country. We reached out to a wide assortment of groups: American Friends Service Committee offices, Women Strike for Peace, Women's International League for Peace and Freedom, SANE, Mother's for Peace, theological schools, Unitarian–Universalist churches, even recently returned participants from the Paris Peace Conference.

Looking back at our endeavor, it seems even more amazing since these were the days of phone calls and letter writing; email and all the other forms of instant messaging were still far in the future.

Our intention to create a vast network of contacts completely overrode any hesitance we may have had about calling complete strangers out of the blue.

Many of our calls went out to people who had as yet heard nothing about Louise's walk. Even when we had to start from the beginning and describe the whole story, without exception, the response was overwhelmingly positive. In one press release, the organizers declared,

"The response to our phone calls has been heart-warming and at times overwhelming; people are deeply moved by the thought of this determined woman making her way along in an effort to reach the 'anaesthetized' people of her country." We heard comments such as,

"This is incredible. We've all been waiting for something like this."

"I'm so glad you called us. We'll spread the word and organize an event to coincide with Mrs. Bruyn's arrival in Washington."

"How wonderful! This is the answer to a prayer—some way for us to respond to what has felt like a hopeless situation."

A week later, our small group of determined mothers had accomplished the inconceivable; we'd found contacts, sometimes four or five or more, in all fifty states of the union. That was miracle enough, but furthermore, we'd found someone ready to organize some peace action either in support of Louise's walk or some other form appropriate to their state. Although plans varied from state to state, most of them followed closely the spirit of Louise's action—an effort to reach citizens and government officials by direct, personal means.

Louise's action had by now touched the hearts of many thousands of people. We felt as though we were witnessing a thrilling variety of peace fireworks—sparks flying out in every direction to ignite responses across the country. Four weeks after we'd begun our initiative, we sent an update to Louise letting her know the spreading impact of her walk:

> If only you had an extra set of ears to have heard some of the reactions! It would give you the encouragement to walk another 450 miles! Judging from our feedback, you really are reaching people who have never been touched this way before. And they are *doing* things. Bless you on your way. Only twelve days left of a beautiful, beautiful trip.

(Olivia and Sharon for the Mother's Group)

On April 1st, those of us who were able flew to Washington to walk the last two days with Louise, a thrilling culmination to our efforts to support her. (She tells the story of her arrival in this book.) Meanwhile, on April 2nd, as she arrived on the Capitol steps, thirty-eight states were engaged in some form of peace action while the remaining twelve were in the process of talking and organizing.

When the press clippings began pouring in, we learned of the moving events that had happened in state capitals across the country. By far the most groups planned to march in silence to their state houses to present the Five Theses and the People's Peace Treaty to their legislators, including their Governor when possible, collect signatures, and talk with bystanders as well as state employees.

April 2—Over 600 women demonstrated in Boston

To give a few examples, all the New England states had organized major events, as in Vermont where a newly formed citizen group described their action as "a citizen effort to bring to the attention of our elected officials the necessity of immediate withdrawal and a reordering of priorities on the domestic and foreign policy fronts."

RUTLAND DAILY HERALD, SATURDAY MORNING, APR

Mrs. Longin Ambros of Hartland Friday taped the five anti-war theses carried by Mrs. Louise Bruyn of Newton, Mass., to Washington, D.C., onto the door of the State House in Montpelier. The action was part of a protest against the Vietnam War and in sympathy with Mrs. Bruyn. In the background is the statue of Ethan Allen. (Herald photo — Slayton)

A Benedictine monk from Weston Priory spoke eloquently:

My purpose in being here today is to affirm the supremacy of life over death, of love over evil, of an American conscience over the desire for power. I want to ask of you, Governor, that you affirm these qualities and give us the sort of moral leadership and encouragement that Mrs. Bruyn and others prophetically give.

Looking directly at Governor Davis, he continued, "It is because I believe you to be a human person who is free that I ask this of you."

Although the Governor was a hawk who supported President Nixon's Vietnam policy, it was the first time that he had agreed to meet officially with leaders of the anti-war movement, an event and dialogue widely covered by Vermont media.

In Juneau, Alaska, a representative from Clergy and Laymen Concerned about the War made a formal presentation of the Five Theses and the People's Peace Treaty to the Governor and Legislature on April 2nd, saying,

> Mrs. Bruyn's walk has motivated us to call upon our Governor whom we had previously left alone. Our task will be to inform him and as many other people up here as possible.

In Baltimore, Maryland, there was "A Solemn March to support Louise Bruyn and the People's Peace Treaty." According to the state coordinator, "this is an effort to reach out to the people of America 73% of whom no longer support the war but don't know how to end it. One person can do something and all the one persons together can bring the will of the people to bear upon a government gone wrong."

In Columbus, Ohio, about forty people gathered to march through Columbus to the Federal Building. They called it a "Walk for Life" and carried signs that read, "We support Louise Bruyn's Walk to Washington," "Peace Now," and "If we kill our brothers, with whom then shall we live?" They gathered signatures for the *Five Theses* and delivered Louise's two documents to their two Representatives and Senators Saxbe and Taft. Their final letter said, "Thanks to Louise Bruyn and her ingenious action and to her friends for organizing so many of us."

One of the most dramatic actions happened in Bloomington, Indiana where a group planned to walk to Indianapolis, the state capitol, a distance of sixty miles. To show how seriously the government regarded anti-war actions, the organizer responsible for calling the State Police in Indianapolis to get permission for the gathering at the state capital had been asked to give her name and address as a contact person. She described what followed:

> You can't imagine my terror at watching an unmarked, drab, olive-green car cruise at four-and-a-half miles an hour past our house several

times. The two men in the car looked so sinister and totally out of place that I dropped down below the windows so they couldn't see me and cowered there only peeking out carefully to see if their surveillance was over. I assume they were state or federal government agents out to intimidate us or at least case the joint. A friend at I.U. who knew about such things also noticed that our phone was tapped.

Such was the atmosphere of distrust and fear that prevailed in this and many other states at the time. Meanwhile, in a press release about the proposed action, one of the leaders said to the assembled walkers,

> I emphasize that the walk will be a rough ordeal. We leave at 5 a.m. on Thursday, April 1st. Planned arrival at the Statehouse is 1 p.m. on Friday, April 2nd in order to correspond with Louise Bruyn's arrival in Washington, D.C. We will be walking ALL NIGHT, twenty-five minutes walk and five minutes rest each half hour of the time.

The Indiana group, about sixty strong, walked through snow and sleet for thirty-two hours. They posted the *Five Theses and the People's Peace Treaty*, proceeded to a reception at the Statehouse, dialogued with legislators and citizens, and ended up with a large rally of several hundred people composed not only of peace groups, but a cross-section of people from all walks of life. As one of the organizers wrote to Louise, "I wish you could have seen how your courageous walk has inspired people back into action around here."

The reports poured in describing peace actions in support of Louise's walk. Specifically they were coordinated for April 2nd—the date of her arrival on the steps of the Capitol. About fifty Maine citizens talked to their legislators; Forty-five assembled on the steps of the State Capitol Building in Cheyenne, Wyoming; More than fifty people stood in silent vigil for fours hours at the State House in Sacramento, California—to name but a few. Twenty-six states had organized significant peace actions, whereas ten more had engaged in quieter forms of action, going door-to-door, writing their legislators, contacting the media, and so on.

Now that the history of this period has been written, we know that the widespread opposition to the Vietnam war, with actions by countless individuals and groups, like Louise's walk for peace, contributed to

250

the shift in United States policy that led to U.S. withdrawal from the Southeast Asia war.

After the walk, the Young Mothers Group wrote to Louise.

Why was your action so compelling? In your walk you were confirming that which so many of us had unconsciously started to doubt: our ability as individuals to change things, particularly big things like the course of the war in Southeast Asia. But you were telling us that if everyone who opposed the war took an action, the war could end. It was an act of hope, a reaffirmation of the power of one person to move many others and thereby change the course of events in a positive way.

So your walk was a positive action; that is what distinguishes it from all the other protests. Whereas many of those were negative, your action inspired people to reach out to one another in a new way. You were walking toward people, extending a kind of promise that if only they would take some action, it would make a difference. Apathy is a defense against anxiety and despair; your walk not only invited others into action, it was as though you carried a banner of hope.

Because the idea of the walk was so beautiful, positive—ennobling, if you will—you somehow called out that which is positive and hopeful in all of us. That is one reason why so many responded. It is a testimony to the extraordinary impact of your walk.

Sources Of *New York Times* Quotes

2/17	p.1 col.1	"Laird Expecting 'Some Tough Days Ahead' in Laos Campaign" by Terence Smith.
2/18	p.10, col.1	"Defense Says Calley Regarded Victims as an Enemy" by Homer Bigart.
2/19	p.1, col.2	"Laird Picks Panel to Curb Army Spying on Civilians" by William Beecher
	p.3, col.3.	"American War Deaths Double to 51 in Week" AP
2/20	p.9, col.1	"Mansfield Warns on Drive in Laos" by John Finney
2/21	p.1, col.2	"Nuclear Alert' Proves False" by Paul L. Montgomery
2/22	p.12, col.3	"M'Govern Assails Nixon War Policy" Special to *The New York Times*
2/23	p.9, col.1	"Harriman Calls for Nixon Defeat" by Joseph B. Treaster
	p.6, col.1	"Heavy Fire Continues to Slow Saigon's Laos Drive" AP
2/24	p.20, col.2	"Calley Concedes Some Killings But Says He Acted on Orders" by Homer Bigart
2/25	p.14, col.3	"An Expert in Counterintelligence" by Richard Halloran
	p. 15, col.1	"A Shift Reported in Surveillance" Special to *The New York Times*
2/26	p.8, col.3	"Ex-Agents Tell of Duplication and Competition in Army 'Watch' on Civilians" by Richard Halloran
2/27	p.1, col.6	"Democrats Say President Indicates an Endless War" by John W. Finney
2/28	p.7, col.1	"Protest Diverts Telephone Taxes" by Bill Kovach
3/1	p.3, col. 1	"Nixon Aides Reported to Debate Setting of a Definite Date for Ending War Role" by Max Frankel
	p.4, col.4	"US Moves Tanks to Seal Laos Frontier" by Craig Whitney
3/2	p.37, col. 2	News Summary, Major Events of the Day International
3/3	p.3, col. 1	"Copters Return from Laos With the Dead" by Gloria Emerson
3/4	p. 1, col. 1	"FOE SAID TO FIRE ACROSS THE DMZ AT U.S. AIRCRAFT; ACTION IS FIRST OF KIND" by Alvin Shuster
3/5	p. 1, col. 4	"Snowstorms Lash Northeast Region" by Paul L. Montgomery
3/6	p. 3, col. 5	"U.S. Discloses Figures on P.O.W.'s and Missing" Special to *The New York Times*
3/7	p. 16, col. 4	"Pilots Over Laos Question the Risks" by Iver Peterson AP
3/8	p.1, col. 6	"1000 U.S. Planes Bomb foe in Foe in Laos and in Cambodia" (AP)
3/9	p.1, col. 8	"Draft Exemption Barred to Critics of a Single War" by Fred P. Graham
3/10	p. 1, col. 2	"Nixon in Interview, Says This Is Probably Last War" by C.L. Sulzberger
3/11	p. 1, col. 6	"Aide to Mitchell Opposes Any Curb on Surveillance" by Richard Halloran (actual date 3/10)

3/12 p. 1, col. 5 "Saigon Is Said to Abandon Big Refugee Resettlement" Special to *The New York Times*

3/13 p. 1, col. 2 "New Drives Swell Number of Vietnam War Refugees" by Tad Szulc

3/14 p. 3, col. 4 "Army Judge Fighting Bias in Germany Is Called Home for Talks at Pentagon" by Thomas Johnson

3/15 p. 1, col. 1 "Kennedy Puts Vietnam Civilian Dead at 25,000 in 1970" by Neil Sheehan

3/16 p. 1, col. 5 "Saigon's Troops Reported to Quit Outpost in Laos" (AP)

3/16 p. 18, col. 1 "Richardson Says Data Banks Must Be Controlled" by Richard Halloran

3/17 p. 21, col. 3 "Veterans Plan a War Protest in Capital" Special to *The New York Times*

3/18 p. 1, col. 4 "Saigon's Forces Quit Fourth Base in Laos Fighting" (AP)

3/18 p. 1, col. 5 "Funds Said to Be Key to G.I. Pullout Rate" by Iver Peterson

3/19 p. 2, col. 1 "Week's G.I. Death Toll in Indochina Put at 45" (AP)

3/20 p. 1, col. 4 "Divinity Students May Be Drafted" by David Rosenbaum

3/20 p. 1, col. 5 "End of Laos Drive Hinted in Saigon; 2000 Withdrawn" by Alvin Shuster

3/21 p. 10, col. 1 "Monitors Urged for Army Reform" by Thomas Johnson

3/21 p. 10, col. 1 "Calley to Lecture Against All Wars If He Is Acquitted" (AP)

3/22 p. 1, col. 6 "2000 Retreat from Laos, Pursued by Hanoi Units; U.S. Planes Bomb in North" by Alvin Shuster

3/22 p. 1, col. 6 "2 G.I. Platoons Near Laos Refuse Orders to Advance" (AP)

3/23 p. 3, col. 1 "Pentagon Defends Use of Tear Gases" Special to *The New York Times*

3/23 p. 5, col. 1 "A 'Week of Concern' for P.O.W.s Opens" Special to *The New York Times*

3/24 p. 1, col. 1 "Plan for Full Voting at 18 Sent to States by House" by Marjorie Hunter

3/25 p. 1, col. 1 "F.B.I. Files Tell of Surveillance of Students, Blacks, War Foes" by Fred Graham

3/26 p. 10, col. 8 "Foe Lists Raid Casualties" Agence France-Presse—Hanoi

3/27 p. 14, col. 4 "Spirit of Saigon's Forces Shaken in Drive Into Laos" Gloria Emerson (actual 3/28)

3/28 p. 15, col. 1 "Foe Shells Bases Near Laos; Signs of Khesanh Pullout Grow" by Alvin Shuster

3/29 p. 1, col. 4 "Foe Kills 33 G.I.'s, Wounds 76 in Raid South of Danang" by Iver Peterson

3/30 p. 1, col. 8 "Calley Guilty of Murder of 22 Civilians at Mylai; Sentence Expected Today" by Homer Bigart

3/30 p. 1, col. 8 "Nixon's Aides Insist Drive In Laos Was Worth Price" by Max Frankl

3/31 p. 1, col. 2 "Calley Pleads for Understanding" by Homer Bigart

3/31 p. 1, col. 4 "Fullbright Plans Hearings on War" by John W. Finney

4/1 p. 1, col. 7 "House Democrats Ask Pullout by '73" by Marjorie Hunter

4/1 p. 1, col. 5 "Casualties Heavy As Enemy Burns Town In Vietnam" (AP)

4/1 p. 1, col. 6 "Calley Sentenced to Life for Murders at Mylai 4; Lengthy Review to Begin" by Homer Bigart

4/1 p. 10, col. 3 "Reports by Saigon on Toll Inflicted on Enemy in Laos Are Arousing Doubts" by Alvin Shuster

4/2 p. 1, col. 5 "Draft Until 1973 Is Voted By House" by David Rosenbaum

4/2 p. 1, col. 6 "2 Georgians in House Shift to Opposition to the War" by John W. Finney

4/2 p. 1, col. 8 "President Orders Calley Released from Stockade" by Linda Charlton

CPSIA information can be obtained
at www.ICGtesting.com
Printed in the USA
FFHW022127250719
53860912-59566FF